Portfolio, Programme and Project Offices

London: TSO

Published by TSO (The Stationery Office) and available from:

Online
www.tsoshop.co.uk

Mail, Telephone, Fax & E-mail
TSO
PO Box 29, Norwich, NR3 1GN
Telephone orders/General enquiries: 0870 600 5522
Fax orders: 0870 600 5533
E-mail: customer.services@tso.co.uk
Textphone: 0870 240 3701

TSO@Blackwell and other Accredited Agents

First edition Crown copyright 2008
Second edition AXELOS Limited copyright 2013
Second impression 2014

ISBN 9780113314225

Printed in the United Kingdom for The Stationery Office
Material is FSC certified and produced using ECF pulp, sourced from fully sustainable forests.

P002566784   c12   09/13

Contents

List of figures

List of tables

Foreword

In today's ever-evolving business environment, it is vital to maintain a high level of confidence in the delivery of an organization's portfolio of programmes and projects. Organizations put at risk their investment in change if they fail to implement and maintain appropriate business support structures. Deployed properly, the various elements described in *Portfolio, Programme and Project Offices* (P3O®) act in a coherent and coordinated manner to give a source of reliable, accurate and up-to-date information as the basis for sound and transparent decision-making.

P3O is applicable regardless of individual circumstances because it helps organizations to develop, and where necessary re-energize, business-appropriate support structures. Organizations across both the public and private sectors are under increasing pressure to manage projects and programmes in order to deliver the best possible value-for-money outcomes, and P3O provides the structures, processes and techniques to enable them to do so. During these uncertain economic times, the achievement of successful outcomes has become even more important than before.

By advocating the use of proven support structures, roles and responsibilities in its processes and techniques, P3O facilitates effective portfolio, programme and project management (PPM). The provision of linkages to all the other products within the AXELOS suite for PPM places P3O at the very heart of that suite. For an organization, these structures bridge the gap between the development of its strategy and its delivery. They also serve as a trustworthy source of advice and guidance on the organization's standard way of managing projects and programmes through to the delivery of benefits.

P3O brings together the real-life experiences of practitioners working in both the public and private sectors and distils them into practical guidance to support senior management in the successful delivery of programmes and projects across an organization. It also ensures that the organization's investment in change is on track and aligned with its business objectives. There will never be a one-size-fits-all solution, but by identifying the common characteristics in a diverse range of situations, P3O provides a flexibility of approach and the necessary rigour to help an organization derive the best possible value for money from its investment.

Peter Hepworth
CEO, AXELOS

Acknowledgments

2013 EDITION

This second edition of *Portfolio, Programme and Project Offices* updates the 2008 edition following a review of changes proposed through the Best Management Practice change control system and a user survey. AXELOS and The Stationery Office (TSO) would like to thank the following for their contribution to this update.

Authoring team

Eileen Roden	QA	Author
Sue Vowler	Project Angels Ltd	Mentor

Project governance and quality assurance

The update was directed by a project board comprising:

Mike Acaster	AXELOS	Project executive
Janine Eves	TSO	Senior supplier
Neil Glover	TSO	Project manager
Richard Pharro	APM Group	Senior supplier
Chris Walters	PPSO SIG	Senior user

Reference group

The board are grateful to the members of the reference group who advised in the development of the product description for the update:

Sarah Briggs, Department of Health; Kevin Brooks, Treetops Training Ltd; Richard Caton, London Borough of Hackney; Lenny Descamps, APMG-International; David Dunning, Corporate Project Solutions Ltd; Tim Ellis, Royal Borough of Kensington and Chelsea; Alan Ferguson, AFA; Stephen Harris, Australian Government Information Management Office; Chris Hobson, CITI Ltd; Emma-Jane Houghton, Turner & Townsend Infrastructure; Stephen Jenner, Portfolio Solutions Ltd; Craig Kilford, Cansoti; Petra Rona, Creative Inn – PMO Consultancy; Steve Simister, Henley Business School; Dr Neil Turner, Cranfield University; Nick Walker, Department for Education; Mike Ward, Outperform (and BPUG coordination)

Reviewers

Quality of the new edition was assured by the efforts of the reviewers including members of the examination panel:

Anne-Marie Byrne, A-M Byrne Consulting; Caroline Clarke, Harmonic Ltd; David Crawford, Think-Link Ltd; David Dunsmuir, Scottish Government; Ralf Finchett Jnr, PMO Planet; Angelika Hamilton, APMG-International; Jo Harper, management consultant, Australia; Pat Heymann, Office for National Statistics; Andy Jones, Friends Life; Jurgen Lackinger, Lackinger-Consulting ; Krzysztof Małus, OMEC; Martin McCann, PMO contractor; Dave McLachlan, BAE Systems Australia; Ronald Middelkamp, Alliander N.V; Rose Milburn, DWP Change; Jamie Murray, DWP Change; Mala Murton, i2i Projects Ltd; Tomasz Nędzi, skills® sp. z o.o; Brian Phillips, Yellowhouse.net Pty Ltd; Michelle Rowland, A&J Project Management Ltd; Steve Salvini, Heriot-Watt University; Graham Shreeve, Target Practice; Paul Summers, Portsmouth City Council; Steve Tatler, HM Revenue and Customs; Sue Taylor, P3O chief examiner; Shelagh Turnbull, Scottish Borders Council; Colin Whaley, DWP Change

Change control panel

Making sure that the new edition kept to the brief was the change control panel, comprising:

Stuart Dixon, QA; David Dunning, Corporate Project Solutions Ltd; Kevin Ling, University of Essex; Sue Taylor, P3O chief examiner

2008 EDITION

AXELOS and TSO thank the following for their contribution to the original work.

Principal contributors

Sue Vowler	Project Angels Ltd	Lead author
Anthony Close	SMS Management & Technology	Authoring team member
Craig Kilford	Project Angels Ltd	Lead reviewer/mentor

P3O concept viability workshop

Colin Bentley, PRINCE2 chief examiner (1998–2008); Sarah Branwhite, Docklands Light Railway; Anne-Marie Byrne, OGC; Chris Churchouse, Mindshift Ltd; Neil Glover, OGC; Andrew Godfrey, 1st Milestone Ltd (Primavera Systems authorized representative), representing Best Practice User Group Ltd; Chris Hobson, CITI Holdings Ltd; Dominic Joyce, CLM Delivery Partner Ltd (London 2012 Olympics); Catherine Locke, Land Registry; Richard Pharro, APM Group Ltd; Chris van der Hoven, Cranfield University; Sue Vowler, Project Angels Ltd

P3O guidance pilot group

British Geological Survey (NERC); NHS National Programme Office; NHS South Central Strategic Health Authority; Programme Office, Workforce Directorate, Department of Health; Scottish Borders Council; Tameside Metropolitan Borough Council

Reviewers

Colin Bentley, PRINCE2 chief examiner (1998–2008); Sarah Branwhite, Docklands Light Railway; Kevin Brooks, Treetops Training Ltd; Anne-Marie Byrne, A-M Byrne Consulting; Chris Churchouse, Mindshift Ltd; David Crawford, Think-Link Ltd; Steve Daniels, Siemens plc; Alan Ferguson, AFA; Melanie Franklin, Maven Training Ltd; Chris Hobson, CITI Holdings Ltd; Nick Johns, Research Councils UK; Dominic Joyce, CLM Delivery Partner Ltd (London 2012 Olympics); Don Kavanagh, Griffiths Waite; Daniel Keller, Swiss Federal Strategy Unit for Information Technology (FSUIT), Swiss Federal Administration; Dr Piotr Kotelnicki, Centrum Rozwiązań Menedżerskich S.A.; Stuart Ladds, OGC; Duncan Leeks, Sellafield Ltd; Geof Leigh, Goaldart Ltd; Laurence Lemee, Clarion Consulting (UK) Ltd; Catherine Locke, Land Registry; Martin McCann, Tameside Metropolitan Borough Council; Wendy Mills, NFU Mutual; Michael Mooney, Civil Nuclear Constabulary; Cezary Paprocki, Centrum Rozwiązań Menedżerskich S.A.; Michael Pears, Department for Children, Schools and Families; Stefan Plocki, BBC; Tim Reeks, HM Revenue & Customs; Ian Rimington, Vodafone UK; Michelle Rowland, A&J Project Management Ltd; Steve Salvini, Heriot-Watt University; Ian Santry, Home Office; Claudia Schulte, PA Consulting; Andrew Schuster, Department of Health; David I. Shepherd, Consultant; Jonathan Simcock, OGC; Gary A. Smith, Cancer Research UK; Rod Sowden, Aspire Europe Ltd; Jennifer Stapleton, Outperform UK Ltd; Liz Underhill, Government Olympic executive; Peter Weaver, The Programme Support Office Ltd; Glenn Webb, P&PM Group, Fujitsu Services Ltd; Mike Weston-Burt, KPMG; Gerald Williams, Project Labs Ltd; Sébastien Wingerter, NGR Consulting

Introduction

1

1 Introduction

Purpose of this chapter

This chapter provides an overview of the guidance, explaining its purpose and summarizing the chapters within this publication. It provides a context for the guidance within the suite of AXELOS Best Management Practice publications and examines its potential value to various audiences.

1.1 PURPOSE OF THIS GUIDE

The purpose of *Portfolio, Programme and Project Offices* (P3O®) is to provide universally applicable guidance, including processes and techniques, along with hints and tips, that will enable individuals and organizations to successfully establish, develop and maintain (or in some cases re-energize) appropriate support structures that will facilitate:

- Informing senior management's decision-making on prioritization, dependencies, risk management, and deployment of resources across the organization to successfully deliver their business objectives (portfolio management)
- Delivery of programmes and projects within time, cost, quality and other organizational constraints
- Identification and realization of outcomes and benefits via programmes and projects.

P3O will provide a focal point for defining a prioritized and balanced portfolio of change and ensuring consistent delivery of programmes and projects across an organization, division, function or department. Three forms of P3O support structure are given as examples in this guidance:

- A single, all-encompassing physical office
- An organization portfolio office supported by permanent hub portfolio offices or temporary programme/project offices
- A decentralized office where P3O functions and services are provided by their functional role/department and no physical P3O office exists.

In summary, the guidance seeks to answer the following questions:

- What is a P3O?
- Why have a P3O?

- How do we design a P3O?
- What functions and services can and should be offered?
- How do we implement or re-energize a P3O?
- How do we operate a P3O?

1.2 HOW TO USE THIS GUIDE

This guide has been written to answer a variety of questions that are often asked about P3Os. Different roles within an organization may have different interests and perspectives. The whole publication should be read to understand these different perspectives; however, Table 1.1 may be used as a navigation aid to quickly locate the answers to specific questions the reader may have.

Please note:

- Throughout the guide PPM is used as the abbreviation for Portfolio, Programme and Project Management, and also includes value and risk management.
- PPM maturity is a reference to an organization's capability to deliver a portfolio, projects and programmes. P3M3 maturity is an assessment of an organization's PPM capabilities using the Portfolio, Programme and Project Management Maturity Model (P3M3®, see Appendix E).

1.3 ORGANIZATIONAL CONTEXT OF PPM

Many organizations operate in a complex environment, with investment being made in many programmes and projects to deliver change at any one time. It is recommended that readers of this guidance have a basic understanding of PPM principles. The guidance does not set out to replace existing guidance on portfolio, programme and project management; it has been developed to enhance and build on the challenge, enablement and support structures referred to in existing AXELOS Best Management Practice guidance.

Table 1.1 Publication navigation guide

Audience/role	Questions asked	Where to look – chapters/appendices
Corporate/portfolio/senior management	Why have any form of P3O?	Chapter 2
	What value does it add to the bottom line or overall organizational performance?	Chapter 3
		Appendix B
	How will a P3O enhance and improve the effectiveness of programme and project delivery?	Appendix E
	What P3O model would be appropriate for this organization?	
	Where is the plan to create the right P3O model for an organization with our level of PPM maturity?	
Senior responsible owners (SROs)/ programme directors/programme managers/project managers	What are the elements of a P3O model?	Chapter 1
	How can I use existing services within the individual offices of the P3O to best advantage?	Chapter 3
		Appendix A
	Do I need to set up a temporary office to serve my programme/project? If so:	Appendix C
	■ What should it look like? ■ How will it add value? ■ How should it be set up? ■ How big should it be? ■ What roles will it need?	
Portfolio/programme/project office manager	What elements of a P3O model should be adopted?	Chapter 1
		Chapter 2
	How will the choices be influenced by the organization's level of P3M3 maturity?	Chapter 3
		Chapter 4
	What functions and services should be offered?	Chapter 5
		Appendix A
	What roles does the P3O need and how big should it be?	Appendix B
		Appendix C
	How do I set up the office?	Appendix E
	How can the value of the current P3O be increased?	Appendix F
P3O staff/roles within P3O Programme and project managers	What is the profile for my role?	Chapter 3
	What functions and services do we offer?	Chapter 5
		Appendix A
	Where do I go to learn more about the standards we use?	Appendix D
		Appendix F
	What tools and techniques will help me do my job?	

1.3.1 What is a portfolio and what is portfolio management?

Definition: portfolio

The totality of an organization's investment (or segment thereof) in the changes required to achieve its strategic objectives.

The process of developing a portfolio will require decisions to be made on how the scarce resources (i.e. money, people, infrastructure and other facilities) can be deployed to best effect. Consideration will need to be given to both the operational and strategic priorities when determining where investment should be made. In defining the portfolio, existing operational programmes or projects that are not aligned with the strategy may have to be realigned or terminated. Programmes or projects that are already under way may also be put on hold while higher-priority programmes and projects supporting the strategy are delivered.

Definition: portfolio management

A coordinated collection of strategic processes and decisions that together enable the most effective balance of organizational change and business as usual.

The focus of portfolio management is delivery of the organization's strategy. It achieves this by ensuring that:

- Changes to business as usual are agreed at the appropriate management level and contribute to at least one strategic objective
- Strategic decisions are based on a clear understanding of cost, risk, impact on business as usual and the strategic benefit to be realized
- Resources and changes are prioritized in line with the current environment, existing changes, resource capacity and capability
- All changes are reviewed frequently in terms of progress, cost, risk priority, benefits and strategic alignment.

Portfolio management aligns the delivery of programmes and projects with strategic objectives, business requirements and the organization's capability, its capacity for change and its PPM maturity. Portfolio management is an active and iterative process and requires the collection and analysis of timely, relevant information about the organization's investment initiatives (programmes and projects) in one place.

Portfolio management should consider not just those programme and project commitments comprising the organization's change agenda, in terms of resources, but should also consider the wider business picture, taking account of business as usual. Only by understanding and appreciating the organization's full suite of commitments, i.e. corporate, programme, project and business as usual, can a fully balanced business portfolio be achieved.

Definition: business as usual (BAU)

The way the business normally achieves its objectives.

In the context of P3O, business as usual describes the things done to keep the business operating on a day-to-day basis. By understanding the demands on business as usual, its lifecycles and key events, the delivery of change through programmes and projects can be timed and managed to ensure the least disruption.

Many organizations segment their portfolio by business unit, division, department or geography, allowing local portfolio management in line with the organization structure and governance framework. Best Management Practice's related guidance *Management of Portfolios* (MoP®) should be referred to for detailed guidance on the management of portfolios (Office of Government Commerce, 2011).

1.3.2 What is a programme and what is programme management?

Definition: programme

A temporary, flexible organization structure created to coordinate, direct and oversee the implementation of a set of related projects and activities in order to deliver outcomes and benefits related to the organization's strategic objectives. A programme is likely to have a life that spans several years.

Definition: programme management

The coordinated organization, direction and implementation of a dossier of projects and transformation activities (i.e. the programme) to achieve outcomes and realize benefits of strategic importance.

The focus of programme management is the delivery of outcomes and benefits that contribute to achieving the organization's strategy.

The Best Management Practice publication *Managing Successful Programmes* (MSP®) should be referred to for detailed guidance on the management of programmes (Cabinet Office, 2011).

1.3.3 What is a project and what is project management?

Definition: project

A temporary organization that is created for the purpose of delivering one or more business products according to an agreed business case.

Projects can stand alone; they do not need to be part of a programme.

Definition: project management

The planning, delegating, monitoring and control of all aspects of the project, and the motivation of those involved, to achieve the project objectives within the expected performance targets for time, cost, quality, scope, benefits and risks.

The focus of project management is the delivery of one or more products that can be used by the organization to deliver an outcome that contributes to achieving the organization's strategy.

Best Management Practice's related guidance *Managing Successful Projects with PRINCE2* (PRINCE2®) should be referred to for detailed guidance on the management of projects (Office of Government Commerce, 2009).

1.3.4 Relationship between business as usual, change and PPM

The relationship between PPM and business as usual is represented in a simple concept – 'Run the business, change the business'. Figure 1.1 shows how PPM and business as usual are integrated and collaboratively realize strategic objectives.

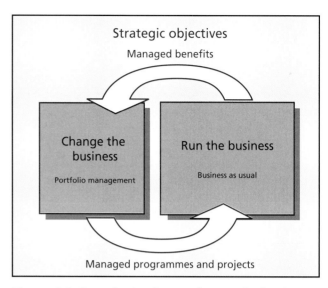

Figure 1.1 'Run the business, change the business'

Portfolios, programmes and projects are undertaken to deliver change to an organization's business operations environment and the correct level of engagement with the wider business (i.e. corporate and operational levels) is vital for success. The engagement may be accomplished by ensuring the change delivers what business operations needs and wants (strategy, business planning and scoping) and at a pace and to a timescale (planning) that ensures the least disruption to business as usual. Any function such as P3O that provides support to change portfolios, programmes and projects must therefore engage with business operations as effectively as it engages with the PPM community. Two key stakeholder groups within an organization are senior management and the operational delivery teams that will run the changed organization through and after transition. The latter group includes service management teams, which are often forgotten in many change initiatives until the latter stages of delivery; these may include IT, human resources (HR) or finance.

Whilst change and business as usual may be regarded as separate activities, they cannot survive without each other; also, the transition from one state to the other must be actively managed. Therefore, any decisions relating to change (programmes or projects) or business as usual need to be made collaboratively by the appropriate people at the correct decision-making level within the organization.

Proposed changes should be assessed to ensure they contribute to the organization's strategic objectives (or enable other changes to contribute). If they do not, the change should not be started or allowed to continue. 'Must do' changes, including regulatory and statutory changes, contribute to the organization's strategic objectives as they are necessary to ensure that business as usual can continue to operate (i.e. the replacement of obsolete IT or other business systems or infrastructure). In these cases the objectives may need to be changed and priorities reviewed.

One of the key benefits of having a P3O is that it provides the mechanism to ensure decisions are made at the correct level in the context of business as usual and that the right mix of programmes and projects is delivered.

1.4 WHAT ARE P3Os?

Definition: Portfolio, Programme and Project Offices (P3O)

The decision-enabling and support business model for all business change within an organization. This will include single or multiple physical or virtual structures, i.e. offices (permanent and/or temporary), providing a mix of central and localized functions and services, and integration with governance arrangements and the wider business such as other corporate support functions.

The P3O guidance provides a joined-up approach to the design, implementation and operation of these offices.

Programme and project offices have been in existence in some form (and under many different names) since the introduction of project management as a disciplined approach to managing change. Initially this began in construction and engineering projects; however, the biggest growth in programme and project support came through the development of project management in IT and technology departments. With the advent of PRINCE2 in 1996 and the shift of emphasis to business-based change programmes and projects, the remit of project offices was expanded. Originally, programme and project offices provided support for disciplines such as planning, risk management, issue management, change control and administration and reported directly to the programme or project manager. As the remit expanded, the role began to include standards and assurance for these disciplines. With the requirement for assurance to be independent of the programme or project, additional reporting lines were introduced, running directly from those

involved in standards and assurance in the programme or project office to those responsible for PPM governance. Business units also saw the value in using programme or project offices to assist in the prioritization of limited spending and the more effective use of resources.

PRINCE2 and MSP have contributed to increasing numbers of centre-of-excellence services, such as providing consistency of approach through standards, and temporary programme and project offices, established to support a specific change initiative.

More recently, MoP has contributed to the increase in organization portfolio offices (see Table 1.2). These ask the questions 'Are we doing the right things?' and 'Are we getting the benefits from our investment?' During the same period, there has been a maturing of the markets for PPM tools and methods and for organizational performance management tools. There are now a wide variety of tools that consolidate and summarize PPM performance data to allow strategic and business-level analysis to be undertaken.

Without a structured approach to implementation, P3Os will often have an unclear vision and scope and be under-resourced or resourced with the incorrect skill sets. In many cases the office will be led by a 'champion' with a personal vision of what the office needs to achieve; the champion then has to find resources to help deliver that vision. Individuals brought into the P3O are often selected simply because they are available or have an interest in PPM, not necessarily because they have been trained for the role.

The most effective P3Os have a vision and scope agreed with senior management within the organization and are led by experienced PPM or strategic/business-planning professionals (depending on the focus of each individual office of the P3O) that have the influence, experience and credibility to gain commitment from all levels in the organization.

P3Os evolve over many months and years. The best have been planned to lead the improvement of PPM maturity across an organization (or department) and similarly evolve their own individual competencies, functions and services as the PPM maturity increases.

An example of a P3O model is shown in Figure 1.2, with the elements described in a P3O context in Table 1.2.

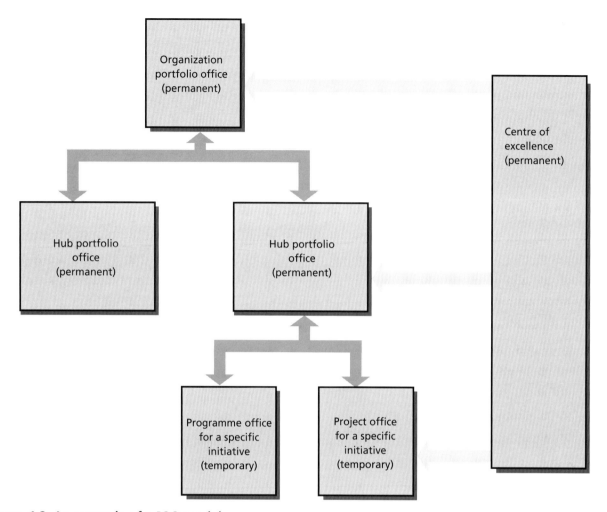

Figure 1.2 An example of a P3O model

Each organization will need to design an appropriate P3O model to suit its own requirements (see Chapter 3). Table 1.2 provides an explanation of the potential elements of a P3O model.

Due to its strategic nature and focus on investment, a portfolio office is very different from a programme or project office.

Portfolio offices differ from programme and project offices in that:

■ They are primarily concerned with ensuring that investment is made in the right changes, whereas programme and project offices are primarily concerned with implementing the changes correctly.

■ They define the right changes as those changes that contribute best to the strategic objectives and, at that particular time, attract acceptable levels of risk, complexity, cost and impact on business as usual.

■ They are usually permanent and align with corporate financial governance structures and decisions. Ideally they should have direct contact with the senior management board.

The element definitions help to identify the functions and services that can be provided by the P3O. However, there is no 'one size fits all' approach, and not every organization will have all the elements. The P3O model to be deployed in any organization will depend on many factors, including:

■ The aims and goals of both the organization and the P3O sponsor (see Appendix A for a role description)
■ The business needs
■ The PPM maturity of the organization
■ The capabilities and capacity of the resource pool
■ The number of programmes and projects being undertaken
■ The wider organizational, political and cultural environment

Table 1.2 P3O model elements

Element	P3O context
Organization portfolio office	A permanent office set up to support the definition and delivery of a portfolio of change across the entire organization or enterprise
Hub portfolio office	A permanent office set up to support the definition and delivery of a portfolio of programmes and projects within a department, division, geographical region or business unit
Programme office	A temporary office set up to support the delivery of a specific change initiative being delivered as a programme
Project office	A temporary office set up to support the delivery of a specific change initiative being delivered as a project
Centre of excellence (COE)	A portfolio, programme and project management standards office, which defines standards (processes, templates and tools), skills and training, manages knowledge and may provide independent assurance. The COE may be part of a portfolio office or exist as a separate independent office

- The business divisional/departmental structure and the geographical location of staff
- The effectiveness of matrix management structures.

An organization may choose to combine functions and services from a number of the elements of the P3O model to create a P3O which is a single permanent office. Conversely, an organization can separate functions and services from the various elements and have a linked set of offices, both permanent and temporary, providing a mix of central and localized services.

1.5 HOW THE P3O MODEL ELEMENTS ALIGN WITH PORTFOLIO, PROGRAMME AND PROJECT LIFECYCLES

This section provides examples of how each of the P3O model elements can add value at different stages of the portfolio, programme or project lifecycle. These are just examples and will vary within organizations depending on the structure, functions and services implemented. The lifecycles as described in MoP, MSP and PRINCE2 are shown in outline in Figure 1.3.

1.5.1 Organization portfolio office/hub portfolio office

The portfolio office advises on and enables decisions around defining and delivering the portfolio, asking questions such as 'Are the right things being done?' and 'Are they achievable?' If not, 'What should be added, removed or changed?' or 'Can the time-to-decision cycle be speeded up?' In some organizations the key question to ask may be 'How can we stop doing the wrong thing?' or 'How can we stop doing things in the wrong way?'

The portfolio office will be responsible for advising senior management on the composition of the portfolio and its progress against plans. It should also provide information on decisions to be taken in respect of any conflicting priorities (including impacts on business operations) and risks and issues. The senior management board may have to make difficult choices about programmes, projects and resources in the light of changing priorities. The portfolio office provides challenge and scrutiny of portfolio information and recommends options/decisions to support those choices. A portfolio office can add real value by focusing decisions on the things that matter most to the organization or departmental board.

Ideally an organization portfolio office would report directly to a main board director (or, in the case of a hub portfolio office, to the highest layer of management within its remit, typically a divisional director). If this is not the case, the portfolio office may have limited visibility of investment decisions and insufficient authority to undertake the required functions and services. If there is no commitment or ongoing support from senior management, the portfolio office will not be effective.

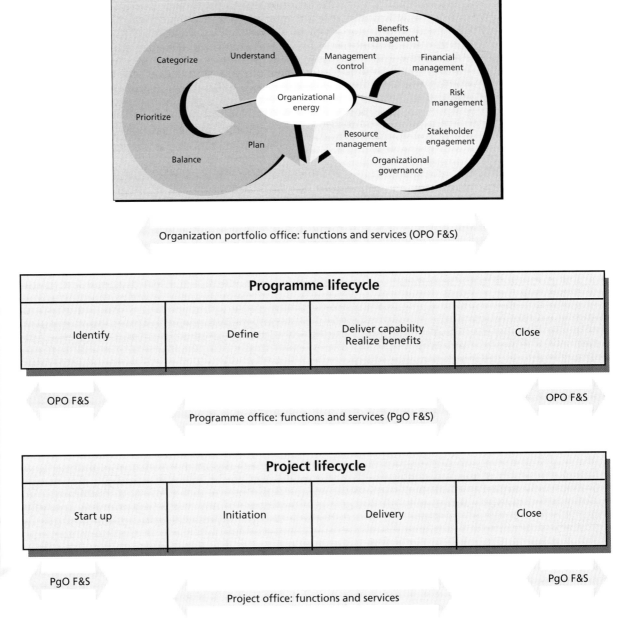

Figure 1.3 P3O model elements aligned with portfolio, programme and project lifecycles

A typical portfolio office provides the means to:

■ Ensure robust project and programme investment processes are embedded across the organization

■ Ensure ongoing programmes and projects contribute to strategic objectives and targets, and undertake the forecasting and tracking of benefits to be realized

■ Assess whether new requirements can be accommodated within existing organizational capability, capacity and PPM maturity

■ Allocate the right resources to the right programmes and projects

■ Scrutinize and challenge investment decisions

■ Identify and manage dependencies between programmes and projects

■ Resolve conflicts and contentions for scarce and costly resources, such as technical, business or change resources

■ Identify threats and opportunities, and evaluate the true implications of the aggregate level of programme and project risk

- Identify, evaluate and deal with portfolio-level/ strategic issues
- Monitor the progress of programmes and projects against key objectives
- Ensure the ongoing successful delivery of programmes and projects
- Adopt value management by actively managing the portfolio to optimize value, realize benefits and feed back learning into the investment selection and portfolio prioritization process
- Achieve value-for-money savings and efficiency gains from programme and project rationalization
- Ensure the organization has a balanced portfolio, with consideration given to the ability of the organization to absorb change with the least disruption to business as usual
- Link the benefits of change (programmes and projects) to the performance management structure
- Ensure investment in research and development activities for the long-term survival of the organization
- Facilitate continuous improvement by ensuring lessons from across the portfolio are captured and implemented.

The portfolio office also provides services at programme set-up and close, such as initiating programmes as part of business planning/ prioritization, and triggering post-programme reviews to assess return on investment/benefits for the portfolio and capture lessons for sharing.

When a specific change initiative is launched as a programme or project, it may require its own temporary programme or project office. This may be resourced from the organization or hub portfolio office.

1.5.2 Programme office

The programme office provides scrutiny, challenge and support for the programme board. It should also be a valuable source of information in relation to the health of the constituent elements of the programme.

For its respective programme, a typical programme office provides the means to:

- Ensure scope is clearly defined, understood and unambiguous
- Coordinate internal communications

- Facilitate the development of the high-level programme plan and the collation of project and transition plans
- Identify and manage dependencies between projects
- Identify threats and opportunities, and evaluate the true implications of the aggregate level of project risk
- Maintain accurate configuration records of all programme deliverables and administer audits as appropriate
- Forecast future resource requirements
- Forecast and track benefits to be realized
- Maintain sufficient management information to report up to senior management and the portfolio office.

The programme office also provides services at project start-up (such as tailoring advice, guidance, templates, processes etc.) and project closure (such as archiving of libraries, redeployment of resources etc.).

1.5.3 Project office

A project office provides services for the project board similar to those provided by the programme office for the programme board, but at a lower level. For example, dependencies are identified and managed across tasks and activities, rather than projects.

Where the project is part of a programme, the scope and activities of the project office will be heavily influenced by the programme office to ensure alignment and consistency of the processes and systems, thereby enabling easy roll-up of information. Some project office services may be provided by resources from the programme office.

On small projects the project office services may be provided by a multitasking project officer or, in some cases, by the project manager.

1.5.4 Centre of excellence

The centre of excellence (COE) ensures consistency of delivery across the portfolio, programmes and projects. It provides standards, methods and processes, knowledge management, assurance and training across the full portfolio of change. There is a potential conflict of interest between the development and embedding of standards and the assurance of those standards, and care must be taken to ensure that the assurance undertaken remains objective.

When a new programme or project is set up, the COE can provide methods, tools and training, along with advice and guidance from lessons shared during similar, previous changes. The COE will provide the means for programme and project teams to capture lessons that can be used by future teams. In this way, the organization can continuously improve programme and project delivery.

1.6 GOVERNANCE AND THE P3O

The structure of the P3O provides the framework for portfolio, programme and/or project governance and must be aligned with the other aspects of corporate governance. Formal decision enablement rules – who makes what decisions, when, and what information they require – should be developed, and the P3O is responsible for ensuring information is communicated appropriately through the different levels of the portfolio, programme and project management environment. Where portfolio management is implemented, this usually means that decisions about inclusion in the portfolio will lie with the portfolio direction group/investment committee and responsibility for oversight of portfolio progress will lie with the portfolio progress group/change delivery committee. Details of these groups can be found in the Best Management Practice guide *Management of Portfolios* (Office of Government Commerce, 2011).

Where the P3O is a single office, this may be easier to implement. Where the P3O comprises multiple offices, rules should be established regarding: levels of plans; dependency tracking; examination and escalation of risk, issues and changes; monitoring and reporting of benefits realization; and the consolidation and summarization of progress information. Overall, the intention is to ensure the right decision is taken by the right person or group, based on the right level of supporting information. There should be a single source for each piece of data, which is then consolidated and summarized appropriately through the layers of the governance structure.

P3Os should provide a comprehensive set of data to enable governance decisions and should be resourced with individuals with the right level of expertise and competence to advise management boards appropriately. The same rigour should be applied to authorization, ensuring stage gates are not passed through without the appropriate authority and sign-off, by giving management boards the correct information to decide on progress, e.g. progress reports, exception reports and options.

A COE provides a range of services to define the standards and provide appropriate tools across PPM functions. This will include defining the standards for information management and providing an appropriate tool to make it easier to consolidate and summarize information to deliver one version of the truth. Consistency of decision-making can be supported by including a single, agreed approach to the setting of traffic-light alerts across the portfolio of change, based on agreed tolerances to facilitate management by exception.

The COE should also define standard methods of working such as tailored use of MoP, MSP, PRINCE2, *Management of Value* (MoV®) and *Management of Risk* (M_o_R®), and should assure their use across the portfolio.

1.7 AXELOS BEST-PRACTICE GUIDANCE

The P3O guidance is part of a suite of AXELOS best-practice publications (known collectively as Best Management Practice) aimed at helping organizations and individuals manage their projects, programmes and services consistently and effectively (see Figure 1.4). This P3O guidance can be used in harmony with other Best Management Practice products and other international or internal organization standards. Where appropriate, Best Management Practice guidance is supported by a qualification scheme and accredited training and consultancy services. All Best Management Practice guidance is intended to be tailored for use by individual organizations.

Best Management Practice publications include:

- *Management of Portfolios* **(MoP)** Portfolio management concerns the twin issues of how to do the 'right' programmes and projects in the context of the organization's strategic objectives, and how to do them 'correctly' in terms of achieving delivery and benefits at a collective level. MoP encompasses: consideration of the principles upon which effective portfolio management is based; the key practices in the portfolio definition and delivery cycles, including examples of how they have been applied in real life; and guidance on how to implement

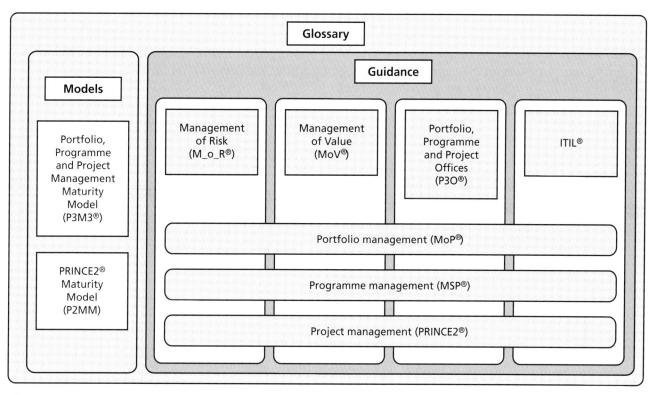

Figure 1.4 AXELOS Best Management Practice guidance

portfolio management and sustain progress in a wide variety of organizations (Office of Government Commerce, 2011).

■ *Managing Successful Programmes* **(MSP)** MSP represents good practice in programme management in successfully delivering transformational change, drawn from the experiences of both public- and private-sector organizations. MSP provides an adaptable route map for programme management, bringing together key principles, governance themes and a set of interrelated processes to facilitate the delivery of business transformation, along with advice on how programme management principles, themes and flow processes can be embedded, reviewed and applied to gain measurable benefits from business change (Cabinet Office, 2011).

■ *Management of Risk* **(M_o_R)** M_o_R offers an effective framework for taking informed decisions about the risks that affect performance objectives. The framework allows organizations to assess risk accurately (selecting the correct responses to threats and opportunities created by uncertainty) and thereby improve service delivery (Office of Government Commerce, 2010).

■ *Management of Value* **(MoV)** MoV provides a cross-sector and universally applicable guide to how to maximize value in a way that takes account of organizations' priorities and differing stakeholders' needs and, at the same time, uses resources as efficiently and effectively as possible. It will help organizations to put in place effective methods to deliver enhanced value across their portfolio, programmes, projects and operational activities to meet the challenges of ever more competitive and resource-constrained environments (Office of Government Commerce, 2010).

■ *Managing Successful Projects with PRINCE2* PRINCE2 (PRojects IN Controlled Environments, V2) is a structured method to help effective project management via clearly defined products. Key themes that feature throughout PRINCE2 are the dependence on a viable business case confirming the delivery of measurable benefits that are aligned with an organization's objectives and strategy, while ensuring the management of risks, costs and quality (Office of Government Commerce, 2009).

■ **ITIL® service management publications** ITIL provides a systematic and professional approach to IT service management (ITSM). Because ITSM is driven both by technology and by the many different organizational environments in which it operates, it is in a state of continual evolution and derives enormous benefits from a best-practice-driven approach. ITIL is based on a lifecycle approach and the core guidance consists of five publications (Cabinet Office, 2011), each representing a stage in the ITIL service lifecycle.

■ For more information on ITIL and the ITSM publications, visit www.itil-officialsite.com

Best Management Practice models include:

■ **Portfolio, Programme and Project Management Maturity Model (P3M3)** P3M3 is a tool for assessing an organization's current capabilities for managing its portfolios, programmes and projects. It helps the organization to implement change and improvements in a structured way. P3M3 consists of a hierarchical collection of elements describing the characteristics of effective processes. It uses a five-level maturity framework and focuses on seven process perspectives, which exist in all three models and can be assessed at all five maturity levels. P3M3 allows organizations to review all seven process perspectives across portfolio, programme and project management or across only one or two of them.

■ **PRINCE2 Maturity Model (P2MM)** P2MM uses the same structure as the P3M3 from which it is derived, but it applies specifically to project management under PRINCE2.

Why have a P3O? 2

2 Why have a P3O?

Purpose of this chapter

This chapter looks at the value of a P3O and answers the questions 'How do I convince senior management of the value that a P3O can add to our organization?' and 'How do I start the process of change?'

2.1 INTRODUCTION

At the very least, an effective P3O provides operational efficiencies in the successful delivery of business change initiatives. At its best, a P3O plays an integral part in ensuring that:

- The strategies and performance requirements of an organization are realized via portfolios, programmes, projects and operational business units
- An integrated set of outcomes and benefits are measured, managed, monitored and refined to ensure that optimal investment and strategic goals are achieved.

These goals may be reached without the involvement of a P3O in strategic change management; however, they are likely to be achieved in a fragmented or unstructured way that may generate significant threats to the best use of scarce resources and achievement of required outcomes.

A P3O can significantly increase an organization's chances of successfully delivering its strategy, maximizing benefits and delivering programmes and projects more cost-effectively.

It can do this in a number of ways. For example:

- Maintaining a 'big picture' understanding of the business change portfolio
- Providing decision support to ensure the right programmes and projects are launched
- Providing standards and processes to ensure consistency of delivery
- Providing independent oversight, scrutiny and challenge to ensure things are done right first time

- Providing assurance, coaching and mentoring to build a competent workforce capable of first-class programme and project delivery
- Providing a 'one version of the truth' reporting function with management dashboards to focus decisions and management interventions
- Reducing the likelihood and impact of events that would have a negative consequence; and, conversely, increasing the likelihood and impact of events that would have a positive consequence
- Improving organizational accountability, decision-making, transparency and visibility
- Identifying, understanding and managing multiple and cross-cutting risks and issues
- Protecting revenue and spend, and enhancing value for money
- Executing change more effectively and efficiently, and improving organizational PPM delivery capability
- Protecting reputation and stakeholder confidence.

Developing a P3O that delivers value from all of the above requires: full senior management support; an investment of both time and money to design and build the most effective, suitable and affordable model for the organization; and investment in the skills required to ensure it is successful.

Senior managers' time is required to understand the challenges the organization faces, what its priorities are, and which programmes and projects will help the managers to deliver the strategy. They need to invest time in attending workshops and meetings with their peers and P3O professionals to understand which model is right for them and to agree a P3O vision for the future.

Getting value out of a P3O will not happen overnight; it takes time, effort, investment and commitment from all stakeholders.

2.2 HOW DO P3Os ADD VALUE?

By putting in place an appropriate P3O model, organizations can improve the delivery of business change and optimize investment to a far greater extent than they could by implementing disciplines within individual programmes and projects on their own. The P3O should be capable of operating and delivering services within the organization's matrix structure, ensuring that temporary structures such as programmes and projects can coexist with and enhance permanent functions and departments that support business as usual.

Whether the proposed P3O model is for a new function or service, a single office or multiple offices, senior-level support and agreement for the required investment will only be achieved if there is a compelling business case. Senior managers need to understand what they will get for their money. If they invest in new functions and a coherent, integrated P3O model, what benefits will they receive and how much will it cost in terms of whole-of-life investment to deliver more successful change?

Hints and tips

In an organization with low PPM maturity, baseline information on the delivery capability of portfolios, programmes and projects may not be available. Anecdotal evidence may be all that can be included within the business case.

Before developing or enhancing a P3O, the organization's requirements for such a model need to be examined. Any model should answer the questions 'What value will it add to the organization?' and 'How will it work across organizational and business divisional boundaries?'

All P3O models require links into a wider organizational business model. Agreeing, understanding and documenting the P3O vision, business operating model and transition plan to achieve it, with all impacted senior managers, is critical to sustained success. Equally, the functions and focus of these interrelated business units will change over time, so careful managing and monitoring is required to ensure the P3O continues to deliver value after it has been established.

Successful implementation of a P3O model requires considerable change management, so there are advantages to it being managed as part of a business change programme, where the establishment of the P3O enables the achievement of the required PPM culture, improves the skills of programme and project managers, or revises business processes to ensure joined-up delivery of strategy. The outcome of the business change programme will be an overall improvement in PPM maturity across the organization, which will

ultimately ensure that the right programmes and projects are delivered to meet the strategy and are delivered consistently and well. The implementation may need to be broken down into several steps. Each step must deliver real benefits, ideally at all levels of management – first to gain commitment, then later to sustain it.

Implementing a P3O that spans an organization will bring widespread change affecting multiple stakeholder groups, requiring changes to relationships and also requiring a shift in mindset and behaviours. This further supports the recommendation that the implementation is run as a programme with the appropriate best-practice management and governance in place, including having a P3O sponsor in place to act as project executive or senior responsible owner (SRO) for the programme.

However, in some organizations, programme management may not yet have been adopted or the change may, in the first instance, be limited to the set-up of a single, small office. In such a case, the P3O design and implementation may be managed as a project. In small organizations where the P3O is simply one or two individuals, implementation of the P3O model may be managed as a series of small incremental business changes, delivered as part of business as usual.

Whatever the approach taken, it is important to have a good understanding of the problems that are intended to be solved and the opportunities to be maximized, supported by a vision of the future P3O provision and a transition plan to achieve that vision. It is also important to engage effectively with stakeholders, communicate well and keep a focused eye on benefits. Even if the P3O model is being implemented as a project or business-as-usual change, some elements of MSP are well worth incorporating in the approach to be taken, including the vision statement, blueprint, benefits management, and leadership and stakeholder engagement.

In the context of implementing a P3O model, the remainder of this chapter discusses possible approaches to understanding the problems to be solved or opportunities to be maximized, and how to engage senior management's attention in supporting a new or re-energized P3O to deliver business value. It sets the scene for Chapter 3, which describes how to design an appropriate P3O model, and Chapter 4, which describes how to implement it.

Hints and tips

Scaling

If you are a small organization with a P3O of one or two people, it is still worth taking the time to assess what your P3O does, who values it, what is offered and what could be offered. Is there support and a viable business case to expand the functions and services? Can further investment be justified?

The phrases 'doing the right programmes and projects' and 'doing programmes and projects right' are often used to describe the role of a P3O or one of the individual offices of the P3O. This can be expanded as in Figure 2.1.

Governance is focused on:

■ **Business change strategy** Are we doing the right things? Is the business investing in those programmes and projects that make the greatest contribution to achieving corporate strategy? Are they correctly prioritized against each other and business-as-usual activities?

■ **Business change design** Are we doing things the right way? Are the programmes and projects (and their outcomes and deliverables) aligned with each other, with the organization's governance, structure and the business-as-usual activities? Are we delivering the programmes/ projects in line with the enterprise architecture/ business roadmap and in the right order/ sequence?

■ **Business change delivery** Are we getting things done consistently and well? Are best-practice delivery methods and governance structures in place for programmes and projects? Are those who are involved in delivering programmes and projects doing so consistently and performing at

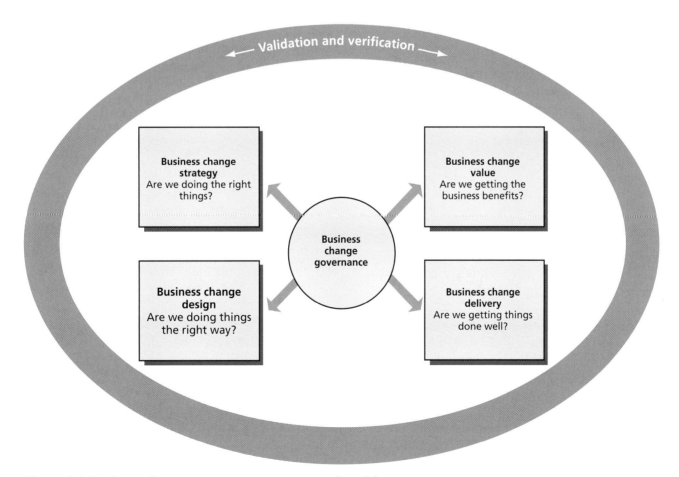

Figure 2.1 Business change governance support and enablement

the required level? Do they have the skills and capability to succeed? Are appropriate tools and techniques available?

- **Business change value** Are we getting the business benefits? Are the programmes and projects delivering the expected contribution to achieving corporate strategy? Is delivery of the strategy still on track?

Governance requirements and the way in which this governance is supported or enabled will vary between organizations. A best-performing P3O will meet all of these requirements; however, organizations may set up an office to focus on one particular aspect and introduce the other aspects over time.

Case study

A government agency set up a portfolio office to fulfil the aim of 'doing the right programmes and projects'. The portfolio office's objective was to provide 'proactive, reactive, knowledgeable, integrated and intelligent strategic decision support'. The key questions it asks and provides answers to are:

- Are we making the right investments and continuing with the best-value programmes and projects?
- Are we serving our stakeholders in the right way?
- How much money will we spend collectively and for what return?
- What programmes and projects under our control are delivering the best value?
- What resources are available to us and what are our options?
- If we have to alter priorities immediately, because of policy or strategy changes, where can we get funding out of our existing portfolio? Which programmes and projects should we stop, and what will be the consequences?
- Are we making the best use of our resources, spending our finances correctly and making the right decisions based on the facts?
- Can we respond effectively to external information requests quickly, efficiently and factually?

The functions and services of the P3O will provide verification and validation of the information supporting the various governance elements.

Verification activities include providing evidence that the governance is in place. Validation activities include providing evidence that the governance is effective.

Best Management Practice guidance is underpinned by six principles for extracting value from programme and project investment (see Table 2.1). An effective P3O provides a range of functions and services to embed these principles within the organization.

2.3 MAXIMIZING THE VALUE A P3O CAN BRING

The P3O can add real value to senior management decision-making and governance capability if it is:

- An appropriate model for the organization
- Adequately resourced
- Interfaces with decision-making bodies
- Has services aligned with other service providers within the organization, such as finance, procurement or audit.

Unfortunately, many P3Os are restructured or closed down within a short space of time because they do not realize the forecasted benefits defined in their business case. Contributing factors to this may be that the individual offices do not exist within a coherent P3O model or the offices within the model do not work together effectively. Consider the following scenarios:

2.3.1 Scenario 1 – Every new programme and project office sets up new frameworks, approaches and tools, and develops skills independently

As new temporary programme and project offices are set up, the resources may bring a mixture of standards and templates they have used previously. In the case of external staff, these may even be tailored to their previous organization. So, when determining what is to be used on the current programme or project, there is the potential for continuous reinvention and inefficiencies. As programmes and projects complete their lifecycle and new ones form, each new set-up involves significant duplication of investment and effort.

It is right that programme and project offices are justified within the respective programme or project business cases and approved accordingly. However, if consideration is given to the full set of services

Table 2.1 Best Management Practice principles for extracting value from programme and project investment

Principle	Description	How P3Os can help
Govern effectively	Governance framework, including SROs for portfolios and programmes, and project executives for projects and associated boards	Provide support to SROs and senior management
	Portfolio governance consistent with the wider organizational governance structure	Support governance – ensure the risks, issues and changes are escalated to the right decision-making authority. Assist in consistency of approach through the levels of governance
	Hierarchy based on achieving scalability with a focus on single points of accountability	
	Governance provided by delegated limits of authority (tolerances) with escalation routes and rules for risks, issues and changes	Provide independent gated review coordination and assurance
	Gated reviews – strategy, business justification etc. through to benefits review	Ensure complete, timely and accurate data is collected at source so that analysis and amalgamation enable quality decision-making
Hold people to account	Accountability of SROs and senior managers for overall portfolio investment decisions	Provide SROs and senior managers with decision support – analysing options and consequences
	Clear accountability of SRO or project executive for programme or project outcomes and benefits	Ensure the right decisions are escalated to the right people with relevant information to support the decision-making process
	Clear accountability of business managers for change transition and benefits management	Provide support, coaching and training for all roles
	Clarity of roles and responsibilities in programme and project teams and the P3O	Provide standard role descriptions and terms of reference for boards
Prioritize investment, align and adjust to business strategy	Prioritization of all business change, ensuring a balanced portfolio of programmes and projects aligned with strategy	Provide senior managers with decision support – analysing options and consequences
	Strategic objectives supported by driver-based analysis	Maintain a register of all programmes and projects in the portfolio, including ideas in the pipeline
	All regulatory, statutory and 'must do' (obsolescence/replacement) programmes and projects have objectives aligned with strategic objectives so they can be prioritized appropriately	Facilitate and support pre-programme and project scoping workshops
		Facilitate and support risk identification workshops across the portfolio of programmes and projects
	All initiatives are clearly aligned with business strategy; and, where appropriate, adjusted to maintain alignment (or reinvest funds elsewhere)	Provide a fast-track mobilization service to programmes and projects, ensuring alignment of scope and plans with strategy and business-as-usual priorities
	Programme and project start-up ensures alignment with organizational or department strategy	Scan the business horizon for upcoming changes to strategy, business issues or delays in decision-making, and analyse the probability and impact of risks on the portfolio of programmes and projects
		Support feedback from programmes and projects to strategy

Table continues

Table 2.1 *continued*

Principle	Description	How P3Os can help
Safeguard value	All investments have a valid business case throughout the lifecycle and investment funds are awarded on the basis of realizable benefits	Support the business-case process
		Provide a benefits tracking service to business owners
	A gated decision process, periodically re-evaluating the ongoing viability of the business case and ensuring benefits continue to be tracked and realized at the planned levels	Ensure benefits aren't double counted and that the measurement process is robust and usable
		Help get more value via benefits from investment across programmes and projects
		Help identify potential opportunities to be realized, exploited or enhanced as part of risk analysis
Invest in people and process	Recognition of portfolio, programme and project disciplines; acknowledgement of the link between strategy and programme and project execution	Develop tailored approaches based on Best Management Practice approaches and ensure they are easily accessible to everybody in the PPM community
	Alignment of reward and recognition strategies with PPM skills and capabilities	Develop training, coaching and mentoring approaches for all roles within the PPM environment
	Standard Best Management Practice approaches in place, e.g. MoP, MSP, PRINCE2, M_o_R and ITIL capability, capacity and risk models that are aligned with organizational maturity and culture	Advise on skills and capability assessments
Track progress through highlight and exception-based reporting	Exception-based management in place for programmes and projects	Provide timely reporting and exception management service from project to portfolio level
	Management time is engaged appropriately, based on risk factors and exception-based reporting	Develop management dashboards that engage and focus senior managers on the key risks and issues that affect delivery of the portfolio
		Make sure the data collection process operates efficiently and effectively

required across the portfolio, there may be greater value in investing in a centre of excellence (COE) that provides a Best Management Practice approach that can be applied to all programmes and projects.

2.3.2 Scenario 2 – Different business units deliver initiatives to improve PPM capability independently of each other

In this scenario, the business units may produce disparate and misaligned initiatives. For example, the IT area may invest in establishing an enterprise project management (EPM) tool or timesheet capability, while the human resources area is identifying and implementing training in

programme and project management methods. Both of these initiatives are operating with no knowledge of (or input from) organization governance policies, organizational risk standards, or performance management and reporting. This may lead to significant process inefficiencies or misaligned governance across these disparate business change initiatives.

It is not unusual to have varying PPM maturity across business units, with different requirements and priorities for improvement. However, consolidating the requirements across all of the business units may identify that investing in an organization-wide programme of improvement may deliver greater value.

Case study

An organization in the energy industry had various independent P3O offices within no coherent structure. As there was no integrated governance and reporting structure, a project manager had to record project-related information in five different IT systems so that individual departments were able to amalgamate and report on different aspects of the project:

- Project registration, planned benefits identification, benefits measurement and benefits reporting were provided for the strategy business unit via a customized database
- Financial management was required for the finance business unit via the organization's enterprise resource management system
- Risk management information for the enterprise risk management business unit was entered via spreadsheets
- IT resource requirements and tracking for the IT business unit were done via an IT resource management system
- Schedule progress and status reporting for project boards was developed using scheduling software and a word processor.

This led to project managers producing a lot of duplicate information and reformatting it for different requirements. This had a severe impact on the time available to project managers to focus on delivery, and increased the cost of delivering projects because of the excessive reporting overhead.

2.4 GETTING INVESTMENT FOR THE P3O

2.4.1 Identifying the stakeholders

As with any change programme that affects multiple stakeholders, it is essential to identify and engage with the members of the community, and determine who will be affected or impacted by the changes – who will be the winners and who may be losers. It does not matter where the idea or mandate (terms of reference for the P3O) comes from to develop, enhance or re-energize a P3O. What is critical is that senior managers who will benefit from the change are identified and engaged. Once they understand and buy into the benefits they will receive, they can use their influence and leadership to champion the change.

Senior managers responsible for providing investment for designing and implementing the P3O model will want to see some personal success as an incentive for supporting the change. They need to see that the P3O will provide clearer information, enabling them to make more effective decisions. They also need to feel comfortable that the planned changes and investment they are agreeing to will address their key concerns, both now and in the future, or they will not support the investment.

A critical success factor is the nomination of a proactive champion for the P3O (P3O sponsor) – a senior manager with authority, influence and charisma who can see the P3O vision and engender commitment from the organization at all levels, particularly at senior manager levels, as well as obtaining investment funds. The level of support will determine the scope of the P3O model that can be implemented. The P3O sponsor should be a manager of or above the scope of the business being impacted. For example, if a portfolio-level P3O is required (i.e. the organization's entire portfolio of programmes and projects is in scope), then the P3O sponsor should be a member of the main board. If a business-unit or divisional-level P3O is required, then the P3O sponsor should be the director or senior manager for that division or business unit.

2.4.2 Identifying the problem

As in all change programmes, success requires: understanding the problems that need to be solved and the opportunities that need to be maximized; recognition of the need for change; and commitment and consensus on how the change will be delivered.

Senior managers need to be asked which issues and problems they rate as critical. Consensus is required, preferably at the main board level. This ensures that the P3O sponsor understands what success looks like across the organization from differing viewpoints and allows them to gain consensus on a common P3O vision. This can be done in a variety of ways.

2.4.2.1 Analysis of recent issues and reviews

Gathering these views and gaining consensus may take the form of a series of interviews, workshops or surveys focusing on recent issues or reviews, such as:

■ We recently undertook a portfolio review and 48% of projects are currently at red-light status in the corporate risk register.

■ We are currently investing in training, tools and methods; however, our programme outcomes are not where we want them to be. Should we consider a more structured approach to P3O investment?

■ Investment in an enterprise PPM tool is being planned. What enterprise business model will need to be in place to integrate with this tool to ensure that we achieve the business value out of the investment?

■ The current P3O is no longer meeting our needs and we need to re-energize it to add value.

■ We have recently aligned our existing portfolio of programmes and projects with the strategic objectives of our organization, and the initial findings are that 27% of our current proposed changes do not support the strategic objectives.

■ Project start-ups always take considerable time and effort to determine the 'new' standards to be used.

■ Too much is going over time; too much is going over budget; we are doing too much at the same time.

By debating the issues in an open session, core problems can be identified and defined. The P3O model should be designed to resolve or limit them through the services provided.

2.4.2.2 The P3O value matrix

A simple technique to assist senior managers in determining their core problems and agreeing the value and scope of the P3O model is the P3O value matrix (see Figure 2.2). The matrix considers portfolios, programmes and projects – and provides a high-level description of the potential role a P3O can play in providing governance over both enabling and restraining activities, across the three levels.

Providing support functions and services (such as the provision of tools, templates and data for decision-making) is often seen as the enabling role of the P3O and therefore welcomed by the PPM community. However, providing assurance functions and services (such as ensuring that no programme or project commences without a valid business case,

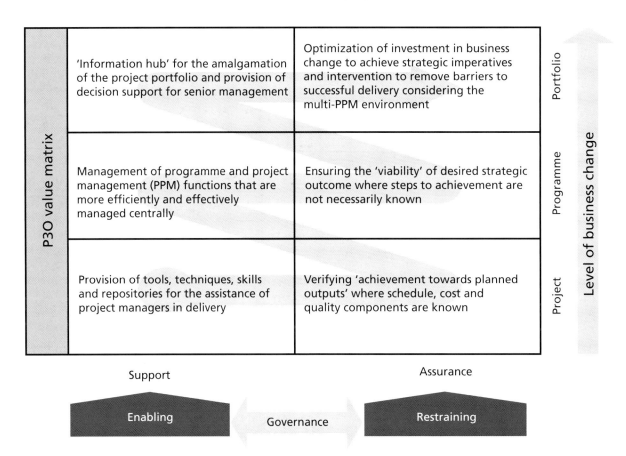

Figure 2.2 P3O value matrix

validated by a relevant governance board, where the outcomes and benefits are aligned with the organization strategy) can be seen as a restraining role. This is often less welcomed by the PPM community (or senior management) as it has the potential to impact on the level of autonomy previously enjoyed. The balance between these two roles – particularly the order in which they are introduced into the organization – requires careful management. Where there is little support or low confidence in the P3O, it may be beneficial to give early focus to support functions and services in order to build relationships with the PPM community and demonstrate the P3O's value, before introducing the assurance functions and services.

One of the benefits of the P3O value matrix is to demonstrate to senior managers that the wider the scope of the P3O, the greater the level of business change that needs to be effected, and that it will not happen overnight.

This matrix can be used to provoke discussion and validation of who the key stakeholders are in the process areas that are affected by the scope of the P3O model and who will get the benefits from

any P3O that is implemented. It is important to understand what value the different stakeholders of the P3O services will get. Stakeholders with differing requirements are:

- **Programme and project managers and the PPM delivery teams** (including those in the assurance and audit function), who need practical hands-on help, start-up support, consistent standards and language, and delivery resources available when they need them
- **Senior managers** with responsibility for prudent investment and strategy realization at the portfolio level, who are looking for timely and concise information to enable them to make appropriate investment decisions
- **Other support business units,** with whom information flows may be necessary
- **The customer/user community** to which change is being delivered, which needs to be reassured that change will happen with minimum disruption to business as usual and that any delivered capability will generate the benefits they require, e.g. they need to understand how

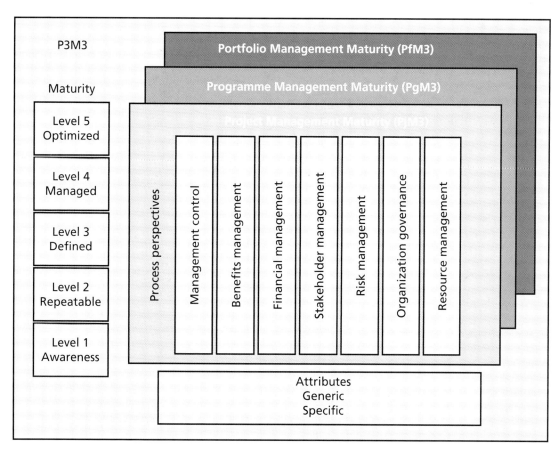

Figure 2.3 Overview of P3M3

operational plans may have to be adjusted to meet the additional demands of business change activities

- **Suppliers** that contribute to the business changes required, who will require a central point of contact for the management of the supplier relationship, especially where the supplier is providing a service across multiple programmes and projects, with forward visibility of requirements to ensure timely provision of external staff and services.

In order to get the full benefits from a P3O, a stepped improvement plan needs to be developed that moves the organization from support at the project level through to assurance and decision support at the portfolio level, building the value over time. Concentrate effort on solving the key concerns and issues up front, followed by a planned series of improvements. The key concern might be that the organization needs to improve its programme and project prioritization to focus on delivery; therefore the improvement plan may initially concentrate on establishing portfolio disciplines (e.g. strategic alignment), rather than improving individual project delivery.

2.4.2.3 Portfolio, Programme and Project Management Maturity Model (P3M3)

A more structured approach can be taken to understand and assess the current PPM maturity of the organization by using P3M3. P3M3 provides a meaningful way to understand the underlying issues and to assess and document the current state of the organization in relation to portfolio, programme and project management (see Figure 2.3). It also provides guidance in terms of the specific outcomes that an organization may wish to achieve to improve capability maturity led by the P3O.

It is important to understand the maturity levels of the environment in which the P3O will be operating in order to build a robust implementation or transition plan with appropriate tranches of delivery, especially where there are different levels of maturity in the various departments/divisions. For

example, there is no point in designing a P3O model underpinned by tools to automate processes from Day 1 if the organization is at Level 1 P3M3 maturity and does not have a basic understanding of the key processes.

Remember that very few organizations will be reaching for P3M3 Level 5 maturity; it is advisable to set a realistic P3M3 level of maturity and the associated outcomes based on a fit-for-purpose approach.

You should also be aware of the P3O's role in addressing the issues raised concerning any failure to deliver, and its role in the ultimate success of portfolios, programmes and projects. Very few 'best-in-class' P3Os appear overnight in a green-field site; an organization often has existing programme or project offices carrying out some, if not all, of the services required by the ideal model. Therefore, in order to create a vision of what the P3O should be providing, you need to understand what is offered now and how effective it is. This involves reviewing the current P3O status: what functions, if any, are performed; who is supported by current P3O services; what are the current organizational skill sets; and whether there are any cultural barriers in place, such as credibility issues. You need to know who values the P3O services, who does not, and why.

Typical questions to ask during data gathering are:

- Is the existing P3O doing the right things?
- What is the current perception from stakeholders – is it favourable, and why?
- Are they doing what they do well?
- Do we have the right people and skills with the correct level of seniority and authority to get things done?
- What should the P3O stop doing?
- What should the P3O start doing?
- How are 'best in class' P3Os operating in similar industries or sectors?

Hints and tips

Where an organization is striving to increase its level of P3M3 maturity from Level 2 (repeatable) to Level 3 (defined), a P3O is essential to provide the following:

- **Common language** Consistent definitions and usage of PPM-related terms, to avoid confusion or misrepresentation.
- **Information management** A central hub for the collection, analysis and amalgamation of information on a highlight and exception basis for all programmes and projects within the portfolio or about a specific programme or project.
- **Organizational focus** A central point of function and service ownership for the development of standards, policies and methods and ensuring they are disseminated, have the commitment of stakeholders, are used appropriately and are continually improved to meet the needs of the different groups. Note that this does not mean that the P3O will own all of the processes (these will be managed by a number of areas), but that the integration of the business processes across the organization is efficient and effective.
- **Training, skills and competency development** A consistent approach for training, skills and competency development, owning a corporate training strategy for PPM and providing logistical support for training courses, coaching/mentoring etc.
- **Centre-of-excellence role deployment** Consistency of approach.
- **Quality assurance** Organization assurance that programmes and projects have suitable quality plans and measures.
- **Tailoring** Guidelines and support for the tailoring of methods and standards to different scales, levels of risk and the complexity of the programme and project delivery.
- **Systems and tools** Design, development and operational management of tools and systems (whether manual or automated) to assist implemented functions or services.

2.4.3 Agreeing the P3O vision

Once it has been agreed what problems the organization is trying to solve and how a P3O could help, the next step is to develop an outline vision statement for the P3O. This should be a clear vision of what the organization's new business model will be, and how success will be measured, with a clear link to the business strategy showing how these changes will contribute to the organization's key objectives. Typically, the P3O vision will be owned by the P3O sponsor and agreed by the key stakeholders.

Hints and tips

If there is an internal communications team within the organization, it can provide valuable input into the publication and promotion of the vision.

The outline vision statement will be supported by the first iteration of the blueprint, defining what the new or revised P3O model will look like in terms of organization and services – a picture of the desired future state. (This is explored further in Chapter 3.)

Hints and tips

Scaling

Even if the scope of your P3O is only at project level or you are a small organization with a P3O of one or two people, consider developing a P3O service catalogue along with your purpose (vision), noting who your customers are and how you serve them, and highlighting recent successes. Often people are not aware of the services you can or could provide and the skills you can bring to help them succeed. By writing this down and publicizing what you do, you improve awareness and continue to build the credibility of the P3O. As demand for your services grows, you can take the opportunity to design an optimum P3O for the organization, based on an agreed vision statement and blueprint.

Example of a P3O vision statement

P3O vision

A fully integrated P3O is operating within the organization. This P3O provides oversight, scrutiny and challenge, enabling full traceability from strategic plans to the investment in delivering new capabilities and the realization of benefits.

Supporting statements

The key value of this investment (and the driver behind functions and services) is the reduction of barriers to the successful delivery of programmes and projects and the optimization of investment in strategically aligned programmes and projects.

In order to achieve this we need to work closely with the following impacted stakeholders: *xxx* and *yyy*.

Success will be measured by:

- Quarterly assessment of the approved portfolio. The approved portfolio represents the optimal investment in programmes and projects required to achieve the strategy that has been agreed to be delivered within the following six months.
- Achievement of Level 3 P3M3 maturity within two years.
- A 10% reduction in costs associated with issue management each year for the next three years.
- The conversion of benefits planned to benefits realized increasing by 15% each year for the next three years.
- The level of defective products delivered by projects being maintained at less than 2%.
- Stakeholder satisfaction surveys undertaken consistently showing satisfaction with programme outcomes of greater than 90%.
- The time to market of new products or services reducing to less than three months from concept stage.

Figure 2.4 shows the proposed P3O model described in the organization section of the blueprint. The example uses the vision statement product outline from MSP as its base, but in this chapter it has been adapted and expanded beyond MSP's requirements, to illustrate how it can be used effectively to gain commitment from senior management.

The following is the first iteration of the blueprint, which will be developed further (in line with the product outline from MSP as the base) before formal approval and before commencing the first tranche of the programme. Further detail on how blueprints are developed is included in Chapter 4.

2.4.3.1 Portfolio level

- There is managed progress towards the achievement of strategic outcomes by maintaining an organization portfolio office to facilitate the translation of strategy into the programmes required.
- An appropriate level of standardization of programme and project planning and controls exists to enable meaningful amalgamated reporting.
- Monitoring and tracking is in place for the enterprise-level portfolio to identify and resolve resource and financial constraints and ensure ongoing optimization of investment to agreed strategies.
- All investment is subject to gated reviews to support successful delivery.

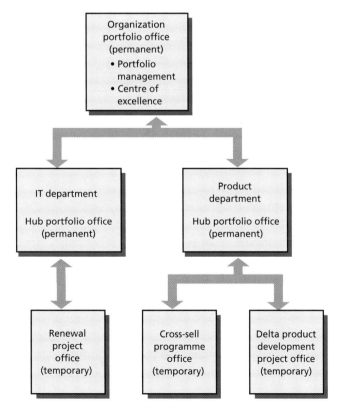

Figure 2.4 An example of a P3O model organization structure

- A register of potential initiatives is maintained to provide input into the development of baseline approved portfolios.
- Dependencies are identified, risks are aggregated and understood against the portfolio, and external factors (e.g. competitors and political, environmental or operational impact) are periodically assessed to enhance the potential for successful delivery.
- The forward planning of resource and capability requirements is proactively managed to balance the supply-and-demand constraints for programme and project delivery.
- Training and the development of skills and competencies are centrally managed for portfolio, programme and project management across the organization.

2.4.3.2 Programme level

- There is a strong focus on the achievement of outcomes and benefits through the use of the MSP framework, supporting processes and systems, skills management, the provision of advisory services and the facilitation of gated reviews at appropriate points in programme lifecycles.
- The programme office acts as the information hub through tracking and reporting, information management, financial accounting, risk and issue identification and tracking, quality control and change control at a programme level to support good governance, and performance management towards required outcomes.
- Strategic governance and senior stakeholder engagement is supported through management reporting at a highlight level or by exception (where required) and gated reviews.
- Excellent leadership and management standards are in place, supporting people at times of change.

2.4.3.3 Project level

- Highly effective project delivery is supported through the use of PRINCE2 project management methodology, with supporting processes and systems, risk identification and management and skills management; advisory services are provided through a COE function; and appropriate accountability for large and complex projects is in place.

- The quality of project management outputs is assured through a flexible governance structure to monitor all significant projects; project health checks, gated reviews and ad hoc assurance of key project management deliverables are in place.
- The transition of new capabilities to business as usual is assured through full integration with service management functions and gating of readiness for service.

Case study

A UK government agency is revising its hub portfolio office to develop a challenge and scrutiny role with an embedded COE, which will work in partnership, within a virtual office, with its government department.

Hub portfolio office vision

The agency hub portfolio office provides professional programme and project management support services to all divisions, project teams and the department. We help projects to utilize skills in the most effective way and repeatedly deliver projects on time, within budget and to a standard that both ourselves and the public can be proud of.

We can provide this service because:

- We are skilled professionals
- We view all divisions as one team
- We believe that our programme management standards, experience and skills are key to our success.

2.4.4 Demonstrating the value

2.4.4.1 The business case

Like any investment decision, implementation of the P3O model, whether by programme, project or incremental business changes, should have a formally agreed business case. The business case is the justification for the proposed investment and should be reviewed throughout the introduction of the P3O. The content and structure of the business case will vary from organization to organization. Appendix B gives an example of a business case for a typical P3O change programme and illustrates the key elements usually found within such a business case. These should be adapted and scaled to meet the challenges the organization may face.

Table 2.2 Elements of P3O capability and linked outcomes

Enabling P3O capability	Outcomes
Selection of the right programmes and projects	Reduced risk, quicker starts, quicker to market, increased confidence in investment
	Pet or rogue projects stopped at the initial investment stage gate
	Business strategy proved or disproved as quickly and cheaply as possible before major investment is committed
Optimization of organizational investment	Money spent on the right programmes and projects, focus on strategic returns and regulatory or 'must do' programmes and projects
	A balanced portfolio, with focus on growth as well as keeping business as usual happy and able to function effectively
Maximization of returns from investment	Forecasted benefits from the programmes and projects are continually reviewed against the current strategy to ensure that investment is optimized
	Forecasts identify that the portfolio will return the right mix of strategically aligned benefits from the overall investment
Allocation of the right resources to the right programmes and projects	Cost savings through correct resource requirements, increasing the likelihood of success by assigning resources to prioritized programmes and projects
Proactive identification and resolution of conflicts and competition for scarce and costly resources	Reduction of management overhead dealing with prioritization conflicts for resources
	Ability to plan the programmes and projects to make the best use of scarce resources, ensuring money is not wasted on expensive 'just in time' external resources
Ongoing alignment of programmes and projects with strategic objectives and targets	Increased clarity of the strategic objectives being met
	Improved decision-making
	Recommendations for programmes and projects to be stopped if they no longer align with changed strategic objectives
	Senior management informed if changes to the business strategy are required for it to be successful
Identification and management of critical interdependencies between programmes and projects	Reduction in delays and failure to deliver, saving money on resources and ensuring predictability of delivery
	Prioritization of critical path activities to optimize effort
Evaluation of the true implications of the aggregate level of programme and project risk	When the true aggregated impact of risk is known, some programmes or projects may not be started, or their scope may be altered to reduce the overall risk exposure of the organization's objectives
Tracking of progress on programmes and projects against key outcomes to ensure visibility and accountability for the delivery of benefits	Success rates of programmes and projects are increased

Enabling P3O capability	Outcomes
Identification of potential duplication of scope, double-counting of benefits or where the outputs of one programme or project will negate the outcomes of another	Achievement of value-for-money savings and efficiency gains from programme and project rationalization
Coordinated change control process across multiple projects, programmes and business operations	The right requests for change (RFCs) are passed to the correct service organization
	Opportunities to bundle multiple related RFCs into a programme or project are identified

There is no 'one size fits all' solution. The business case may be required to set up an organization-wide P3O or an individual office within the P3O model (e.g. a portfolio office or project office), or to re-energize or refresh an existing P3O model or office.

The purpose of the business case is to clearly identify the plan, benefits and risks involved with the implementation of the P3O model. As with every business case, it should answer the questions often asked by senior management: 'Why have any form of P3O?' and 'What value does it add to our investment portfolio?'

The business case should be aimed at the appropriate level of senior management, and if a business-case approval process exists, it should be agreed via that process.

Hints and tips

Scaling

For a small P3O, the formality of a business case may seem a daunting prospect, but by developing one you are simply practising what you preach in respect of programme and project management. By systematically challenging your costs and benefits, you will be able to focus your scarce resources in more effective ways or alternatively attract increased funding to extend the services you offer or improve on those you already deliver.

If the business case does not highlight benefits that are of value to the organization's leadership, and demonstrate its contribution to the organization's strategic goals, it will be rejected. It is essential that the business case demonstrates that the P3O will add value and lead to sustained improvement. It is advisable to take a collaborative approach in developing the business case; this may involve workshops with senior management, as mentioned earlier in this chapter. The key questions to be answered at these workshops are:

- What problems are we looking to solve?
- What will be the scope of the office or model?
- Who will be its customers?
- What outcomes/added value are we expecting?
- How will we measure its success?
- What are the key services?

The output can be summarized as a list of the desired outcomes and the associated P3O capability that can generate them. Table 2.2 shows examples of expected outcomes, linked to elements of P3O capability.

Having answered the key questions, the business case – including options, costs, benefits, constraints, risks and success criteria – will follow. Chapter 3 looks at the various considerations when examining different options for the P3O model.

In constructing the business case and gaining commitment from senior managers, there is a requirement to understand what benefits are achievable. MSP provides guidance on how to develop a benefits map showing the relationships between outputs, capabilities, outcomes and benefits. The structure and content of a benefits map is given in Table 2.3.

When evaluating the expected benefits, consideration should be given to organizational constraints, which may restrain the new P3O capability being achieved and therefore limit the ability to realize the benefits in full. Examples of these constraints are:

- **Pace of change** The implementation of the P3O model must be matched to the organization's ability to adapt to change and will need to take into account any other change initiatives under

Table 2.3 Structure and content of a benefits map

	Output	Capability	Outcome	Benefit
Description	The deliverable, or output developed by a project from a planned activity	The completed set of project outputs required to deliver an outcome exists prior to the transition	A new operational state achieved after transition of the capability into live operations	The measurable improvement resulting from an outcome perceived as an advantage by one or more stakeholders and which contributes towards one or more organizational objective(s)
Rationale	Answers at least in part the fundamental question 'What do we need to create to enable a change?'	Answers the question 'What will we need to have in place to enable the new operating state?'	Answers the question 'What is the desired operational state of the organization using these new things?'	Answers the question 'Why is this justified?' (i.e. it explains what a programme delivers)
Example	Portfolio benefits management framework	Consistent approach to benefits management, including the identification of the contribution of each programme and project to corporate strategy	Unnecessary or inappropriate programmes and projects are not started	Elimination of 10 projects at an average annualized cost of £600,000, for a total expected saving of £6,000,000

way. There is little point in creating a vision statement that seeks to achieve P3M3 Level 5 maturity for portfolio management across the organization within 18 months if the organization is currently at P3M3 Level 1 maturity.

■ **Culture** The culture of the organization will either facilitate or inhibit its ability to adopt a P3O approach. An organization in which individuals work autonomously and where there is little consistency of process will need a different timescale and approach from one in which there is a high compliance culture. Anyone seeking to develop a new P3O model or enhance an existing one should not underestimate how difficult it may be to change the culture; it can slow the desired pace of change by months or even years.

■ **Capability and capacity** Depending on the funding available, the new or revised P3O model may have to be delivered using existing organizational capability and capacity. An assessment will need to be made as to whether its requirements can be accommodated. If they cannot, then an alternative plan and business case will be required.

In some cases, external consultants may be brought in to fast-track some quick wins to finance future expansion of the P3O role. If consultants are brought in to design the P3O model and get it off the ground quickly, then an early deliverable should be the recruitment of a permanent head of P3O, who can be involved at an early stage to influence the development and benefit from an early skills transfer from the external consultants.

■ **Budget restrictions** The source, as well as the value, of the available budget will constrain the scope of the P3O model to be implemented. If the budget is being provided by a single division or strategic change, it is unlikely that an organization-wide P3O model will be possible.

Case study

The chief information officer (CIO) of an international logistics and transport organization was keen to establish a P3O in a short period of time to support the timely integration of strategic acquisitions. An assessment of the IT staff determined a significantly high level of resistance to change of this nature, resulting from multiple failed attempts at implementing fragmented parts of an unstructured P3O model, such as methods, tools and project offices. When interviewed as to whether a corporate project management methodology existed, the respondent, a career project manager with the organization, replied, 'Oh yes, we have at least five gathering dust on the network.'

Accordingly, the approach was altered and external consultants/contractors were engaged to develop and operate an effective P3O model, achieve the rapid pace of change required by the CIO and allow for the longer-term transition to existing staff.

2.4.4.2 Key performance indicators

The full benefits of a P3O will not be realized overnight. In order to maintain buy-in and ongoing commitment from stakeholders, it may be helpful to use some key performance indicators (KPIs) – quantitative and qualitative measures – to track progress at regular intervals.

The KPIs chosen will depend on what the P3O was set up to achieve. However, all measures of success for the P3O should be aligned with overall portfolio, programme and project success and with the benefits forecasted within the business case.

As a minimum, improvement targets and associated KPIs should be set for the following areas:

■ Overall programme and project success rates in relation to capital cost, duration, operating cost and benefits realization for each portfolio

■ Improved portfolio balance – in terms of overall risk, programme and project lifecycle stages, strategic alignment and investment type

■ Enhanced contribution to strategic objectives.

Improving the portfolio balance will involve not only developing the right mix of programmes and projects but also avoiding the scenario where multiple programmes and projects:

■ Are in the start-up process at the same time

■ Are intended to deliver key outputs into a business function simultaneously

■ Require limited resources at the same time.

KPIs should be SMART: Specific, Measurable, Achievable, Relevant and Time-bound.

Three sample KPIs and associated targets are included in Table 2.4.

Care should be taken over the targets and KPIs set, as they will drive the behaviour and focus of the P3O and the PPM community. KPIs may change over time as the organization changes, so, for each period, select a small number that relate directly to the expected outcomes that are of the most value to the key stakeholders.

Table 2.4 Examples of P3O KPIs

Programme and project success	20% of all capital projects completing in Q4 will be within 10% of budget and timescale
Portfolio balance	Spend on short-term contractors in Q1 will be less than £25,000 (by matching delivery to organization capacity)
Enhanced contribution	70% of projects completing in Q1 will have benefits tracked against the benefits realization plan and will be reported on monthly

Case study

A large private-sector organization implemented an organization portfolio office to support the delivery of a £60 million portfolio of change to deliver the new business strategy. The portfolio was governed by a portfolio review group, which met monthly to consider additions to the portfolio, prioritize existing programmes and projects against new initiatives, review the progress of approved programmes and projects, and track the delivery of benefits.

The things that mattered most to the senior management team were getting its products to market within an acceptable time window in order to compete effectively, and improving the predictability of delivery timescales for new projects to ensure that the operational teams could plan their business as usual.

The combination of the portfolio review group, an effective portfolio management process, and timely and concise progress reporting (under the control of the portfolio office) led to a significant increase in the predictability of project delivery timescales and a decrease in time to market for new product launches. Project delivery to time and cost as predicted in the project initiation document improved from a 24% success rate to more than 80% in one year. There was a similar decrease in the time it took to bring a product to market, from 13 months to between three and six months.

2.4.5 Agreeing an appropriate cost model

The business case should cover both set-up and ongoing costs. The P3O functions and services will incur both operational and enhancement costs and an early decision will need to be made regarding funding policies to appropriately reflect P3O costs to their users. There are many ways in which this can be done.

In some organizations the P3Os are moving away from being simple cost centres and are charging business units or programmes and projects for their services. In other organizations, P3Os are seen as an integral component of the key corporate performance management and governance function, and are therefore funded from central budgets. In yet others, the basic services are centrally funded but the P3O has to recoup some delivery costs through a cross-charging regime.

2.4.5.1 Temporary offices

The set-up and operational costs of temporary offices that support individual programmes or projects are included in the business case that justifies the respective programme or project and are funded accordingly. The categorization of expenditure will follow the financial rules set up for the programme or project.

2.4.5.2 Permanent offices

For permanent offices, various cost models are available. The P3O may charge some or all of the costs associated with its services to the various business units that undertake programmes or projects. Where this is the case, based on estimated usage levels, metrics are designed to determine the proportion of cost associated with each service. These metrics may include:

- The financial value
- The number of programmes and projects
- Resource numbers used in the delivery of programmes and projects
- Weighting against historic business benefits achieved.

Some of the variations are:

- **Fully absorbed costs** The P3O is treated as an organizational overhead and may be set up as one or more cost centres (or considered part of a larger cost centre).
- **Cost allocation – forecasted usage** The costs of the P3O are estimated at the beginning of the financial period. Each business unit is provided with a fixed charge for that period, based on an agreed metric such as number of programmes and projects. The business units pay the amount agreed, regardless of the actual usage.
  This model requires no special recording systems and processes other than those in place for regular cost-centre reporting.
- **Cost allocation – actual usage** The costs of the P3O are estimated at the beginning of the financial period, and a price for each service is agreed. These prices can vary between fixed price, per-hour usage, per-day usage, per-project usage etc. Business units are charged only for the services that they use.

This model is the most sophisticated and requires consistent recording of programme and project metrics (possibly including timesheet completion for the P3O resources), along with processes and systems aligned with the organization's financial systems and governance. It is also desirable that there is some stability in usage to ensure that supply continues to meet demand.

Organizations may choose to use a combination of these approaches. For example, an organization may choose to centrally fund (i.e. absorb the costs for) the development of standards/methods and the provision of standardized toolsets, but may divide the other P3O costs across the business units, based on the budgeted value of their programmes and projects.

Case study

A large services organization developed a portfolio office that was composed of two teams: the centre of excellence (COE) team responsible for standards, methods, best practice, facilitated workshops and health checks; and a delivery-focused team of project coordinators providing delivery support to individual programmes and projects through planning, risk, issue and change control, as well as quality review support and undertaking the role of configuration librarian.

The head of the portfolio office and the COE team were centrally funded, along with the accommodation for both teams, but each project coordinator's time was cross-charged to the individual project budget. This meant that the team of project coordinators could flex in size to meet demand from projects without affecting headcount restrictions.

Over time the demand on the small COE team expanded through requests for workshop facilitation, and a charge was introduced to manage demand. Unfortunately this led to a drop in demand from the areas of the organization that had not really embraced good project management, thereby discouraging best practice in the areas that needed it the most.

To reverse this trend, in the following financial planning year a decision was taken to stop charging for workshops and to increase the headcount for the COE team through the centrally funded pot.

Case study

The P3O for a large banking and finance organization was a centralized portfolio office and was assessed as having greater than Level 3 P3M3 maturity. The P3O had two key areas of value:

- A **COE** with P3O staff providing standards, methods, toolsets, knowledge management, communities of practice, resource competency and capacity management, continuous improvement, portfolio and strategy translation services
- A **project delivery area** with P3O staff providing project investigations, project initiation, the provision of a centralized resource pool for project management and business analysis, project accommodation and project assurance services.

The staffing for this P3O across both of the areas numbered more than 120.

Following analysis of project costs by the P3O, the SROs and project executives were concerned at the highly variable project costs depending on whether the project manager was a resource from the P3O permanent resource pool or an external consultant or contractor. The cost differential between these two options could be as much as 375% and would sometimes determine whether or not a project's business case would meet the required return-on-investment hurdle rates.

The P3O relied on external organizations to supplement its own staff to more effectively match supply and demand to the normal peaks and troughs of resource forward planning and thus provide a lower overall cost for project delivery. Unfortunately, the existing funding model of cost allocation for the COE and the direct allocation of project delivery costs to the projects was creating this problem.

A secondary issue was that, in some cases, the SROs and project executives were then using their own business operations staff (against corporate policy) to undertake project management, without understanding the need to match competencies to the complexity of the project, and the level of successful delivery was being negatively impacted.

Following an analysis of the issues, the P3O moved to a centrally managed internal resource pool supplemented by external resources (when necessary) with a full charging model. A blended rate was developed for project delivery services: each project was charged the same rate for project delivery staff, regardless of whether they were sourced from the internal pool or externally contracted. This blended rate was determined by the average cost of project delivery staff across the portfolio and included the underlying overhead of COE staff to create a zero-based cost centre.

With a carefully managed implementation plan and stakeholder engagement, the outcome of this change in funding approach was an overall saving in project delivery. Projects were charged rates for project delivery that were always better than if they were to engage externally contracted project resources by themselves (reflecting value back to the SROs and project executives). The P3O was able to continue its remit to operate a centrally managed project delivery service and set the number of permanent project management resources against the inherent level of demand, and was therefore more cost-effective across the organization. Additionally, the cost of developing and maintaining COE services (which was previously seen by senior management as an overhead) was offset against the savings that were always in place but not previously understood by the business because of the constraints of the previous funding model.

2.5 OVERCOMING COMMON BARRIERS

Getting to an agreed mandate is not always straightforward. Here are a number of common barriers you may need to overcome.

2.5.1 Lack of focus on the full P3O model

Often there is no appetite among senior managers in the business to consider the full requirements of establishing an effective P3O model for the organization. There can be a reluctance to look beyond a single component, such as training, PPM tool implementation or framework development. This can result in partial delivery of P3O functionality, which ultimately leads to restrictions on the value of the P3O to the business and failure to deliver the forecasted benefits. If it is not possible to achieve consensus at this level, then it is critical that the

head of P3O maintains the vision, intermediate blueprints and plans but looks to gain acceptance of the components of the P3O model through tranches of delivery.

In many organizations there are two problems that inhibit gaining the consensus of senior executives:

- Many executives do not understand how change management should work; they do not recognize that it is any different from any other form of management.
- Executives who do have some understanding of change management do not understand what is in it for them.

Case study

A major bank addressed this problem of a lack of consensus, led from the top (chairman of the group), first by better education, and second by ensuring that a significant part of each executive's remuneration was dependent on them personally realizing operational improvement through the successful implementation of strategy via programmes and projects.

2.5.2 Funding the P3O model

Another significant barrier when building consensus at the senior management level is the perception of the overhead associated with P3O operation. Some stakeholders may think that the current situation, where programmes and projects are completed without a structured P3O model, is satisfactory. Others may simply be reluctant to fund the overhead, so expect resistance.

The goal of developing the vision statement and the business case is that focus is applied to the value provided by the P3O services, not simply to the cost. Tangible success measures that demonstrate achievement of the planned vision and value should be documented and agreed. Useful techniques that will help to document value profiles and associated metrics such as value for money are detailed within the Best Management Practice guide *Management of Value* (MoV) (Office of Government Commerce, 2010).

Once the P3O is operational, reporting on achievements towards these success measures against the cost of the P3O business unit(s) is an effective way to maintain focus on 'added value' and balance the threat/opportunity equation.

2.5.3 Challenging current culture or approaches

The proposed P3O model may challenge the current culture or 'ways we do things around here'. This may threaten the ability of the P3O to realize the forecasted benefits, because of a lack of commitment at best or sabotage at worst. If the embedded culture is at senior management level, then the potential for failure is higher.

Undertaking stakeholder analysis and developing a communications plan aimed at addressing the required changes to the culture will help to break down barriers. However, aligning individuals' performance measures and rewards may be more effective.

2.5.4 P3O costs seen as unnecessary overhead

Some organizations do not see the value in providing support to individual programmes or projects either at start-up or during their lifetime. This means the programme or project manager takes on support tasks that could be more efficiently and cost-effectively delivered by a programme or project support officer or through a hub portfolio office. This may lead to a slower pace of change, exhaustion of the programme or project manager, or delay in the realization of planned outcomes and benefits.

2.5.5 Perceived bureaucracy of the P3O processes and standards

A common barrier when building consensus at the senior management level is the perceived bureaucracy associated with compliance with repeatable processes and governance arrangements for the delivery of business change. In addition to noting the requirement for minimalist processes, an early deliverable should be the development of tailoring guidelines to allow standards and templates to be flexed to meet the requirements of the programme or project.

Wherever possible, keep processes simple and align any new processes with existing processes and activities that are already seen to add value. Consider a stepped approach by concentrating on those processes that are visible to senior managers, e.g. building a portfolio register of programmes or projects to illustrate the breadth and value of the portfolio. It is also worth considering strengthening formal sign-off for business cases and implementing a gated sign-off approach to stop rogue projects at inception or at the earliest sign of non-viability of the business case.

Most of the services described in the P3O model have to be carried out if programmes and projects are to be successful. The question to pose to senior management is not whether the P3O services are needed, but where is the most cost-effective place for them to be managed?

2.5.6 Other barriers

Other common barriers include:

- Lack of authority for the P3O to provide the governance and control arrangements
- Inadequate use of the individual P3O offices or lack of integration with other functions within the wider organization
- Lack of clarity in the role(s), responsibilities and accountabilities of P3O staff
- Lack of clarity in the scope of individual P3O offices
- Lack of senior management sponsorship/ commitment to the P3O concept.

Case study

A senior manager in the financial sector identified the need for stronger PPM discipline to achieve more successful delivery of business change. To address this, he recommended the introduction of an organization portfolio office and repeatable approaches for programmes and projects based on Best Management Practice. The key area of concern, in terms of the cultural aspects of the programme, was the minimalist approach used in the organization.

In designing the P3O model, governance arrangements were developed that minimized additional effort but refocused decision-making on the basis of more targeted information. For example, the senior manager held fortnightly direct-reports meetings; the agenda associated with these was modified to include portfolio monitoring, tracking and requests for changes to the approved portfolio, and the business planning cycle was modified to shape the outputs of the process to become the input to the portfolio identification process. This did not add any overhead to the management effort of the senior manager, but it brought portfolio management and decision-making into a controlled state to enable more proactive decision support and improved delivery rates.

2.6 TIMESCALES

The timescales required for a programme to develop and implement a P3O model will differ depending on the level of value to be achieved and the level of activity to be undertaken.

Expect an 18-month to two-year business timescale for a typical change programme to move an organization from Level 1 P3M3 maturity (awareness) to Level 3 P3M3 maturity (defined).

This may be varied with different levels of investment (such as investing more in external consultants to shorten the timeframe) or slowing down the throughput of programmes and projects while the P3O implementation programme is running (to enable more PPM community involvement in the P3O programme).

The key requirement here is to allow for a stepped approach to change, where the introduced capabilities are allowed to fully embed and become natural ways of working.

The timescale will also be driven by senior management's ability and appetite for making decisions on the way forward.

Hints and tips

When designing a transition plan, the outcomes of the P3M3 capability assessment are a good way of prioritizing the specific order of capability development and implementation to ensure early value is delivered.

Designing a P3O model

3 Designing a P3O model

Purpose of this chapter

This chapter explains how organizations can design an appropriate P3O model to implement portfolio, programme and project office concepts and support processes through physical offices and typical roles and responsibilities. Some organizations may implement a P3O model through a single office supporting both the needs of senior management at the portfolio level and the needs of individual programmes and projects. Other organizations may seek to distribute support across the organization so it is physically located with the teams it supports, or aligned with business functions or departments. There are many different ways of doing this and there is no 'one size fits all'.

This chapter presents various design considerations for the P3O. These will require mapping against scope and the organization's desired outcomes for the P3O (as stated in the mandate). This will determine the most appropriate model, functions and services to be implemented and the roles required to operate the P3O.

3.1 INTRODUCTION

The design of the P3O model (a key input into the blueprint) should address:

- The P3O model to be deployed
- How many separate offices there should be
- The functions and services they offer
- Where the component offices are physically located.

Variations on the models may arise out of different organizational factors, including:

- Economic sector, whether public, private or voluntary
- Size of organization
- Approach to organizational governance arrangements
- Number, size, complexity and duration of projects
- Organizational portfolio, programme and project management maturity

- Centralization versus decentralization of core services
- Whether the business is driven by local or central investment decisions
- Whether the organization provides opportunities for growing its staff, with a strong coaching and support ethos, and thereby values a formal centre of excellence (COE)
- Whether there is a culture of 'quality and assurance' and a mindset of continual improvement in the organization
- Whether programmes and projects are undertaken as internally focused initiatives or the organization delivers programme and project management services to a client base
- Whether there are distinct geographical divisions of the organization.

Another dimension that drives the P3O model is the business goals of the organization. Typical business goals will include the following:

- Improve quality and/or quantity of service provision
- Reduce time to market
- Increase revenues
- Reduce costs
- Improve quality of product.

For example, there is no point in building a model that is focused on supporting a high level of governance if 'time to market' is critical to the organization and additional governance would cost the organization significantly in sales if it delayed the implementation of a critical programme or project.

A P3O provides a decision-enabling/delivery support structure for change within an organization. Chapter 1 introduced the concept of the P3O model as the total structure put in place to deliver functions and services across an organization through a single office or multiple offices. The example P3O model in Figure 1.2 demonstrates the three functional areas in which the P3O can provide services:

- **Strategic planning/portfolio support functions** This functional area focuses on supporting management decision-making. It may include alignment with strategy, prioritization, benefits management, reporting through management dashboards, support for escalated risks, issues, changes and information and the provision of oversight, scrutiny and challenge.

These are key services at the portfolio level but rely on supporting information from programmes and projects. They may be provided by a separate team within an organization portfolio office or exist in a separate business-planning or strategy support office. In large organizations where decision-making is decentralized to local business units, departments or geographical units, the services may be provided by hub portfolio offices supporting local decision-making.

■ **Delivery support functions** This functional area focuses on supporting the delivery of change. These services may be provided through a central flexible resource pool of delivery staff, with capacity planning and human resource (HR) management processes. The central resource pool may be permanent or contracted, depending on local resource management policies and how work is planned. The delivery staff within the central pool may be programme or project resources deployed to support specific programmes and projects as they are launched. Alternatively, they may be internal programme or project specialists who are deployed at programme or project start-up to ensure a fast-track and consistent start-up or deployed throughout a programme or project's lifecycle to provide inputs of expertise, e.g. planning and workshop facilitation.

In some P3O models, the central resource pool may also include a pool of professional programme and project managers, deployed temporarily to specific programmes and projects to manage their delivery. In large organizations, delivery staff may be deployed through local hub portfolio offices, building on local or business knowledge, ensuring co-located teams and reducing travel time and cost.

■ **Centre of excellence functions or services** This functional area focuses on the development of standard methods and processes, developing consistent working practices and ensuring they are deployed appropriately and well. It may include capability support through training and coaching, internal consultancy (the creation of

standards and help, advice and guidance in their tailoring), knowledge management, tools support and independent assurance.

The functions generally exist in an organization portfolio office but may have evolved as a separate independent COE office. In a large organization, COE functions may exist in local hub portfolio offices, deployed within business units or departments or to support a geographical area of an organization. In such cases, there should be a single source of standards (provided through a central COE) within the organization, but training and coaching in their use, tailoring for local need and assurance of their use may be provided through a local hub portfolio office.

These three functional areas require different competencies, skills and experience. Offices within the P3O model may be set up to focus on a particular functional area, or a large office may be split up into functional teams. The range of services provided by each office may evolve over time: it is essential for the head of P3O to develop the services in line with business requirements and continually demonstrate the value of the services provided.

An organization with low PPM maturity, introducing a P3O model for the first time, may decide to focus on one particular function.

It is worth noting that organizations will often use generic terms for the various offices within the P3O model, which do not always clearly indicate the role of the office. For example, 'programme management office' can be used to describe a temporary programme office or an organization portfolio office.

Case study

The board of a struggling retail organization, with low PPM maturity, identified a portfolio of change they believed was required to turn the business around. A programme office was set up, initially to ensure all projects were delivered in a consistent way (COE function). Following successful implementation of a project management method, the services were expanded to focus on project assurance services (delivery support).

3.2 DESIGN CONSIDERATIONS FOR A P3O MODEL

The following design considerations are relevant for a single office or a full organization P3O model consisting of multiple offices. Examples of all the various options can be found in both public and private organizations.

3.2.1 Reporting lines

'Where should a P3O sit within the organization?' and 'Where should its component offices report in terms of line management?' are questions that are often asked. If a programme office has historically sat within an IT department, it may struggle to prove its worth as an organization portfolio office for all programmes and projects across the organization.

There is no single answer to these questions; a P3O model is often made up of multiple offices, each serving a particular business need. However, for the P3O model to add maximum value to an organization, it should ultimately report to a main board director, preferably the strategy or business change director. If the P3O model is to provide support to the organization's governance for all change programmes and projects, its final point of escalation for decisions, priorities, risks, issues and changes should be the main board.

Where an organization portfolio office exists, it should report to a main board director, the chief executive officer (CEO), chief operating officer (COO), chief financial officer (CFO) or chief information officer (CIO). If the portfolio office is a hub portfolio office in a decentralized model, aligned with a division or department, it should report to the divisional director.

Where a COE exists (in a separate office from the portfolio office), it often reports to a corporate services function or directorate, aligned with other cross-organizational standards and assurance departments such as audit, finance, procurement or communications.

Reporting lines should also be considered at programme and project office level: Should the office be self contained within the programme or project, with direct reporting lines to the programme or project manager? Could the services be provided more effectively by a programme office or hub portfolio office reporting to a programme manager or projects director, with the same services being provided to several projects?

3.2.2 Centralized versus decentralized offices

In many organizations there will be a single P3O office, sitting in a central corporate function or department, that will perform one or all of the portfolio support, delivery and COE functions. In other organizations there may be central offices set up specifically for portfolio support, delivery or COE functions. In large organizations or functionally focused organizations, with decentralized decision-making and a policy of deploying local resources closest to business delivery, there may be a small central office with portfolio support and COE functions, with delivery and local portfolio and COE functions operating out of hub portfolio offices. Decentralized models focus support on local need, but care must be taken to ensure adherence to a consistent organization-wide set of standards, albeit with local variations. A number of example models are detailed in the following sections.

3.2.2.1 P3O model with an organization portfolio office

In this model there is one permanent P3O office (see Figure 3.1), which may be called the organization portfolio office. (Other possible variations of its name include portfolio management unit, enterprise portfolio office or corporate portfolio office.) This office has a variety of purposes, including one or more of the following:

- **Strategic planning/portfolio support** Enabling strategy, prioritization, senior management decision support
- **Delivery support** Flexible resource pool of delivery support staff – specialists, coordinators, support officers etc.
- **Centre of excellence** Standards, assurance, competencies and training.

The services that this model offers are often linked to the PPM maturity of the organization and where the office reports within the organization structure. In an organization with low PPM maturity, the office's services may be limited to providing standards or project management handbooks. In a mature organization, it may offer strategic support, internal consultancy and a flexible delivery support pool. It may also work with other organizational departments, e.g. strategy or business-planning unit, internal audit, finance or HR, to provide a virtual P3O.

As programmes or projects are launched, temporary programme or project offices may be set up and support staff can be provided from the central flexible resource pool to help the programme or project manager fast-track the start-up and initiation stages. Where there is no flexible resource pool, contract staff may be recruited. These staff need to be inducted into the standards recommended by the organization portfolio office. As the programme or project progresses into implementation, the support staff roles should be revisited to ensure that the central expert pool is being used appropriately and that the programme or project has sufficient (not excessive) support resources.

Support staff within the temporary programme and project offices may be line-managed through the organization portfolio office or the business units themselves.

This is a centralized model that can occur in any size of organization, but it is more often found in small to medium-sized organizations with centralized decision-making and key functions co-located geographically. In Appendix C, Case Study 2 (government agency) and Case Study 3 (food manufacturing) illustrate practical applications of this model. Case Study 5 (services) illustrates an organizational model with central flexible resource pools of programme and project managers and project coordinator staff.

The organization portfolio office model often starts its life in the IT or technology division or department and then has its remit expanded to provide support to all key programmes and projects across an organization, as well as IT programmes and projects. It may still be located in the IT division and its services cross-charged across the organization, or it

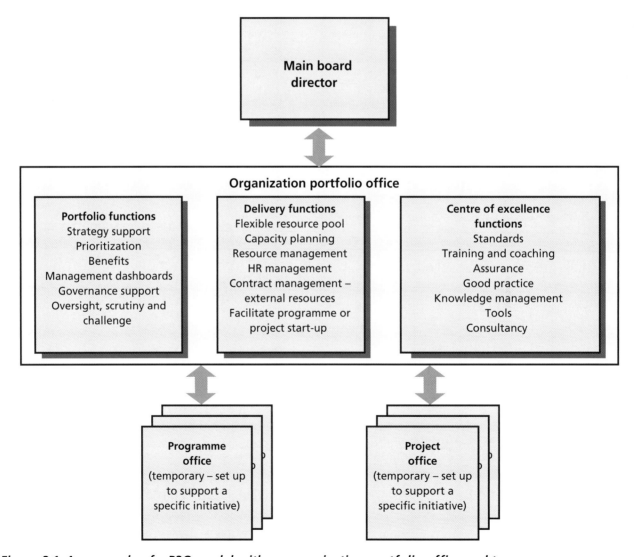

Figure 3.1 An example of a P3O model with an organization portfolio office and temporary programme and project offices

may have matured and be located within corporate services or report to a strategy or business development director (on the main board), which is the ideal position.

Figure 3.1 shows a single office responsible for the three functional areas of strategic planning (portfolio functions), delivery support (flexible resource pool) and COE functions (standards and capability support). However, in some organizations the strategic planning support functions may have evolved in a separate office under a strategy director (see Figure 3.2). Where this occurs, the ideal scenario would be a merging of the two offices under a single director. If this is not possible, then the two offices should work closely with each other.

In Appendix C, Case Study 6 (telecommunications) illustrates the separation of the strategic portfolio functions from the COE and delivery functions, a variation on a P3O model with an organization portfolio office, as illustrated in Figure 3.2.

The underlying success factors in a P3O model with an organization portfolio office are listed in Table 3.1.

3.2.2.2 P3O model with hub portfolio offices connected by spokes

A P3O model with hub portfolio offices describes a system of organizational design where there is a permanent central organization portfolio office connected to a number of permanent decentralized offices with a subset of the centralized office's business objectives, functions and services.

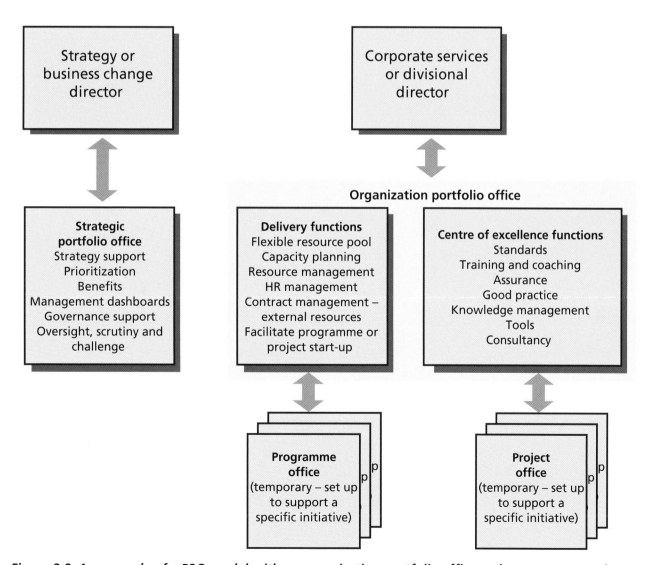

Figure 3.2 An example of a P3O model with an organization portfolio office and separate strategic portfolio office

Table 3.1 Underlying success factors for models with an organization portfolio office

Underlying success factor	Advantages	Consequences of not doing it
A P3O champion representing senior management continuity of support	Decision-making at senior levels Drives action through other management teams	P3O is not recognized Processes are not used Processes are not embedded in the culture and the initial roll-out effort is wasted
Clarity of strategy and direction for management of change	Gives direction for prioritization and capacity planning	The organization does not have a portfolio of programmes and projects aligned to the organization's goals Too many programmes or projects are started that do not add real value to the organization Pet or rogue projects are allowed to develop, driven by whoever shouts loudest
A head of P3O who is highly respected, charismatic and is comfortable working and influencing at all levels within the organization	Gives the P3O units gravitas across the organization The head of P3O is invited to senior planning meetings and is able to influence organizational direction	P3O requirements are not considered when key restructuring decisions are taken Rolling out standards and methods across an organization is difficult
A portfolio office that is staffed with highly competent senior staff, who have practical experience of running programmes and projects, including the 'war stories and delivery scars', and who are also excellent coaches and mentors	Ability to empathize with delivery programmes and projects Knowledge of what works and the challenges involved Ability to tailor standards and approaches appropriately Respected and listened to	P3O seen as admin office or a 'post box'
An established programme/project management forum/community of practice (COP) – where professionals across the company come together to learn from each other	Lessons shared 'in context' – of how enterprise standards translate into reality The organization portfolio office learns directly from programme and project managers what changes are required to maintain standards that are fit for purpose within the operational environment Changes in industry best practice and how it may be applied within the organization can be easily communicated to the full PPM community	Potential for local programme offices or cliques to form, with no sense of corporate identity No face-to-face forum to discuss and debate issues and updates to organizational best practice
A blueprint for the P3O which is regularly reviewed and updated in line with improvements in Best Management Practice or changes in organizational focus, structure or business drivers	Structure and focus for P3O development and delivery Used to focus senior management's attention on the added value of the P3O and challenge attempts at cost cutting	The purpose and services of the P3O model are vulnerable to constant change as senior managers champion changes over time and personal visions intervene

Underlying success factor	Advantages	Consequences of not doing it
An intranet or collaboration zone where all PPM staff can access best practice and standards	Single source of access for standards, periodically updated Lessons and emerging industry good practice can be centrally applied and easily accessed by all	Local standards evolve and develop Individuals save templates etc. on local drives and do not keep up with changing best practice

These decentralized offices in their turn act as hub portfolio offices to the temporary programmes and projects they service. This model is often referred to as a hub-and-spoke model. It provides the benefit of scalability for large organizations and supports business ownership by maintaining a level of decentralization.

The information hub refers to the centralized element of the hub-and-spoke model for P3O in terms of information flows. All information flows and processes are arranged so that they move along spokes to the organization-level office at the centre. The central office owns the portfolio, programme and project information and also the data amalgamation processes that support highlight and exception-based reporting.

This model tends to be an option for larger, more complex organizations, possibly with a multinational reach. It is similar to the model with an organization portfolio office; however, the size of the organization, the divisional split of business interests or the geographical spread of sites may necessitate the setting up of separate hub portfolio offices to focus support at the point of local delivery.

As in the model with an organization portfolio office, individual temporary programmes and projects may be staffed from the hub portfolio office's flexible resource pool or embedded resources, provided from within the business division or geographical location.

Programmes and projects will use standards and assurance from the corporate COE or the local hub portfolio office (acting as a local COE), depending on its size and maturity.

Where the hub portfolio office services a geographical area, division, department or business unit, it may also perform local prioritization of programmes and projects that feed into the organization-wide prioritization process. This will include developing divisional management dashboards and carrying out capacity planning for scarce technical resources and PPM resources.

An example of this is illustrated in Figure 3.3. The model comprises a permanent central organization portfolio office with hub portfolio offices, supporting individual business units, and temporary programme and project offices set up to support the delivery of individual programmes and projects.

In Appendix C, Case Study 4 (retail) and Case Study 6 (telecommunications) illustrate practical applications of models with hub portfolio offices. The underlying success factors in this model are the same as for the organization portfolio office model (see Table 3.1), with the additional factors outlined in Table 3.2.

3.2.2.3 Virtual P3O model

The ultimate decentralized model is the virtual P3O model, where there is no permanent office. P3O functions and services are embedded in the organization's business delivery units, with portfolio activities undertaken by a central strategy or business-planning office or within the finance department. Temporary programme and project offices are established to support initiatives as they are launched, and these offices are staffed and supported from within the business units themselves.

This model generally exists in organizations with a high level of PPM maturity, where consistent standards are embedded, the PPM resources are highly competent, and P3O functions and services can be provided across the organization without the need for a physical structure to support them. There is often a head of profession for portfolio, programme and project management, who liaises with all the professional staff embedded within business teams. This role also provides the link to strategy and business planning, and ensures that internal standards remain aligned with good practice through attendance at best-practice events, seminars etc. A key feature of this model is its use of programme, risk and project management forums/communities of practice, where all PPM professionals come together at regular events to share best practice and learn about new methods and ways of working.

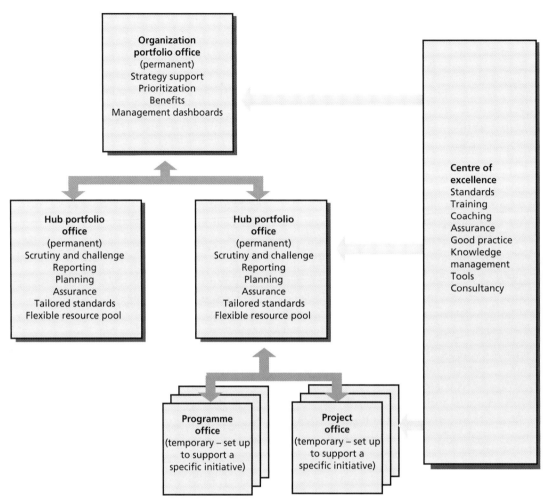

Figure 3.3 An example of a P3O model with hub portfolio offices and temporary programme and project offices

Table 3.2 Additional underlying success factors for hub portfolio offices

Underlying success factor	Advantages	Consequences of not doing it
An effective capacity planning and flexible resourcing model	Geographic clustering of resources Resources familiar with local business model and working practices, e.g. IT or marketing focus	Resources continue to be bought in or asked to travel over a large geographical area
Availability of good heads of portfolio offices using core standards and methods and the ability to tailor them appropriately to local need	Flow down of good practice and standards with localized tailoring and application	Local hub portfolio offices develop their own standards and do not share best practice Transfer of staff between hub portfolio offices (across divisions) requires constant retraining
An established heads of portfolio/programme offices forum, where key staff from hub portfolio offices meet to ensure consistency of approach	Consistency of application of enterprise or corporate best practice Learning from each other how best to apply enterprise or corporate standards	Local hub portfolio offices develop their own standards and do not share best practice Transfer of staff between hub portfolio offices (across divisions) requires constant retraining

It is becoming more common for a virtual P3O to be developed using external resources and internal collaboration tools. This allows a more community-based involvement, with a smaller core team. With the trends in cost reduction, this could be a useful model for an organization to explore further as its PPM maturity increases.

The underlying success factors in the virtual office model are outlined in Table 3.3.

Hints and tips

A virtual P3O may evolve in an organization with low PPM maturity as disparate parts of the organization recognize the value of P3O services. However, without having the underlying success factors in place, it will not realize the potential benefits for the organization. In this situation, it is recommended that a re-energization programme or project is considered to review the structure and the products and services provided to identify the optimum model for the organization.

Table 3.3 Underlying success factors in the virtual office model

Underlying success factor	Advantages	Consequences of not doing it
The organization has a P3M3 maturity level of 3 or above	Consistent working practices, and a culture of review and continual improvement Centralized training and centralized access to standards (a key feature of a consistent approach)	There is no consistent way of working and there is the potential that multiple methods will develop across the organization
Established programme/project management forums	Sharing of best practice and a collaborative approach to the updating and embedding of these practices	The base standards and practices stagnate Any updates without consultation are seen as an imposition and consistency of approach disappears over time
A single point of ownership by a senior PPM professional (head of profession for PPM) for portfolio, programme and project standards	Senior professional is outward-facing to look for and consider advances in best practice, but with a good understanding as to how the advances may be applied pragmatically within the organization	Local variations creep in and the previous good work is undone
Standards are continually developed and embedded through reference to external best practice	A single point of reference for virtual teams to access, which is updated regularly	Local variations creep in and the previous good work is undone
A strong underlying PPM culture	Those involved in delivering change, including the project executive, senior responsible owner (SRO), programme and project board, programme and project manager, and business teams, understand their roles and the benefits of a consistent approach	Programmes and projects act individually and do not deliver consistent good working practices The training overhead for programme and project managers to bring boards and business resources up to date is excessive

3.2.3 Permanent versus temporary offices

A P3O can consist of permanent offices, temporary offices or a combination of both.

It is recommended that permanent offices are established to provide functions and services that support ongoing portfolios, senior management decision-making and the setting of generic standards for all change initiatives. These are likely to be organization portfolio offices, local hub portfolio offices and COEs, resourced by permanent staff trained to perform specific functions. In some permanent offices there may be a core of permanent staff supplemented by contract staff to meet peaks and troughs of workload or to provide an input of expertise to develop new standards etc.

When a new programme or project is launched, it may require its own temporary programme or project office. If there is a permanent office (portfolio office or hub portfolio office) with a central flexible delivery team, resources may be requested from there. This has the advantage of ensuring that staff trained in organization standards and ways of working are deployed, start-up is fast-tracked and costs are kept to a minimum (economies of scale and reuse). However, in some organizations the central pool may not exist or may not be big enough to cope with demand, in which case business staff may be seconded to project roles with support from a COE (where one exists), or contract staff may be engaged. Some organizations may develop a framework agreement with a partner organization to provide all programme and project staff, both managers and support staff. However, whenever contract or framework staff are used, they should, wherever possible, be inducted into the organization's standards and ways of working.

Organizations that have no organization portfolio or hub portfolio offices, where temporary programme or project offices are established to support initiatives as they arise, generally have low PPM maturity (Level 1 or 2 P3M3 maturity). In these organizations, a 'programme or projects culture' has not yet been established. As each new programme or project is launched, it is staffed with local business people, sometimes supplemented by contract staff to bring in additional expertise. Although there is no organization portfolio office, there may be an underlying project method, defined on the company intranet or inherent in the company's culture, in that individuals may have been sent on programme or project management training courses such as PRINCE2 or MSP. This model suffers from inconsistency of approach on programmes and projects, with extreme variations in terms of delivery success, dependent on local business managers' competence.

The underlying success factors in the temporary office model are defined in Table 3.4.

Table 3.4 Underlying success factors for temporary offices

Underlying success factor	Advantages	Consequences of not doing it
Centrally documented programme or project standards and templates	All programme and project managers have a central point to refer to for standards, templates etc. and don't have to invent their own Consistency of approach and terminology across the organization	All programme and project managers act individually and use their own templates Where there is a large contract PPM pool, external staff bring their own familiar standards and ignore any internal enterprise or corporate ways of working
A consistent approach to programme and project management training through the procurement of an approved set of courses and training providers	All staff advised to go on similar courses through a standard set of providers Consistent training messages and language	Staff select which courses they wish to attend, and there are inconsistencies in language and messages Training providers are not able to tailor courses to local company culture
An established heads of programme/project offices forum, including key staff from (hub) portfolio offices, to ensure consistency of approach	Consistency of application of enterprise or corporate best practice Learning from each other how best to apply enterprise or corporate standards	Local offices develop their own standards and do not share best practice Transfer of staff across programme and project offices requires constant retraining

3.2.4 Co-located versus distributed models

The ideal scenario is to have a permanent organization office with staff physically co-located, ensuring team cohesion and consistency of approach. However, in some organizations, as a result of a lack of physical office space, or an adherence to work/life-balance policies that allow individuals to work near their homes, or the location of functional experts with other teams, the team will work in a distributed model. Where a distributed office or team exists, it is essential that there is an acknowledged single set of standards, albeit with separate owners for components of the standards. It is also vital that the distributed team communicates often and well, through the use of meetings, central information portals and collaborative working practices.

It is most likely that a virtual model (see section 3.2.2.3) will have a distributed team.

3.3 WHAT FUNCTIONS AND SERVICES SHOULD THE P3O OFFER?

3.3.1 High-level functions and services

There are many functions and services that the P3O can provide. Those provided should contribute directly to the outcomes required by the organization and should be based on the business drivers, levels of governance and customer demands. Although every office may deliver all of the functions and services, each office may have a different functional emphasis – planning, delivery or COE. Organization portfolio offices primarily focus on strategic planning/portfolio support services, whereas temporary programme and project offices focus on delivery support services. COE services may be provided by a separate office or may be integrated into portfolio, programme or project offices.

The focus for each functional area is shown in Figure 3.4.

3.3.2 Services at the point of delivery

A function or service may have a different emphasis in different offices within the P3O model and at different levels of governance, with the key driver being 'adding value at the point of service delivery'. Some functions and services exist only at portfolio level, whereas others may exist at portfolio, programme and project level but require different input/support requirements.

An example of how the function of planning and estimating may be delivered through services within the various functional areas is detailed below:

- Within the **strategic planning/portfolio support** functional area, portfolio planning is done in terms of designing the programmes and projects and their impact on business operations to meet the strategic objectives of the organization, incorporating them into business plans and then providing support through ongoing prioritization, capacity and resource planning. It answers the questions 'What should we deliver?' and 'Do we have the capacity to deliver and adopt it?'

- Within the **delivery support** functional area, programme planning is concerned with understanding the new capability that will be required to realize planned business benefits, how it will be delivered and when, whilst ensuring that delivery resources are available and economic. It also covers dependency management, both within the programme and to other external factors. Project planning is concerned with developing a plan to deliver the outputs in a timely and cost-effective manner to the required quality, managing dependencies and ensuring transition plans to business operations are in place.

- Within the **centre of excellence** functional area, planning is concerned with the provision of standards, tools, techniques and expertise to enable roll-up of milestone data and dependencies.

Another example is the function of risk management:

- Within the **strategic planning/portfolio support** functional area, risk is considered from a strategic viewpoint, looking at risks that may inhibit the organization's ability to deliver its strategic objectives and opportunities to exceed them. The P3O should develop a risk management policy for compliance by programmes and projects based on the organization's own corporate risk policy, identify and manage portfolio risks, and liaise with the corporate risk department where one exists. It should also review the risks of programmes and projects to look for common risks that should be

P3O	Planning (portfolio)	Portfolio build, prioritization, analysis and reporting
		Programme and project set-up and closure
		Stakeholder engagement and communications
		Planning and estimating
		Capacity planning and resource management
		Benefits management
		Performance monitoring
	Delivery (programme and project)	Planning and estimating
		Monitor and review
		Reporting
		Risk management
		Issue management
		Change control
		Finance
		Commercial (including supplier management)
		Quality assurance
		Information management (including configuration and asset management)
		Transition management
		Secretariat
	Centre of excellence	Standards and methods (processes and tools)
		Internal consultancy
		Organizational learning and knowledge management
		People and skills (PPM competencies)

Figure 3.4 High-level functions and services of a P3O model

managed at the portfolio level rather than individually by programmes or projects. The P3O would be best placed to evaluate the net effect of these threats and opportunities when aggregated, and to escalate this information to the board or corporate risk management.

■ Within the **delivery support** functional area, programme-level risk is considered with regard to the ability to achieve the planned outcomes and benefits for a specific business change, and the P3O should develop and maintain the programme's risk register, recommending escalation or cascading of risks as necessary. The P3O may also look at risks to stakeholders, benefits, delivery, dependencies and external supplier risks, and proactively review risks across the individual projects to seek out those that should be managed by the programme rather than by individual projects. At project level, risk is considered with regard to the delivery of the project's outputs to meet the required objectives on time, cost, benefits, quality and scope. The P3O may also provide resources to manage the risk process in support of the project manager and project board.

■ Within the **centre of excellence** functional area, the P3O should provide a standard risk management strategy, process and templates (aligned with corporate and programme standards if they exist) to ensure consistent application of risk management, and standardized risk registers to enable monitoring of risks. The P3O may also provide resources to run objective risk identification workshops.

See Appendix F for a detailed breakdown of the potential services for each of the functions listed.

Hints and tips

Scope and scaling

When deciding on the services to provide, it is worth remembering that not every service offered needs to be provided for every project. For example, health checks might only be provided for the top 20% of projects.

Hints and tips

Scaling

If you are a very small office, these models may seem daunting. The key thing to consider is what these models offer in terms of functions and services and who they serve in terms of stakeholders. If you are not carrying out the functions and services highlighted in the models, ask who is doing those things within your organization. The outcome may be the discovery of a network of people who could work more effectively together as a virtual P3O.

3.3.3 Integration with the wider organization

The P3O will not exist in a vacuum. When considering the functions and services to provide, it is essential to understand how these will integrate into the wider organization. A frequent reason for the failure of permanent P3Os is a lack of integration of the P3O model with the wider organization model. The head of P3O needs to understand who is responsible for the various functions and how the model, and the various offices within it, will interact with them. These other functions include:

■ Strategy development and management, including business planning
■ IT service management (release, change, configuration etc.)
■ Human resources
■ Marketing/public relations
■ Procurement/purchasing/commercial, including bid management
■ Finance
■ Corporate risk management
■ Corporate information assurance (see section 3.3.6 for further information)
■ Audit
■ Quality
■ Business operations.

Just as P3O resources may exist in a matrix management environment with local business line management but a professional link to an organization portfolio office or COE, so will other professional resources.

Clarity is required in terms of roles/responsibilities for delivering functions and services across business areas. For example, financial functions and services may be provided through a temporary programme office, but the person delivering the service may be embedded in the programme office, with their line management and the standards for financial reporting developed and specified by the finance department (see Figure 3.5). Embedded resources are temporarily assigned to a programme or project (either full-time or part-time), but their originating department still controls the processes that they will follow and is responsible for normal line management activities.

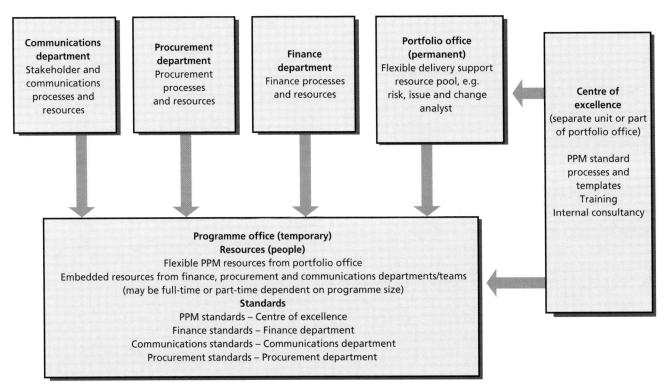

Figure 3.5 *An example of the embedding of resources from an organization portfolio office, COE and business functions into a temporary programme office*

Hints and tips

Scaling

In a small P3O, or if you carry out programme or project support for a small organization, review what you do and do not offer in terms of functions and services – you may find you are delivering functions that may be better delivered by others, including the programme and project managers themselves. Are there functions you feel may make better use of your time and competencies? If so, challenge your job description and daily, weekly and monthly task lists. If there are functions or services missing that may benefit the organization but you do not have the skills to provide them, seek investment in focused training that will be of benefit to yourself and the organization.

3.3.4 Independence of P3O assurance services

Independent assurance services are often included within a P3O service offering. These may take many forms, such as coordinating or facilitating gated reviews, stage reviews (e.g. in the UK government,

the OGC Gateway™ review process), regular health checks, internal or independent audits, and lesson reviews.

Assurance teams may also provide quality assurance to programmes and projects by providing an assurance resource (full- or part-time) or independent advice/guidance on the tailoring of processes in the start-up stage.

Whatever the level of assurance service provided, it is essential that it is independent of the programme or project delivery and that there are no conflicts of interest.

The P3O itself should also be subject to independent assurance and external audit, in particular the external review of COE functions and services, to ensure that good practice is being kept up to date with changing industry standards and trends.

Within a multi-programme/project environment, staff across the P3O may carry out assurance at appropriate checkpoints and at gated reviews, as well as providing ongoing oversight, scrutiny and challenge. Independent assurance external to the delegated assurance from the programme or project board may be requested by senior management boards and may be focused on fulfilment of strategy, impact on business operations, management of dependencies or other areas of concern.

Case study

A programme office servicing a large, complex programme within a UK government department offers an independent standards and assurance function. This office consists of three individuals who are assigned to projects within the programme. Each assigned assurance resource provides advice/guidance on the standard processes to be used and develops an assurance approach tailored to the individual project – this may consist of gated review coordination, health checks, intermediate and final lesson reviews, and advice or guidance on quality criteria and quality reviews. The assurance team is separate from the delivery support team within the programme office, ensuring its independence.

Hints and tips

An assurance function should always be forward-looking and action-oriented (either specific or systemic) to improve the potential for successful delivery, rather than simply auditing what may have happened.

3.3.5 Alignment of governance services provided by the P3O

Chapter 1 introduced the concept of the P3O supporting governance in an organization by enabling and challenging programme and project data and in some cases scrutinizing the impact of programme or project delivery on business as usual (through achievement of strategic goals or the least disruption to operational working).

The P3O model seeks to provide the governance backbone for all change within an organization, ensuring all decisions are made at the appropriate level, with the right facts and in a timely manner. This means that the P3O needs to work effectively with all bodies across an organization that either make decisions or provide facts and information to allow a decision to be made. The PPM governance cannot be developed in isolation from the business-as-usual decision-making bodies. The relationship between the P3O and these bodies should be defined and rules of engagement established.

Governance must be agreed and defined in terms of:

■ Who makes what decision and when
■ What delegated limits of authority are in place
■ The rules and routes for escalation and cascading of information, risks, issues and changes.

The agreement should reflect the governance and information needs of all stakeholders.

The terms of reference for all the offices within the P3O should detail their specific governance responsibilities.

3.3.6 Information assurance

The value of information assurance (IA) varies from organization to organization. Organizations such as the Ministry of Defence, the banking industry and others working with personal or sensitive information understand that it is critical to their business, and they invest significant time and money to maintain robust processes, procedures and systems in this area. The Data Protection Act and the Freedom of Information legislation define minimum statutory guidelines for all organizations. This has implications for all portfolio, programme and project information.

IA is based on the three concepts of confidentiality, integrity and availability. These terms mean that: information is only available to those who have a need and the authority to see it; only those with the correct authority are able to change information; and the information is available whenever and wherever the business requires it to be.

The P3O has a crucial cost-effective role in providing a number of IA-related resources and management functions for the support of all areas of the PPM environment. Consideration of the IA requirements for the project and its outputs must start at the beginning of the project. Trying to build in IA measures or take remedial action to deal with identified IA issues at the end of the project will never be as cost-effective or as efficient as building them in during development. The P3O can ensure that an appropriate initial assessment of the IA issues is carried out during the initiation stage of any new activity.

For portfolios and programmes, the role of the P3O is more about setting the overall objectives (in line with the business objectives) and then ensuring they are followed. This might be the establishment of a standard (perhaps using the ISO 27000 series on information security matters and similar national guidance in information assurance) or simply a general security policy statement. The role can also include responsibility for developing a consistent filing structure for programmes and projects.

In the scenario where there is a separate IA function or department within an organization, the P3O should engage appropriately with the experts within it and follow a process of embedding IA resources and processes into portfolio, programme and project offices or teams, as previously discussed with reference to finance or commercial staff.

Hints and tips

The programme to implement or re-energize the P3O model will need to consider IA for all PPM data used for governance and reporting in the operational P3O. This will impact all aspects of the P3O blueprint.

3.3.7 Non-PPM functions and services

It is sometimes necessary for a P3O to undertake functions and services outside the PPM area of operations, either in the interests of business efficiency or because the functions have no other logical home. This may mean providing a secretariat service to management boards, looking after travel and accommodation (operational accommodation in addition to project accommodation) or liaising with procurement regarding the acquisition of equipment or resources.

Hints and tips

Where the P3O provides non-PPM functions and services, it is important to ring-fence these administration resources away from the professional PPM functions in a separate team. If the P3O is seen as nothing more than an administration office, it may discourage people from deciding on a potentially rewarding career within a P3O.

3.4   ROLES AND RESPONSIBILITIES WITHIN A P3O

There are 21 defined P3O roles, and any P3O will be made up of a combination of these roles. Some are specific to a level of organizational governance (e.g. portfolio analyst), while others are specific to a function or service (e.g. risk manager). When each of the offices within the P3O model is designed, job descriptions detailing the required skills and

competencies should be defined for each position within the office. Individual job descriptions may combine elements from a number of different roles.

The role descriptions in Tables 3.5, 3.6 and 3.7 should be treated as a 'pick and mix' set to create custom job descriptions tailored to the organization's business and customer requirements.

Full role descriptions appear in Appendix A and examples are given in Appendix C. Case Study 2 (government agency) provides examples of functional role descriptions, and Case Study 6 (telecommunications) provides examples of generic role descriptions.

3.4.1   Skills and competencies of P3O staff

The tone and approach of a successful P3O component office within the P3O model is set by the person at the top, so the head of P3O is a key role. This individual must have the right experience, have influence, credibility and charisma, and be able to lead 'from the middle'– manage up, down and sideways. They need to be a good 'people person', have a good understanding of methods, be a decision-maker, be capable of following a vision and have first-hand experience of programme and project delivery. It is a difficult job to do right and these people are hard to find. Some of the best heads of P3O have come from varied backgrounds, including business operations management, strategy development and business planning. An extensive knowledge of PPM is not necessarily a key competency.

In staffing an office of the P3O, there should be a matching of roles to individual strengths. Some people are better at detailed work; others will have strong interpersonal and coaching skills. One way for individuals to develop the breadth and depth of their skills is by rotating the P3O functions or roles among the staff.

Although good PPM skills and competencies are essential for some P3O roles, others will require more generic business skills, functional competencies (such as finance or procurement) and generic personal skills such as coaching, mentoring, facilitation and presentation skills.

There should be a clear emphasis on P3O as a career path in its own right, rather than as a stepping stone to becoming a programme or project manager. P3O staff should have a clear career path mapped out, underpinned by mandatory and desirable skills and competencies, with personal and role-focused development plans. Qualifications in P3O-related disciplines are to be encouraged so as to improve the skills, competencies and credibility of the P3O function.

In developing more professional P3Os, staffed by individuals with the right skills, organizations need to understand that an investment in high-calibre individuals is required. It is more important to have a small number of appropriately skilled people who can interpret and challenge data, than to have a large number of administrative staff who collate data without interpreting it and without making the necessary recommendations to the decision-makers.

The skills and competencies of portfolio office staff will need to include investment management, strategic planning and implementation, and benefits management. These staff will also need to have the ability to see the 'big picture', what is often referred to as the 'helicopter view', and make recommendations based on insightful information. They will need to have political awareness and stakeholder engagement skills, be capable of operating and influencing at senior management board level, and have an understanding of the business challenges and changes required. They should also have credible delivery experience (i.e. they should have run large programmes and projects, managed risks at a strategic level or operated a business unit) and understand the challenges that change will bring and how to balance change with operational working. Such people are hard to find and should be valued and developed.

Hints and tips
Scaling

In a small organization with only a single person or a few people dedicated to P3O functions in a central office, where there are skills gaps, consider how you can expand your headcount and talent-spot for the organization through the use of secondments.

Case study

An organization portfolio office had a headcount of nine people to support all the programmes and projects across a large multi-division organization. Demand rose significantly as the organization portfolio office began publishing its successes and achieved a reputation for fast-tracking projects through start-up and providing pragmatic help.

Increasing the headcount was not an option, so the head of the organization portfolio office sought secondments from across the business, talent-spotting good people and gaining agreements from their line managers to fund a six-month secondment within the portfolio office. These six-month secondments were invariably extended to a year, or 18 months in some cases, as the value of the practical experience was recognized.

The business units gained by having their people intensively trained, coached and given practical experience. The portfolio office gained by increasing its pool of resources without increasing its headcount. When the staff returned to their units, they provided hub portfolio offices or local programme or project support to their business units, which took the pressure off the organization portfolio office and also provided a flexible resource pool that the organization portfolio office could tap into when workloads peaked.

The secondment process was formally agreed with the HR team and officially sanctioned. Overall business benefits included a general improvement in programme and project management skills across the business and a more successful delivery of change.

3.4.2 Role types

The roles within a P3O can be considered as management, generic or functional.

3.4.2.1 P3O management roles

An outline of the three management role descriptions is provided in Table 3.5. Further details of the roles and responsibilities can be found in Appendix A.

Table 3.5 Outline of P3O management role descriptions

Role name	Outline description
P3O sponsor	The P3O sponsor is a senior manager who directs and champions the establishment and evolving operation of the P3O. They will ideally be a member of the main board.
	The P3O sponsor is accountable for developing and maintaining a viable business case to secure the investment required to implement and run the P3O model. The P3O sponsor may also fulfil the role of portfolio director.
Head of P3O (permanent office) – may be called head of portfolio office	The head of P3O establishes and runs the office(s).
	The role requires strong leadership and management skills, coupled with strong PPM or strategy/business-planning skills to ensure the integrity of the portfolio and programmes and projects. The individual will need to develop and maintain robust relationships with all parts of the business to ensure that all initiatives meet the requirements of the portfolio direction group/investment committee and the portfolio progress group/change delivery committee. They will also need to work with business areas to identify any gaps in initiatives and to understand what activities are planned to fill those gaps.
	The individual will need to understand the wider objectives of the portfolio, have credibility within the environment and be able to influence others. They must be able to develop and maintain effective working relationships with senior managers, the programme and project teams and any third-party service providers.
	The role will also provide strategic challenge, overview and scrutiny, ensuring alignment with wider policy and strategic initiatives.
	In some organizations the head of P3O may be a strategic or business-planning manager or director.
	The head of P3O may also fulfil the role of portfolio manager.
Head of programme or project office (temporary office)	The head of programme or project office establishes and runs the office.
	The role requires strong leadership and management skills, coupled with strong PPM skills to ensure the integrity of the programme or project. The individual will need to develop and maintain robust relationships with all parts of the business to ensure that all initiatives meet the requirements of the programme or project board. The individual will also need to work with business areas to identify any gaps in initiatives and to understand what activities are planned to fill those gaps.
	The individual will need to understand the wider objectives of the programme or project, have credibility within its environment and be able to influence others. They must be able to develop and maintain effective working relationships with senior managers, the programme and project teams and any third-party service providers.
	They may deputize for the programme or project manager.
	The role will also provide strategic overview and scrutiny, ensuring alignment with wider policy and strategic initiatives.

P3O management roles all require significant business experience and knowledge, as these roles are required to understand how the current portfolio contributes to the strategic direction of the organization and provide an appropriate level of scrutiny and challenge. Staff will not be able to undertake their roles successfully unless they have credibility with the senior management and board. Their roles contain key responsibilities for maintaining relationships within the business and ensuring the P3O continues to add value to the organization.

3.4.2.2 P3O generic roles

An outline of the three generic role descriptions is provided in Table 3.6. Further details of the roles and responsibilities can be found in Appendix A.

As the name implies, the generic P3O roles require a broad understanding of PPM. The generic roles are amongst the most common roles within a small P3O.

3.4.2.3 P3O functional roles

Outlines of the 15 functional role descriptions are provided in Table 3.7. Further details of the roles and responsibilities can be found in Appendix A.

Functional roles do not need to be performed by individuals who are line-managed within the P3O structure. These roles are usually managed from the originating function, such as finance, HR, marketing/PR or procurement. The individuals who undertake these roles may be embedded within the P3O (see section 3.2.2.3).

In a large P3O, these roles may be shared across multiple individuals, e.g. the risk role may be shared by a risk lead and a number of risk managers. Conversely, in small P3Os, a single person will take on multiple roles from Table 3.7, aligned with their skills and competencies and the requirements of the organization, programme or project.

Table 3.6 Outline of P3O generic role descriptions

Role name	Outline description
Portfolio analyst	The role facilitates the development and ongoing management of an optimized portfolio, ensuring senior management decisions lead to the fulfilment of strategic objectives through the delivery of programmes and projects (aligned with business-as-usual objectives).
	They develop and maintain management dashboards.
Programme or project specialist (internal consultant)	The specialist provides hands-on support for programme and project managers and plays a proactive knowledge management role in the promotion of programme and project management methods, and the roll-out of Best Management Practice.
	They provide a consultancy service to programme and project managers or programme and project boards, delivering hands-on assistance to support the successful delivery of the programme or project. This consultancy may take the form of coaching, help, advice and guidance, or may be of a specific nature in the form of facilitated workshops.
	At the beginning of a project, the specialist will work with the programme or project manager and the business to help define an appropriate level of governance and structure for effective management of the programme/project and decide on the level of support and the type of services required.
	They may provide a tailored series of workshops, which may include elements of programme/project start-up advice, risk analysis, project scoping, planning, tailoring of methods etc.
Programme or project officer (may also be referred to as programme or project coordinator or administrator, depending on level of responsibility)	The purpose of the programme or project officer is to improve the planning and delivery process by collecting and maintaining data in a consistent form. It is the responsibility of programme or project officers to implement guidelines, procedures and templates to collect and maintain this data and provide hands-on delivery support to a programme or project.

Table 3.7 Outline of P3O functional role descriptions

Role name	Outline description
Benefits and value role	The benefits and value role ensures that a consistent 'fit for purpose' approach to benefits and value management is applied across the portfolio or programme and that benefits realization is optimized from the organization's investment in change.
Commercial role	The purpose of the commercial role is to ensure the organization carries out the role of informed customer and all commercial/procurement practices and decisions meet designated standards and offer the organization 'value for money'.
	The role may be a P3O role but is more likely to be embedded in the P3O, with formal line management from the commercial, procurement or purchasing function.
	It may also exist within a virtual P3O model.
Communications and stakeholder engagement role	The communications and stakeholder engagement role ensures stakeholder analysis is undertaken regularly and a communication plan is designed and implemented successfully. In high-profile P3Os this role may manage relationships with the media.
Information management role	The information management role is the custodian and guardian of all master copies of the portfolio, programme or project's information. The role encompasses configuration management duties.
	This role should work closely with any information assurance (IA) department or function, as well as with those in the issue and change control roles.
Consultancy and performance management role	The consultancy and performance management role provides internal consultancy and expertise in PPM and organization processes focused on maintaining minimum standards and achieving target performance across the organization.
	It seeks to continuously improve performance of the portfolio, programme and projects within an organization.
	It also creates, maintains and disseminates good practice.
Finance role	The finance role establishes a professional finance function within the portfolio, programme or project to ensure the timely provision of funding and effective financial control.
	The role may be a P3O role but is more likely to be embedded in the P3O, while maintaining formal line management from the corporate finance function.
Issue role	The issue role takes the lead in ensuring that the portfolio, programme or project has effective processes in place to identify, monitor and resolve issues. It should be closely aligned with the information management, risk management and change control roles.
Change control role	The change control role takes the lead in ensuring that the portfolio, programme or project has effective processes in place to identify, monitor and deliver changes. It should be closely aligned with the information management and issue roles.
Planning and estimating role	The planning and estimating role is responsible for facilitating the development and maintenance of the portfolio, programme or project plan and dependency logs.
Quality assurance role	The quality assurance role leads the work to ensure that the new products or services delivered by the portfolio, programme or project are fit for purpose and are capable of delivering the benefits required by the relevant board/management level.
Resource management role	The resource management role ensures that current and future programmes and projects are equipped with enough staff with the right skills, at the time they are needed, and that those resources are used as efficiently as possible.

Role name	Outline description
Risk role	The risk role takes the lead in ensuring that the portfolio, programme or project has effective processes in place to identify and monitor risks, has access to reliable and up-to-date information about risks, and uses the appropriate controls and actions to deal with risks.
	The role should ensure that all risk management practices are consistent with the corporate risk management policy and strategy.
	It is closely related to the issue role.
Reporting role	The reporting role provides a reporting service to the portfolio, programme or project – it collates base data and generates reports to multiple audiences through aggregated data.
Secretariat/administrator role	The secretariat/administrator role provides portfolio, programme or project administrative support.
	It may also provide a secretariat function for the relevant boards.
Tools expert role	The tools expert role is an expert in software tools to support the change environment. The role may provide support to the PPM community to configure software or provide training and coaching in its use.
	Examples of tools may include enterprise PPM software, planning, risk, document management or collaboration tools.

Hints and tips

Scaling

In a small P3O, the roles are more likely to be generic and multifunctional, so consider whether the generic role descriptions fit what your organization requires of you. If not, build your own job descriptions by picking the key elements from the functional role descriptions. The role descriptions can also help you refine your own job descriptions, or help you refocus on tasks and activities that would make better use of your skills and time. Also, if your small team is not carrying out all the functional roles, find out who in the organization takes on those roles and build links with them or their departments.

3.5 SIZING AND TAILORING OF THE P3O MODEL

A common question asked when designing a P3O model is 'How many people will the P3O need?' followed by 'What level should they be at?'

The key drivers for the size of a P3O are:

- The number and size of the programmes and projects to be serviced by the P3O

- The number of functions and services to be provided by the P3O
- The size of the organization.

However, there are many other factors to consider.

A P3O may service a single programme, a number of programmes or the organization's full portfolio of change. The detailed design and size of individual offices within the P3O model will need to take account of the PPM maturity of the organization and the characteristics of the programmes it will serve or enable. The design and size will also depend on the P3O vision and the business drivers it is set up to serve.

Staff numbers within a P3O across an organization may vary from a single person to more than 100 people (when including delivery resources), but on average the figure is between five and ten people, with individuals undertaking a generic role or a composite functional role. High-performing organizations with mature P3Os are more likely to have larger offices, with specialized functional roles allied to a specific function or service.

Sizing a permanent organization portfolio office or hub portfolio office will be different from sizing a temporary programme or project office. When putting in place services for a temporary office, resources may be: taken from a flexible resource pool within a hub portfolio office; engaged on a temporary basis from the contract market; or engaged as a work package through a framework agreement with a management or PPM consultancy company.

The structure of the P3O model will have an impact on the number of resources required.

It may be more cost-effective to provide services to a small programme or project by upgrading an existing programme office to a hub portfolio office (for instance where the programme does not justify enough support resource to form a viable programme office in its own right) rather than establishing a dedicated programme or project office.

Consideration should also be given to which offices could be partly or wholly virtual by making use of existing corporate resources.

Where an organization has a mature organization portfolio office or hub-and-spoke model in place with flexible resource pools, the number of staff and costs are likely to be lower as experienced P3O staff are not required to go through the organizational processes learning curve and will provide a more cost-effective and efficient service.

Designing the shape and size of a P3O model completely by formula should not be attempted, as no formula can fully cater for the nuances of any given organization or programme. However, it is possible to develop a starting point for debate using the portfolio or programme value and size characteristics in the models that follow.

3.5.1 Sizing option 1 – by budget

The first model is based on the size of the financial investment in the portfolio or programme. Typically, the overall cost of the P3O will range between 3% and 5% of the total financial investment (the total investment, not the annual investment). Within this figure the level of P3O provision will vary as the portfolio changes or the programme progresses.

3.5.2 Sizing option 2 – by size

The second model is used to calculate the size of a temporary programme office and is based on the headcount of the programme. The overall headcount of the programme office is taken as a percentage of the programme headcount, as detailed in Table 3.8. The numbers in Table 3.8 represent average numbers at the point when the programme is established and going through to implementation; numbers may fluctuate during initiation and throughout the life of the programme, depending on the number of projects being supported at any moment in time and where they are in their lifecycle.

The numbers in Table 3.8 assume the programme office:

- Produces some management reporting
- Uses some basic IT tools
- Works within an environment where the level of P3M3 maturity is between 2 and 3.

Adjustment to these numbers will be required for the following situations:

- A higher or lower level of P3M3 maturity
- Additional services provided (e.g. any COE functions)
- Programmes spread over multiple locations
- Complex or novel programmes
- Programmes with a large number of third parties
- Programmes with complex finances or complex benefits management plans
- Programmes with large numbers of projects
- The need for short-term resources required for peak loading, e.g. set-up, acceptance, ends of tranches
- Programmes with complex stakeholder and communications requirements.

Table 3.8 Average headcount in temporary programme office based on size of programme

Unit	Headcount						
Programme	30	60	120	200	300	500	1000
Programme office	3	4	7	9	12	17	25
% programme office staff	10	7	6	5	4	3	3

Table 3.9 An example of a P3O sizing model (option 3)

Background information	
Working days per month	20
Portfolio board meetings per month	2
Average number of projects in the portfolio	280
Average number of complex projects in the portfolio	9
Number of programme offices in the P3O model	8
Programme office meetings per month	2
Business planning effort (days per annum)	40

Functions and services		Effort (days per month)	FTE time required	Basis for calculation
1	Planning – portfolio build, prioritization, analysis and reporting	10	0.5	5 days' planning for each of the portfolio board meetings per month
2	Planning – programme and project set-up and closure	11.2	0.6	2% of projects in set-up and closure each month, each requiring 2 days' effort
3	Planning – stakeholder engagement and communications	10	0.5	2.5 days per week to prepare and respond to communications
4	Planning – planning and estimating	42	2.1	15% of projects requiring support each month, each requiring 1 day's effort
5	Delivery – monitoring, reviewing and reporting	32	1.6	2 days' preparation for each of the programme office meetings per month
6	Delivery – risk, issue and change management	18	0.9	2 days' support for each complex project per month
7	Delivery – assurance and quality	28	1.4	5% of projects requiring assurance activity each month, each requiring 2 days' effort
8	Delivery – secretariat	6	0.3	3 days' planning for each portfolio board meeting
9	COE – internal consultancy	18	0.9	2 days' support for each complex project per month
10	COE – standards and method	20	1	20% of total effort to be spent on process improvement
	Business planning	3.3	0.2	

| *Total FTEs required* | | | *10.0* | |

FTEs per functional area (see Figure 3.6)	*FTEs*	*% effort*
Planning (including business planning)	3.9	39
Delivery	4.2	42
COE	1.9	19

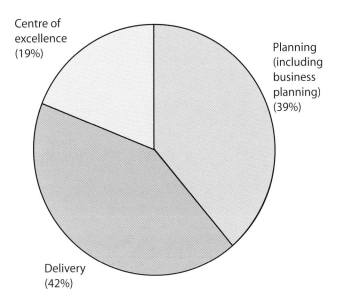

Centre of excellence (19%)

Planning (including business planning) (39%)

Delivery (42%)

Figure 3.6 FTEs per functional area for a P3O sizing model (option 3)

3.5.3 Sizing option 3 – by function

The third model uses a bottom-up approach to size the P3O. For each service the P3O plans to deliver, an estimate is made of the number of hours or days required per month to service the portfolio or programme. This can then be converted into the number of FTE (full-time equivalent employees) required for each service. Totalling up provides you with an initial estimate of the number of resources required for the P3O. (A worked example is given in Table 3.9 and Figure 3.6.)

The size of the office and the activities it carries out will vary through the project or programme lifecycle, so the exercise should be carried out at least twice, once in definition and second at the start of implementation. The sizing for some functions, such as reporting, may be driven by the number of programmes or projects within the portfolio at any point in time, whereas other functions may be driven by the governance structure and input required.

3.5.4 Additional considerations for a temporary programme or project office

The size of a temporary programme or project office will also vary throughout its lifecycle, which is where the use of flexible resource pools through hub portfolio offices can add real value.

In the mobilization stage (start-up/identification and initiation/definition) of a programme or project, there is a need for internal consultancy to facilitate establishing and tailoring standard processes, initiate the reporting cycle, develop plans, and fast-track the team and facilities set-up. This could be provided through the temporary engagement of planners, internal consultants (to facilitate collaborative start-up, planning and risk workshops) and assurance staff (to establish a quality strategy and plan) to work alongside the programme and project managers.

As the programme or project progresses into implementation and delivery, the need for a full-time planner reduces as the programme or project manager takes responsibility for the updating of the plan; however, some planning support may still be required. The need for internal consultancy reduces to a coaching role (where required), but the assurance role should continue on a part-time basis to provide continuity, support through lesson sharing, ongoing health checks, gated reviews and advice. During the delivery stage, depending on the size, complexity and innovative nature of the programme or project, there may be a need for generic support from specialists or support officers or functional-based support from a finance, communications, commercial, risk, issue or change perspective.

As the programme or project progresses into closedown and post-implementation review, the delivery resources are no longer required, but internal consultancy may be needed to facilitate independent lesson reviews and evaluations. Also, HR professionals may be asked to ensure that all professional development/appraisal information has been captured and programme or project staff are returned to their 'day jobs' or back into the flexible resource pool with the least inconvenience to individuals.

One of the most common problems found when reviewing temporary programme offices is that their programme support staff pool is too big. This is often because the number of staff is established at mobilization (initiation/definition) and then instead of releasing some of these staff as the programme or project manager takes ownership of delivery, they are kept and 'found work to do' or they do the project manager's job for them.

There are various solutions to this problem, depending on local culture and staffing policies:

- Set up hub portfolio offices with flexible resource pools, which can be used to mobilize programmes and projects and provide delivery support throughout the lifecycle. The advantage of this is a trained core of people who understand 'the way we do things around here' and require little or no training.
- Engage consultancy support in the mobilization stage (initiation/definition) of a programme or project. This may be from a COE or through work packages procured from external management or PPM consultancy companies (through a framework agreement). This approach may also ensure adherence to standards, but it requires any external consultancy company to be trained in and familiar with local standards.
- Engage contract staff to assist in the mobilization stage (initiation/definition). This is the least preferred option, as these staff are not trained in local standards and often bring their own set of templates and processes, leading to a lack of consistency across programmes and portfolios.

Additional case studies can be found in Appendix C, with a variety of organizational models and solutions.

Case study

A large temporary programme of change was operating within a government agency. The programme had a programme board (with SRO), programme manager and six discrete projects, delivering key strands of the capability. There was also a strong business change implementation team, a design authority and a separate stakeholder engagement and communications team (see Figure 3.7).

The programme office supported the programme through its lifecycle and engaged additional external consultancy support through a management consultancy for the crucial first 100 days to:

- Fast-track start-up
- Establish procedures
- Develop a programme plan (with dependencies)
- Initiate the reporting cycle
- Establish information management
- Develop a strategy for quality output
- Initiate risk, issue and change management
- Engage with the departmental COE to provide good-practice standards and templates
- Provide facilitation support for kick-off workshops.

While the external consultancy team supported the mobilization of the programme with the programme office manager, a parallel internal recruitment exercise took place to build the core support team. This team had to carry out a set of functional activities on behalf of the programme and the projects. However, the projects were providing administration resources to support themselves. The programme office therefore recruited senior individuals to fulfil the functional roles. These individuals were also permanent members of staff who could be made available, so the functional roles were tailored to meet their strengths and expertise.

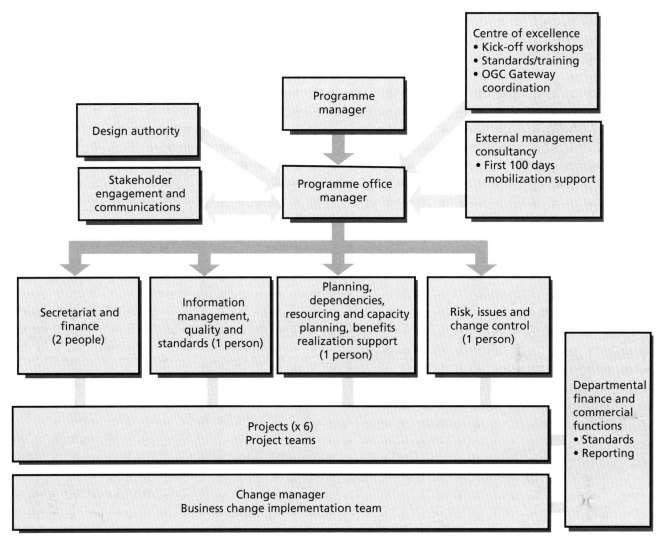

Figure 3.7 Government temporary programme office with external mobilization support

How to implement or re-energize a P3O

4

4 How to implement or re-energize a P3O

Purpose of this chapter

Chapter 2 was about understanding the value of the P3O to the organization – the problems to be solved and the opportunities to be maximized. It also looked at ways to engage senior management to get their commitment and support for a new or re-energized P3O. It set the scene for this chapter by producing the mandate along with the outline vision statement, the first iteration of the blueprint and an outline business case for the future P3O model.

Chapter 3 took the business case and vision statement created in Chapter 2, developed them through the design process to identify the most appropriate P3O model for the organization, and identified the functions and services to be provided. The design of the P3O model, along with the current and target levels of P3M3 maturity of the organization, will determine the most appropriate implementation approach.

This chapter provides guidance on the best-practice approaches to programme and project delivery that are recommended to implement or re-energize the P3O, with a particular focus on *Managing Successful Programmes* (MSP).

4.1 INTRODUCTION

There are many checklists, techniques and processes that can help an organization to design and implement a P3O or re-energize an existing one. These include:

- A P3O implementation lifecycle for establishing/improving capability and the role of the P3O model, based on MSP principles and processes
- How to use the results of a P3M3 assessment to set targets to enable the establishment and prioritization of the projects dossier or project deliverables (for start-up, improvement and recovery of underperforming P3O models)
- Guidance on example timeframes for the various levels of P3M3 maturity and projects (e.g. P3O start-up) within the programme

- An understanding of implementation success factors and key threats to delivery
- Consideration of organizational change issues, including how to engage P3O stakeholders effectively
- The need for ongoing periodic review and recording lessons
- The requirement to integrate with the yearly business planning cycle for a permanent element of the P3O such as a portfolio office.

Whatever the approach taken, it is important to have a good understanding of the problems you are intending to solve or the opportunities you want to maximize, supported by a vision of the future P3O provision and a time-phased plan to achieve that vision.

In some organizations, where there is insufficient stakeholder buy-in for a programme or project, the initial formation of the P3O and early improvements are often delivered with an evolutionary approach, using small incremental business changes delivered by a P3O enthusiast. Without appropriate funding and buy-in, the services provided will be of limited scope, and effort must be focused on building credibility through the value of these services offered in order to gain the required investment in time and money to design and deliver an appropriate P3O model for the organization.

Due to the significant level of business change involved (including the need to change mindsets and behaviours), it is recommended that the implementation or re-energizing of the P3O is managed as a programme using MSP, with:

- A defined budget, expected outcomes and timescales to deliver
- Appropriate governance, including a P3O sponsor to act as project executive or senior responsible owner (SRO) for the programme
- Adherence to an appropriate lifecycle and processes.

Hints and tips

Demonstrating the benefits of applying Best Management Practice standards and procedures to the programme or project to implement or re-energize the P3O is an ideal way of gaining recognition of the value a P3O can deliver.

However, it is recognized that in some organizations, programme management may not yet have been adopted or the change may be limited to a simple office set-up or introduction of a new system or service, in which case the design and implementation or re-energizing of the P3O may be managed as a project.

Hints and tips

A best-in-class P3O comprises a portfolio office that provides a realistic overall picture of the organization's portfolio, with standardized reporting rolled up into management dashboards. This is supported by centre of excellence (COE) functions and services, assurance (not audit) and delivery services that are accessible to all across the business. The most successful P3Os are proactively working with business leaders to jointly determine the services they should offer to maximize value from investment in programmes and projects.

An optimal, mature P3O is unlikely to be achieved through a single-tranche blueprint: there may need to be multiple tranches of benefit delivery with intermediate blueprints along the journey to maturity.

In this situation, the key activities and documents used within the lifecycles are still valid, though they will obviously be scaled down in terms of size and complexity. It is essential that there is a P3O sponsor at an appropriate level within the organization, there is buy-in from all the necessary stakeholders, and the changes to be implemented can be demonstrated to add value to the organization.

4.2 IMPLEMENTATION LIFECYCLE FOR A PERMANENT P3O

Figure 4.1 shows a typical lifecycle for implementing or re-energizing a permanent P3O. As discussed earlier, this lifecycle is compatible with MSP themes, principles, processes and products. This guidance covers the key activities only. An experienced programme manager should be engaged to deliver the programme and develop a detailed plan containing all the activities required for programme delivery.

Hints and tips

The implementation or re-energizing of a P3O may be only part of a larger programme, e.g. a programme to introduce effective portfolio management into the organization.

4.2.1 Identify

The key activities within this process are covered in Chapter 2.

The current-state assessment covers two aspects: the current P3O capability and the level of PPM maturity of the organization.

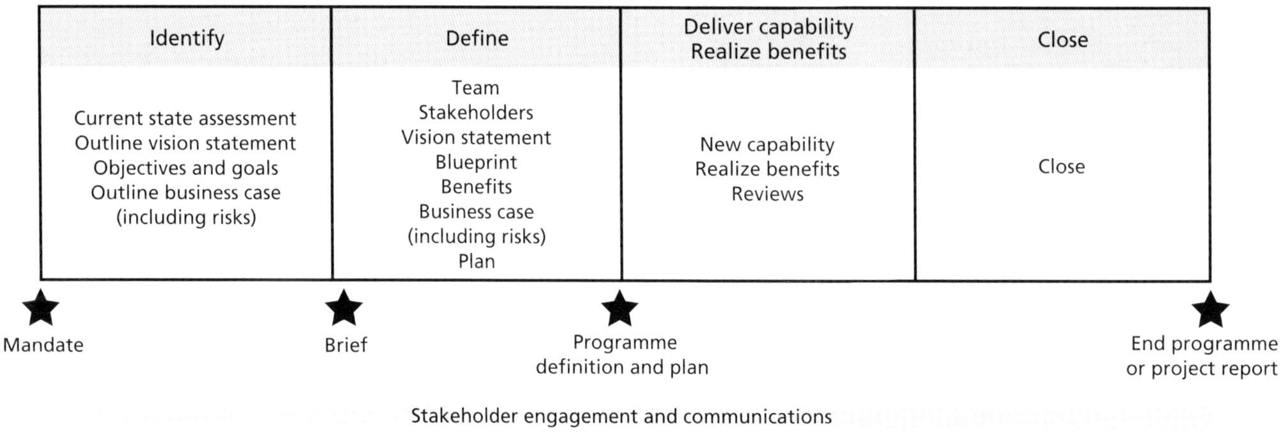

Identify	Define	Deliver capability Realize benefits	Close
Current state assessment Outline vision statement Objectives and goals Outline business case (including risks)	Team Stakeholders Vision statement Blueprint Benefits Business case (including risks) Plan	New capability Realize benefits Reviews	Close
★ Mandate	★ Brief	★ Programme definition and plan	★ End programme or project report

Stakeholder engagement and communications

Figure 4.1 Implementation lifecycle for a permanent P3O model

Assessing the current P3O capability will provide information on the functions and services already provided by the business and the resources that are currently involved in providing them. If there is a recognized P3O, the programme or project to be undertaken will be focused on moving from the current P3O model to a new P3O model – a re-energizing programme or project. Additional time and focus may be required to engage with those who are currently receiving functions and services from the existing P3O, as these functions and services may not be provided in the new P3O model. Additionally, the current perception of the quality and value of the functions and services will have an impact on the support for the programme or project. The analysis will also provide an indication of the current skills and experience available that may be utilized in the implementation team or in one of the offices within the new operational P3O.

Assessing the PPM maturity of the organization, using P3M3 or some other framework, provides information that will influence the proposed model (see Chapter 3) but will also influence the implementation method (as discussed in section 4.1).

Outputs from the Identify process include the objectives and structure of the future P3O model through an outline vision statement and programme brief, and guidance on developing a business case to justify the investment in the P3O and provide an ongoing reference point for the value it will add to the organization. These will be developed further in the next phase.

4.2.2 Define

Activities associated with the Define process need careful planning in order to design the detailed future-state P3O blueprint and develop governance strategies to ensure that it continues to align with strategic objectives.

The key activities within the Define process are as follows:

1   Team – establish the implementation team

2   Stakeholders – identify and analyse stakeholders

3   Vision statement– refine the vision statement

4   Blueprint – develop the P3O blueprint

5   Benefits – develop, model and validate the benefits

6   Business case (including risks) – develop the business case, risk register and risk management strategy

7   Plan – identify stages/tranches of delivery and develop the implementation or transition plan.

Note that these activities are not sequential and often happen in parallel with one other. All definition activities are scalable, and for a small organization or small P3O operation, the approach should be tailored to suit local need and available resources.

4.2.2.1 Define activity 1 – Establish the implementation team

It is critical that the implementation team has the right mix of skills and experience (or has access to them) to ensure that a pragmatic P3O model is defined and implemented. Fundamentally, a core team with capabilities in strategic and business analysis, and portfolio, programme and project management is required, with associated specialist knowledge of processes, tools and techniques.

The members of the team set up to establish or transform the P3O may also be the individuals who will form the core team working within the operational P3O going forward, or they may be a mix of long-term staff and interim resources. Particular care should be taken in the choice of programme manager. There should be clear separation from the P3O sponsor (who will take the role of project executive or SRO for the programme). Where the programme manager will take on the role of head of P3O, or head of a programme or project office, independent assurance should be engaged to validate the design of the P3O.

Hints and tips

Scaling

In a small organization, or where the P3O office consists of only one or two people, there may not be a formal implementation team. However, it is important that the individuals who will operate the P3O are given appropriate support, coaching or training, including interim external support, to enable them to be effective in implementing the new P3O functions and services. Also, find out who else in your organization has complementary or similar skills and competencies, and work closely with them to develop collaborative working.

The following checklist provides a guide to the additional skills and competencies that may be required:

Processes

- Portfolio, programme and project planning and scheduling
- Financial management
- Enterprise architecture processes and principles
- Portfolio management
- Governance design and implementation
- Procurement
- Contract and supplier management
- Strategic management
- Risk management
- Portfolio, programme and project assurance
- Requirements management
- Benefits management.

Organizational

- Organizational design
- Roles and responsibilities development
- Organizational change management
- Training
- Mentoring.

Technology

- PPM software installation, configuration and training
- Project scheduling software
- Spreadsheet and database design and development
- Knowledge management systems
- Web portal development.

Information

- Performance management
- Management reporting
- Governance secretariat
- Information and knowledge management
- Enterprise architecture modelling
- Strategic planning.

In terms of identifying potential candidates and appointing roles, it is important to have a mix of those with knowledge of the organization's current practices (if these are in place) and culture, and those with specialist skills, to ensure that a balance of new and current ways of working is available to the P3O programme.

Where the P3O model cannot be developed by internal staff, either owing to a lack of the right skills and competencies or because resources are unavailable, it will be necessary to buy in external expertise to fast-track the programme or project through the blueprint design and into implementation. When engaging external consultants or contractors, ensure they will work together as a coherent team, with complementary skills and experience. An early deliverable should be the engagement or appointment of the permanent head of P3O, so a skills transfer can take place from the external supplier and the head of P3O can have input into the design of the P3O blueprint from an early stage.

The use of expert reference or focus groups (both internal and external) is strongly recommended, as it enables input across the multiple specialist areas of knowledge required within the scope of a P3O.

4.2.2.2 Define activity 2 – Identify and analyse stakeholders

As with any change programme that affects multiple stakeholders, it is essential to understand who the members of the stakeholder community are, who will be affected or impacted by the changes, who will be winners and who may be losers. Thus:

- Carry out a stakeholder analysis of all those involved in or impacted by the P3O model development or improvement programme. This will include senior managers, business unit managers, the programme and project management delivery community, P3O staff (old and new), external suppliers and business process owners of linked units.
- A key success factor is to enthuse a champion (P3O sponsor) – a senior manager with authority, influence and charisma who can sell the P3O vision and engage commitment across the organization at all levels, particularly at senior manager level, and who can also obtain investment funds.
- Develop an effective communication plan to educate stakeholders in the value of the P3O, make them aware of the services the P3O will or does offer, and engage their commitment and enthusiasm for the new world that will follow the P3O model roll-out. However, do not underestimate the amount of resistance that is likely to be encountered. Members of the PPM community who deliver change are often the most resistant to change themselves.
- Do not just communicate what is being done (or could be done): develop a marketing plan for the P3O; develop a 'brand' and a slogan or strap

line; use 'selling tactics'; advertise successes (using facts and numbers); and use case studies, leaflets and posters to announce what the P3O does and has achieved. Use all available media, particularly intranets, portals, internal newsletters and team briefings, to get the message across.

■ Finally, don't just communicate once – use regular programme/project management forums to share lessons, coach people in new approaches, tools and techniques, and make the P3O the first port of call when an issue arises.

Hints and tips

Scaling

Even small offices within the P3O with just one or two people need to understand their stakeholders, whom they serve, whom they work with and whom they impact upon. Do other members of the organization understand what you do? Do they recognize your successes? If you don't tell them, they won't know. Raise your profile and develop a clear understanding of your stakeholder community: you might be surprised where future support may come from. However, be aware of the consequences. One organization successfully marketed itself across a new division and was overwhelmed by the response and increased requests for help – this led to bringing in temporary staff for the short term while a formal business case was developed to ensure the office continued to add value.

4.2.2.3 Define activity 3 – Refine the vision statement

Ensure that the outline vision statement developed at the start of the P3O change programme (see section 2.4.3 for an example of a vision statement) is refined to include a high-level view of the outcomes that will be achieved across process, organizational, technology and information areas once the programme is completed. This will be critical as a marketing tool to communicate the goals of the programme across the wider organization and build momentum, as a significant number of staff may be impacted.

4.2.2.4 Define activity 4 – Develop the P3O blueprint

The blueprint will describe the future state of the P3O, to be met either in a single tranche of delivery or through multiple tranches (along with an intermediate blueprint for each tranche). It should include sections on:

1 Processes (including operational costs and performance levels)

2 Organizational structure

3 Technology (including tools and techniques)

4 Information and data requirements.

Blueprint section 1 – Processes (including operational costs and performance levels)

Define and agree which functions and services will be required to address the issues you are facing and to meet future expectations of the P3O. Appendix F provides a useful checklist of functions and services focused on the different levels and types of offices within the P3O model. Use the tables in Appendix F as a 'pick and mix' guide to identify which functions and services are required immediately and which may be aspirations for future tranches of delivery as the organization and staff, both within and outside the P3O, gain maturity over time. This will help to develop a phased implementation plan.

In terms of delivering the functions and services, it is important to understand how they will be implemented and operated, i.e. whether a manual process or automated processes/tools will be used. This may evolve over the various implementation tranches, with an initial manual business process moving to a simple tool approach using spreadsheets and eventually evolving into an organization-wide integrated tool. At this stage it is important to define 'what' functions and services the P3O will contribute to and 'which' functions or services the P3O will own as part of the P3O model.

Consider using pictures, process models or swimlanes (see section 5.6.8) to demonstrate processes, interfaces, roles and responsibilities. You are more likely to gain the attention of senior managers and other users of the P3O if the key processes defined within the P3O model can be described on a single page.

It is also important to design and implement P3O metrics or performance indicators to measure how successful the P3O is in delivering the functions and services, and to show their value to the organization. These measures should be linked to the key performance indicators (KPIs) developed to measure the success of the P3O. This is necessary to maintain continued support for the P3O and to justify the investment in its set-up and ongoing operation. Keep the performance measures simple or no one will bother to collect or maintain them. Ensure they justify the ongoing existence of the P3O.

Some general success measures that may be used to determine the effectiveness of the P3O over time are:

- **Number of programmes and projects delivered to plan** Measuring the effectiveness of the P3O in providing decision support and achieving plans
- **Number of programmes and projects rejected, deferred, re-scoped and cancelled by stage** Measuring the effectiveness of governance in ensuring that poor business change investments are stopped in a timely manner
- **Average programme and project delivery timescales** Measuring the effectiveness of the P3O in increasing throughput by reducing average programme and project lifecycles and improving the predictability of delivery timescales
- **Variance between forecasted benefits and benefits realized** Measuring the outcomes of the P3O in facilitating programme and project delivery and ensuring there is a focus on measuring and realizing benefits
- **Cost of risk mitigation against level of residual risk (risk treatment)** Measuring the effectiveness of risk response actions against the reduction in the inherent risk of the portfolio
- **Audits of level of compliance to processes** Measuring the effectiveness of the P3O in having fit-for-purpose approaches that are used by the programme and project community
- **Number of programmes and projects delivering non-red gateway reviews** Measuring the reduction in red gateway assessments, including the reduction in the number of red-specific recommendations in the action plan and delivery confidence assessments
- **Staff turnover** Measuring staff morale and individuals' alignment with the P3O. Exit interviews can also be used to supplement this success measure

- **Staff development** Measuring spending on staff to improve the P3O, qualification levels across the resource pool, and metrics on matching skills to programmes and projects (both within the P3O and within the programme and project delivery resource pool)
- **Stakeholder surveys** Measuring objectively the level of stakeholder satisfaction in the operation of the P3O – is it delivering the services its customers want and need, and is it perceived to offer value for money?
- **P3M3 assessment** Evaluating the change in the organization's level of P3M3 maturity as a result of investment in the P3O model over time
- **Post-programme and project reviews/health checks** Measuring the compliance of programmes and projects to the programme and project management frameworks, strategies and policies, and the achievement of planned business benefits
- **Happiness quotient** Measuring how happy individuals are with how the organization delivers change.

Hints and tips
Scaling

As a small office within the P3O, you may feel that setting up performance measures is not a good use of your time. However, consider using performance measures to justify your existence or your future growth plans. Demonstrating value and attributing it to your team's actions is the best way of justifying increased investment. Also consider using some of these performance measures within your own personal objectives to focus attention on your achievements.

Blueprint section 2 – Organizational structure
GOVERNANCE

The underlying goal in establishing an organization-wide P3O is to bring structure to decision-making and business change practices across an organization, with a clear line of sight from strategic goals down to local change decisions and working practices. It is important to note that practices will already be in place within the organization, which may not be structured to deliver optimum value to the organization.

In designing the P3O model, a key outcome will be a joined-up governance model that enables a clear strategic understanding of priorities, progress, key risks and issues, thereby enabling confident decision-making with points of accountability at all levels.

A simple technique to determine the future governance model is to start with a generic model of portfolio, programme and project organization (see Figure 4.2) and align the organization with these roles and responsibilities. It is important to understand the organization's business governance structures and decision-making bodies, as decisions made within the change environment will impact on business as usual and vice versa. The governance model should describe who makes what decisions and when, who may be impacted by those decisions,

and what the rules for delegation of authority and escalation of risks, issues and changes will be. This will help define the P3O stakeholder community, provide the basis for a communications plan, and provide points of reference and formal accountability when issues arise within the portfolio, programme or project governance structures.

Once the conceptual governance model is developed and agreed within the P3O blueprint, it can subsequently be translated into a functional model (i.e. giving names or positions to governance structures and accountabilities). The component offices of the P3O model should sit within the overall organization governance model.

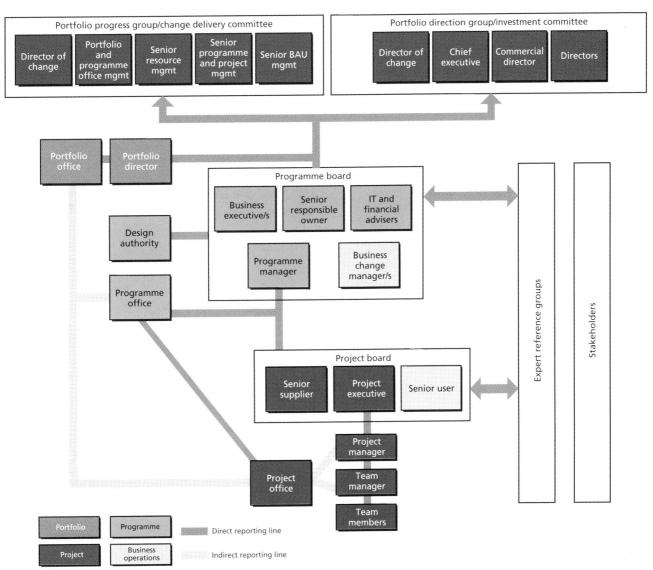

Figure 4.2 Generic portfolio, programme, project and P3O model organization, consisting of the portfolio office, programme office(s) and project office(s)

P3O ORGANIZATION, ROLES AND SIZING

Once it has been agreed where the component offices of the P3O model will sit, where they will report to and whom they will serve in terms of customers, the P3O model itself should be designed in terms of reporting lines, centralized versus decentralized reporting, roles and responsibilities.

The functions and services that are owned by the P3O model, or that the P3O contributes to at portfolio, programme or project level, will drive the role types, the organizational components and the number of staff required to operate the P3O functions and services.

When building the P3O staffing plan, first define the staff skills profiles, assess the current staff (if a P3O exists) or the staff that are available, and define an action or development plan to fill any gaps. Consider options for training, mentoring or coaching for existing or new staff. Buy in short-term help to fast-track the set-up stage.

Finally, don't neglect relevant qualifications for staff within the P3O, to give credibility to the people and the services they provide. Chapter 3 and the appendices of this publication provide useful reference material, as follows:

- For an in-depth look at P3O models, sizing, functions and services, and the roles/responsibilities within them, see Chapter 3
- For roles and responsibilities, see Appendix A
- For case studies, and for examples of P3O models that may be appropriate for tailoring to your organization, see Appendix C
- For an in-depth look at functions and services and how they are implemented in different offices of the P3O model, see Appendix F.

ORGANIZATIONAL RELATIONSHIPS

The P3O will require commitment from other parts of the organization to undertake parts of processes, comply with policies and standards, and potentially integrate their processes with the P3O model.

It is important that any changes to current practices within other parts of the organization as a result of developing or enhancing a P3O model are documented and agreed.

Determine who will be the business process owner and who will be the contributor to the business processes. The P3O may be either, but it is necessary to be clear as to which. See section 3.3.3 for further information on integrating with other business units.

CULTURE

It is important to document and agree the type of P3O culture that the organization should strive for in developing the P3O blueprint. Some characteristics that may be required for an effective P3O model include:

- Information sharing
- Focus on learning rather than blame
- Value focus to all activities
- Innovative
- Service-focused
- Proactive analysis rather than data collection
- Pragmatic approach, flexing where appropriate
- Facilitating rather than directing
- Managing to objectives
- Believing in continuous improvement through recorded lessons.

It is also important to understand the organizational culture into which the P3O model will be delivering, and to adapt the approach and communications to suit that culture.

Case study

A government agency already had in place several programmes that had evolved local processes over time. The agency decided to set up an organization portfolio office to provide overall portfolio-level support and encourage consistency in the way the programmes were managed and controlled.

Taking account of the current culture meant that the portfolio office did not impose strict new processes and templates on the programme offices from Day 1, but allowed them to continue in much the same way as before while setting out a series of minimum principles with mandated elements for investment proposals, business cases and reporting. All mandated elements were those necessary to allow ease of roll-up of information and presentation of that information to the agency investment group by the portfolio office.

Moving towards a culture where all processes and templates were consistent was achieved over time by setting up a working group of all programme office representatives and selecting the best from across all programmes. Because the programme staff felt they were creating their own solution rather than the portfolio office imposing it on them, acceptance and adherence was high.

P3M3 perspectives	P3M3-specific attributes supported by PPM tools
Management control	• Lifecycle control • Gates, stages and tranches • Change control • Issue control and management • Progress monitoring • Clarity of end state • Interventions and redirection • Configuration management
Benefits management	• Benefits management process and workflow management • Benefits management information and benefits realization plans • Benefits profiling, categorization, ownership and measurement • Management of benefits realization activities • Business change management • Business performance management
Stakeholder management	• Stakeholder identification and analysis • Structured engagement cycles • Regular and effective communications • Sophistication in the use of channels and message delivery • Processing and actioning feedback
Organizational governance	• Initiative optimization • Strategic alignment of initiatives • Governance process and workflow management • Existence of control boards • Approvals and authorization • Control and reporting structures • Legislative compliance • Compliance and integration with corporate standards • Assurance for project and programme compliance • Alignment between PPM and organizational hierarchy
Financial management	• Financial reporting and monitoring • Integration to business planning cycle • Actual budget and forecast PPM expenditure • Staged funding release • Financial tolerances setting process • Financial management information on costs and benefits • Investment management process and workflow management • Project proposal management, financial appraisal and business cases
Risk management	• Enterprise-level visibility of risk exposure due to PPM • Tracking of resource and budgetary implications of risks • Risk categorization, assessment and audit • Risk registers, tracking and management • Risk management process and workflow management
Resource management	• Resource optimization of resources across initiatives • Resource management process and workflow management • Capacity and capability building • Supply chain management • Resource monitoring, estimation and forecasting of utilization • Utilization and efficiency • Integration of operational and PPM needs

Figure 4.3 Aligning P3M3 attributes with tool capabilities

Blueprint section 3 – Technology (including tools and techniques)

TYPES

The tools and technologies that support the P3O business processes and information flows may be as simple as documents, forms, spreadsheets and databases, or much more sophisticated. It is important to note that tools and technologies should not necessarily be limited to schedule management or planning-and-control-related software. Consideration should also be given to the level of integration to limit or remove data duplication at the programme or project manager and team levels.

Chapter 5 gives examples of tools and technologies that should be considered when developing the blueprint.

ORGANIZATIONAL MATURITY

It is critical to match the PPM maturity of the organization with the sophistication of the tools and technologies to be employed in achieving pragmatic solutions. It may be that a manual process is more appropriate at the outset than an automated process or tools. Tools may evolve over time, with the initial manual business process or simple spreadsheet tool approach eventually evolving into an organization-wide integrated tool.

Figure 4.3 provides a list of the P3M3 attributes across each perspective where tools may support increasing the level of P3M3 maturity of the organization. It is important to note that this list is not exhaustive, but it may be used to derive specific requirements for the organization.

Blueprint section 4 – Information and data requirements

The blueprint will detail all the data requirements of the P3O to support the various functions and services to be provided. Careful consideration must be given to the three aspects of information assurance (IA) and the additional costs that appropriate controls and processes will incur.

It is also important to document the proposed reporting requirements for the future-state P3O. This will need to integrate with the organizational component of the blueprint and align with the requirements of:

- Governance groups, e.g. senior management board, divisional boards, programme and project boards, steering groups

- Component offices within the P3O (e.g. between portfolio, programme and project offices)
- Programme and project delivery groups
- Corporate support functions, e.g. finance, audit, quality, procurement, marketing and communications
- Benefit owners, business change managers and business change teams
- External (if required).

The blueprint should also describe the need for alignment with the principle of management by exception and the use of highlight and exception-based reporting. At this stage, the detailed content of these reports is not required, but it will be detailed in the subsequent initiatives to deliver the capability. However, a high-level overview of the content of management dashboards will add value and help gain commitment.

Information flows will vary from organization to organization, to align with the specific governance bodies within that organization. An example of an information flow for a P3O model is shown in Table 4.1. It should be noted that this is a case study and contains report and role names used locally within the organization.

4.2.2.5 Define activity 5 – Develop, model and validate the benefits

Even if you are using a project approach (or a series of business process changes being made as part of business as usual) to implement the new or re-energized P3O model, it is essential to focus on the benefits the P3O will deliver and formally track these over time, so take time out to understand and adopt MSP processes and products. Develop a benefits management strategy, benefits map, benefit profiles and benefits realization plan as defined in MSP.

In creating benefit profiles and developing the benefits management strategy, there are significant opportunities to generate commitment and support for the P3O concept and its value to the organization. Once the affected business areas are identified, undertake a series of workshops to determine the initial, interim and final outcomes to be achieved by progressive transition to the P3O model. This can then be used as an input to determine the planned benefits as a result of the new capabilities delivered or more benefits with less investment.

Case study

A European public-sector organization launched a multimillion-euro project, which was more than 70% financed from European restructuring funds. The reporting requirements were extensive, with more than 10 different reports plus 70 other documents for different institutions – including two central government institutions – each month. Each report had to adhere to a strictly defined format, containing various items of information, including extensive financial data. The reports were so complex that the project team designated a separate person to prepare each of them. The designated report owner was responsible for gathering data from five different team managers, report preparation and report distribution.

Soon, problems occurred. Team managers were tired of giving practically the same information to different people. Reports prepared by different people, based on information collected at different times, tended to be incoherent and the lack of joined-up timing meant that there was no single consistent view of progress. The source information was incorrect or inadequate, as team managers tended to give it just to get rid of the people asking for it. As a result, some of the reports were rejected, causing financial problems for the project – payment tranches were suspended.

An external consultant was brought in to examine the issues and propose a solution. The conclusion was to use PRINCE2 reporting formats and processes, supported by the introduction of a project office to manage reporting. Each team manager was obliged to prepare monthly reports in a predefined format (containing all the necessary information to feed the multiple stakeholder reports). Those reports were collected by one person who, using simple IT tools, was able to amalgamate this information into reports in the formats required by the different institutions.

The benefits of this were clear:

- Reduced cost – one person instead of ten
- Better team morale among team managers
- Reports contained accurate and coherent information from a single source, aligned to a single point in time
- Subsequent payment tranches were executed without delay.

Spelling out the specific benefits for each user may encourage them to become champions and help to influence stakeholders across the organization. However, care must be taken in recognizing that some current users or current P3O staff may not benefit from the new or revised model and therefore may resist the change.

Some of the benefit drivers (translatable into benefit profiles) that a P3O may provide are:

- **Increased cost savings** Delivering the same capabilities with less business change investment
- **Increased cost avoidance** Reducing the investment in outputs that do not lead to planned business benefits, and stopping such programmes or projects either before they get off the ground or while they are under way
- **Increased strategic alignment** Reducing investment in programmes and projects that only provide tactical value to the business goals of the organization
- **Increased programme and project throughput** Delivering more change through programmes and projects with the same investment
- **Optimization of benefits** Delivering more business benefits with the same business change investment or, by effectively monitoring and measuring benefits, ensuring business as usual puts the effort into achieving them
- **Increased level of portfolio management maturity** Optimizing investment as the portfolio delivers due to improved visibility, decision support and control
- **Reduction in threats to the organization** Stronger alignment between planned and actual business change investment as a result of reduced expenditure on the mitigation of threats, or issue management
- **Maximization of opportunities** Achieving higher returns on investment in business change as a result of identifying opportunities for additional benefits as new capabilities are delivered
- **More effective use of resources** Less non-productive time for resources and/or a reduction in the reliance on external resources in the delivery of new capabilities.

Table 4.1 An example of a P3O information flow

ID	Report name	Accountability	Report recipient	Meeting and report frequency
Portfolio level				
1	Portfolio report – management dashboard with supporting papers, including benefits reviews	Portfolio director or portfolio office manager	Senior management	Monthly
2	Portfolio risk and issue papers for resolving portfolio conflicts across the business units, and specifying significant assurance-related risks or issues for programmes and projects	Portfolio director or portfolio office manager, with contributions from business units, programmes and projects as required	Senior management	By exception
3	Escalated programme and project risk and issue papers	Programme and project boards	Senior management (tabled through portfolio director)	By exception
4	Mission-critical business cases	Senior responsible owners	Portfolio board	As required
5	Operational business plans (describing core business and changes to core business)	Business unit managers	Strategic planning P3O	Annually or as necessary
Programme level				
6	Business unit portfolio report – management dashboard and supporting papers	Hub (divisional, department or business unit) portfolio office	Business unit senior manager P3O	Monthly
7	Escalated programme and project risk and issue papers	Programme and project boards	Business unit senior manager	By exception
8	Business unit portfolio risk and issue papers for resolving portfolio conflicts within the business unit, and specifying significant assurance-related risks or issues for programmes and projects within the business unit	Business unit programme office with contributions from programme and project boards	Business unit senior manager P3O	By exception
9	Benefit reviews	Business change managers	Business unit senior manager	As documented in benefits management strategy
Project level				
10	Project mandates	Idea generator	P3O	As required
11	Project business case	Project manager	Project executive P3O	On acceptance of project mandate into approved programme or portfolio

ID	Report name	Accountability	Report recipient	Meeting and report frequency
12	Highlight and exception reports	Project manager	Project executive P3O	Highlight reports may be monthly or fortnightly on acceptance of project business case
13	End project report	Project manager	Project executive P3O	On agreed completion of the project
14	Post-project report	Project executive or nominated business owner	Business unit manager P3O	Defined time after project completed when benefits and original business-case investment can be assessed
15	Risk and issues	Project manager	Project executive	As required
Transition management				
16	Benefit profiles	Business-case generator or business change manager	Business unit programme office P3O	In parallel with business case and updated periodically
17	Transition plan	Programme or project manager with contribution by senior user or business change manager	Project executive P3O	When approaching readiness for implementation of business change

4.2.2.6 Define activity 6 – Develop and confirm the business case (including risks)

The development of the outline business case is covered in Chapter 2. At this stage in the lifecycle, more detailed information becomes available as the blueprint develops, and the business case should continue to be revised and refined throughout the Define stage. Detailed costings for the resources and tools required to deliver the agreed functions and services will be more accurate and, along with the proposed implementation plan, a baseline cash flow can be developed. An example of a business case is provided in Appendix B.

As with any other programme, it is necessary to document how risks will be managed and communicated within the risk management strategy and risk communication plan. Each programme will have its own risks. The following are common areas identified as the most likely sources of threats to the achievement of the blueprint for the P3O:

■ **Lack of continued senior management commitment** Success relies on the continued visible support and commitment of investment and required business resources by senior

management. Any reduction in the level of commitment will negatively impact the successful implementation of the P3O model.

Hints and tips

■ Do not proceed if there is no senior management consensus on the P3O vision. Revise the scope to what is acceptable and supportable by a viable business case.

■ Regularly confirm the planned benefits of the P3O model and report performance to these goals.

■ Manage senior management as key stakeholders to programme success.

■ **Insufficient support to utilize or recruit required skills** Functions and services will only realize the anticipated benefits if they are provided by individuals with the right skills and experience. Trying to provide too many services across too wide a community with inadequate resourcing will lead to overstretched resources, poor delivery of services and a reduction in the credibility of the P3O.

Hints and tips

- Use MoV techniques to clearly demonstrate the value of the proposed functions and services to the organization, with clear alignment of the functions and services with the required skills and experience.
- Only commit to the implementation of services that add value in their own right and can be delivered with the skills and experience available.
- Limit the functions and services to those that can be provided competently by the resources available.
- Limit the breadth of services (i.e. to one programme or project) to ensure an acceptable level of service is provided.

- **Resistance to change by impacted staff** Implementation of the P3O model will deliver new and consistent processes with goals of improving productivity and eliminating investment in pet projects. Individual project managers may feel that they are losing control of their projects as a result of this centralized approach. This may result in resistance to change by those staff who are impacted by it.

Hints and tips

Alert the P3O sponsor and other key roles in the programme (such as business change manager, senior users etc.) to the risk of staff resistance to change as early as possible, so they are able to take proactive measures at a senior level to reduce this resistance, or are prepared to take action before it starts to have an impact on the programme.

- **Lack of common language among programme team or impacted staff** Given the multitude of approaches to portfolio, programme and project management, stakeholders may have difficulty understanding the different terms used in establishing the P3O model, which may impact on the quality of outputs or lead to resistance to change.

Hints and tips

Agree alignment with global standards (such as PRINCE2, MSP, MoP, P3M3 and ITIL), provide awareness training and adopt a common glossary to ensure that all staff are at the same level of understanding.

- **Managing the implementation of the P3O model as a project** The complexity associated with the required level of business change may not be recognized if implementation of the P3O model is managed as a project. If the integration across the organization is left to the head of P3O, it may significantly reduce the potential for success. The delivery of the P3O model and the realization of its planned business benefits is a complex business change programme that requires iterative refinement of the capabilities to be delivered and associated activities. It also impacts upon numerous business units and business change principles across the organization.

Hints and tips

Build consensus around the concept of the P3O model across the organization in advance of any implementation activity.

- **Overly focusing on toolsets** Significant benefits can be achieved through the adoption of PPM solutions (and other software applications) to provide process automation and improved visibility and control. Implementing sophisticated tools in an immature organization or implementing tools that need a significant investment in time and money to embed into the organization can severely impact the successful delivery of programmes and projects.

Hints and tips

Investigate existing tools used by programme and project delivery staff (e.g. spreadsheets or Microsoft Project) and investigate a solution that builds on the use of these tools to reduce the investment required to embed new ones. Allow for functionality to be added over time as skills and capability grow.

Equally, recognize when to move away from manual approaches and achieve the benefits of process automation through toolsets, at the appropriate level of PPM maturity.

- **Overly focusing on processes and templates** The introduction of PPM processes and their associated principles at a detailed level may focus programme and project delivery staff on process compliance rather than the achievement of business outcomes. Focusing on whether the right template has been used rather than the quality of the information gathered will have a detrimental impact on its perceived value, as the process will be seen as an additional burden rather than a source of help.

Hints and tips

Focus on communicating process principles rather than detailed process steps (supported by appropriate training in portfolio, programme and project management) to assist staff in balancing what is required to achieve governance (e.g. gating), decision support (e.g. programme or project status reporting) and transition to new ways of working. Develop tailoring guidelines to allow the programme and project delivery community to flex processes based on the levels of risk, complexity and size of programmes and projects, and develop minimum mandatory compliance to key governance principles.

■ **Initial lack of quality of portfolio or programme information** When moving to a higher level of amalgamated information, there needs to be an acceptable level of project standardization or commonality. Generally, moving from an unstructured to a structured P3O model will mean that when information is initially brought together for amalgamated reporting, it is of poor quality or has elements missing.

Hints and tips

Ensure that data quality improvement or alignment activities are included in the transition plan to introduce amalgamated reporting.

Provide health warnings on any dashboards or reports advising on the level of accuracy or completeness of the information.

■ **Lack of capacity of impacted staff to absorb change** As PPM methods focus on numerous principles as well as processes, implementing all at once, or rolling out a toolset in one implementation, may fail because of the inability of impacted staff to understand and comply with all the new ways of working.

Hints and tips

In line with the programme approach and planned benefits, identify opportunities to undertake a number of proof-of-concept studies and prioritize the implementation of processes and impacted users. Develop local experts or champions who really understand the principles and processes or tools, and use their expertise locally as 'super users' to embed the changes.

■ **The P3O becomes the de-facto owner of business change** This is especially relevant where the P3O owns delivery resources (such as project managers or business analysts) that are then provided to the business, combined with weak governance arrangements. Essentially, where the P3O may be providing more efficient resource allocation of skills and competencies across programmes and projects by maintaining a resource pool, the P3O is subsequently blamed for failing to deliver outputs or outcomes or attain benefits management goals, i.e. it takes on an implicit ownership of the business change outcomes.

Hints and tips

Proactively communicate the role of the P3O in facilitating business owners to achieve their required business change outcomes. Ensure that the governance model is clearly defined, with clarity on how the roles of project executive, SRO, business change managers, senior managers and their teams operate effectively together. Ensure that the success measures for the P3O are established and refined with clear contribution to the organization and are regularly communicated to key stakeholders.

4.2.2.7 Define activity 7 – Plan stages or tranches of delivery

Each P3O model implementation or re-energization will have its own unique combination and phasing of initiatives to achieve the future-state business model (as defined in the blueprint). As stated previously, the priority associated with these should be driven by the largest capability gaps identified through a P3M3 assessment and what is of most value to senior management. However, it is worth noting that over half the P3Os created are closed down within a five-year timeframe – potentially before the implementation is fully completed.

Accordingly, it is important to adopt an incremental approach to reduce the adverse impacts of a 'big bang' implementation and to demonstrate early benefits to senior management from the investment. Early benefits can also be used to fund later tranches of delivery, so the evolution of the P3O becomes self-financing.

Design the implementation or re-energization plan so that the first tranche of delivery contains early critical improvement. Go for early benefits that achieve demonstrable improvements, and consider those deliverables that are simple to implement, visible to senior management and increase credibility of the P3O. For example, if implementing an organization-wide P3O model, create a portfolio register – a list of all programmes and projects being undertaken by the organization, their link to strategy, value, key stakeholders and delivery timeframe. For the first time, the senior management team will be able to see all change in the organization. Following on from that, it is possible to carry out a rationalization exercise to identify duplications of initiatives that may be counter-productive. Add exception-based reporting through a management dashboard to the portfolio toolkit, and senior managers will be able to buy into your value and continued existence. The investment cash released by stopping projects that should never have started in the first place will provide funding for investment elsewhere, potentially subsequent tranches of P3O implementation.

A key input to portfolio planning is to develop a balanced portfolio of programmes and projects with a defined investment budget and balanced set of resources. This should be aligned with business-as-usual priorities and strategic objectives. It therefore makes sense to align the development of P3O capability with the normal organization business-planning cycle. In some cases, the P3O may also manage this cycle.

Integrating the P3O processes with the yearly (or three- or five-yearly) business-planning cycle also allows for full integration of the P3O model and its benefits into the business-budgeting lifecycle. If the P3O model is designed to save x% through stopped projects, then the x% saved should be built into next year's budget for use by other initiatives. This adds impetus to making the planned savings, as the P3O staff will be held to account by senior management.

The projects dossier for a P3O programme with the objective to improve PPM maturity within the organization may include projects to design and establish:

- Organization governance model for business change
- Business planning or strategy translation framework
- Physical P3O offices (including functions and services)
- Existing programme and project portfolio identification and optimization
- P3O metrics and reporting
- Programme and project stage-gate model and framework
- Programme and project delivery model and framework
- Portfolio management model and framework
- Management metrics and amalgamated (highlight and exception) reporting model and framework
- Competency management and career management model and framework
- Requirements management model and framework
- Supplier management model and framework
- Functional models and frameworks (such as risk, benefits, information, configuration, quality and financial management)
- Training, coaching and mentoring model
- COE community model – sharing lessons and best practice
- Toolset/s implementation/s
- Assurance model
- Continual improvement model.

Hints and tips
Scaling

- For a small office within the P3O, consider a three-year phased performance improvement plan with single deliverables rather than tranches of change.
- Rather than delivering full processes and templates, consider setting principles and minimum mandated standards that are pragmatic and can be tailored.

By way of example, Figure 4.4 provides an outline plan based on this projects dossier for a P3O model containing a permanent organization portfolio

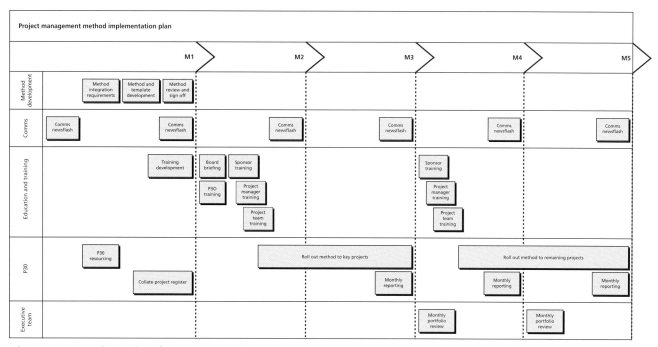

Figure 4.4 Outline plan for a P3O establishment and PPM maturity development programme

office. It operates in the private sector, with a baseline of above Level 1 P3M3 maturity and targeting Level 3 P3M3 maturity.

Key sensitivities that may impact on the development of your own projects dossier include:

■ Existing PPM maturity and targets
■ Priorities for capability development
■ Ability to embed change as a result of the culture of an organization, or other business changes impacting on staff
■ Functions and services to be embedded as a result of the P3O added value
■ Pace of change requirements
■ Resource capacity
■ Management commitment
■ Scale of the portfolio
■ Level of need to achieve early benefits to secure continued momentum
■ Risks to delivery and planned benefits.

Note that all elements of the blueprint are implicit in this plan, i.e. process, organization, tools and technologies, and information and data requirements.

This diagrammatic outline of a plan is also based on achieving early benefits in terms of visibility as to the business change initiatives being undertaken across the organization and justifying their continued investment through business-case development or refinement. Equally, early benefits are achieved

through PRINCE2, MSP, MoP and senior management training (or similar methods) to provide improved potential for successful delivery.

When considering implementing new tools and techniques, take into account the guidance provided in Chapter 5.

The following points should be considered when defining implementation success factors:

■ Consider how capability can be introduced in short tranches of around three months' duration to demonstrate early value.
■ Ensure that a common glossary is used by all design and implementation projects to ensure that a common language is being used.
■ Ensure that a stakeholder analysis is done early and that a communications plan is developed to ensure consistent messages are being given to all impacted stakeholders and there is the opportunity for them to provide feedback.
■ Programme and project delivery frameworks are generally delivered before portfolio management frameworks, as it is often necessary to get a level of project standardization in place to roll up quality decision-support information to the portfolio level. However, if portfolio management is a key priority then consider what elements of

portfolio management can be established without the building blocks of good programme and project information flowing up.

- Obtaining a baseline view of the current portfolio is a key enabler to the majority of subsequent projects. It will help gain visibility and determine the scale of the challenge, and should be undertaken early. Although this information will generally be of poor quality, it will assist in determining gaps for subsequent activity.
- Consider how a 'proof of concept' or a 'pilot' approach can be applied before full implementation, to maximize the likelihood of success. This may involve:
  - Trialling new ways of working on a project or subset of the portfolio
  - Running practices such as revised reporting in parallel to current approaches until confidence is achieved in the quality of the decision-support information
  - Focusing efforts where the most gains are to be made, e.g. the top 20 projects.
- Look for examples of good practice (or pockets of excellence) operating within the organization and develop standards around these to roll out further. Use the programme or project teams as champions to roll out their best practice.
- Consider developing manual processes to validate whether they work effectively and add value, and then automate them as a subsequent step once the process is proven.
- Bring impacted stakeholders along the capability development journey; train them early in key principles such as PRINCE2, MSP and MoP (or similar methods) and then use that knowledge in working groups for alignment and tailoring.

4.2.3 Deliver

4.2.3.1 Deliver new capability, and transition and stabilize operations

Throughout delivery it is essential to develop close links with the impacted business areas to ensure the rate of change is bearable and the required level of ongoing support is maintained. The way in which new processes and tools are implemented and embedded through delivery will have a direct impact on the credibility of, and ongoing support for, the P3O.

Hints and tips
Building relationships during delivery

Delivery offers an ideal opportunity for those in the implementation team who are going to work in the P3O to build relationships with the future customers of the functions and services they will be providing.

4.2.3.2 Realize benefits

Benefits will be realized throughout the programme to implement the P3O model, not just post-programme.

Benefit profiles must be maintained, reflecting the benefits realized and updated with the latest view of expected benefits. It is essential that delivered benefits are aligned with the programme outcomes and organization strategy, and made visible to senior management and other key stakeholders to retain their ongoing support.

4.2.3.3 Periodic reviews

As a minimum, at the end of each tranche/stage of delivery, a review should be undertaken to assess progress to date and to ensure that lessons have been learned and they have informed the approach and plan for the subsequent tranche(s). Use the P3O's gated review process to provide governance through a 'go' or 'no go' gate, demonstrating that you believe in and practise your own processes.

4.2.4 Close

The P3O model implementation or re-energization programme may have a long-term lifecycle or may enter a period of continual improvement supported by a performance improvement plan.

However, where a specific programme has been developed to set up new P3O capability, formal closure and post-implementation and benefits reviews are essential. This offers an opportunity to move from transition to making the P3O capability 'business as usual' and allows time for reflection and review – asking the question 'Was it worth it?'

External consultants or contractors who were brought in to fast-track the improvement programme may be released. The P3O should ensure that full skills transfer is complete before that happens, otherwise the benefits delivered may disappear over time.

After closing the programme, it is essential to maintain the role of P3O sponsor as a champion for the P3O and maintain relationships with the key stakeholders. The P3O needs to continue to provide functions and services that are aligned with the business requirements, and it is likely that support and investment will be required for further changes to be delivered through subsequent programmes or projects.

4.3 IMPLEMENTATION LIFECYCLE FOR A TEMPORARY PROGRAMME OR PROJECT OFFICE

Unlike the permanent P3O model described in the previous sections of this chapter, the temporary programme or project office is designed specifically for a finite lifecycle and with a more focused set of stakeholders, consisting of:

- Upward – programme or project boards
- Inward – programme or project team members
- Outward – suppliers, organization portfolio office or COE, corporate support functions etc.

Accordingly, the requirements will be different and varied depending on the size, scale and complexity of the programme or project to be supported.

All programme and project management methods, such as MSP and PRINCE2, will encompass processes and product outlines that delivery support teams such as the temporary programme or project offices will need to follow. These should be referenced in your organization when setting up a temporary programme or project office.

The following sections focus on the key success factors inherent in the definition and set-up of a temporary programme or project office.

4.3.1 Organizational context

As new programmes and projects are launched, temporary programme or project offices may be established to support them from start-up, through delivery to closure. Where there is an organization portfolio office or hub portfolio office in place, the temporary office may be resourced from central teams with standards and templates provided by a COE function. In this scenario, the start-up, running and closure of the temporary programme or project office will be a standard function or service provided by the organization portfolio office team.

Where the organization has a COE but no flexible central pool of delivery support staff, local business resources may be assigned to provide programme or project office functions or they may be sourced from the contract market or through framework partnerships (see Appendix C, Case Study 4 – retail organization, for a practical example of this). Wherever the resources come from, they should engage with the COE to seek assistance with start-up through facilitated workshops, the provision of standard processes and templates, and ongoing assurance or coaching.

In organizations where there is no organization portfolio office or COE function, the set-up and running of the temporary office will rely on the expertise of the local business team responsible for the programme or project and the maturity of their approach to PPM and the associated processes.

The physical environment will also have to be set up for the programme or project office. This can range from using existing business facilities to setting up a complete programme or project environment requiring a work space, desks, office equipment, communications infrastructure and software etc.

Some organizations support 'collaboration zones', which are specially equipped office areas with team-working tools. These may be used for facilitated workshops or to fast-track the development of plans.

4.3.2 Definition and implementation of a temporary programme or project office

It is generally reasonable to allocate up to 10% of the programme or project lifecycle timescale for the establishment of the temporary programme or project office. See Table 4.2 for sample set-up timescales.

Table 4.2 An example of temporary programme or project office establishment timescales

Programme or project lifecycle	Temporary office set-up time (approx.)
12 weeks	1 week
6 months	2½ weeks
12 months	5 weeks
24 months	10 weeks

This activity is undertaken at the commencement of the project, often in conjunction with other programme or project start-up activities.

The requirements for information flows and processes will have been developed and agreed in governance strategy documents, and the structure and functions of the temporary programme or project office will be determined in the programme or project initiation documentation for which approval is being sought. These requirements will drive the temporary programme or project office model and the processes it uses.

The programme or project office will need to establish a set of processes to be followed, templates to be used, and ways of working with the rest of the programme or project team and the governance board.

The programme or project may require a common set of tools to be established, to ensure all documents produced may be read and updated by the full programme or project team. A key requirement will be to build a configuration library and establish guidelines for the physical and electronic storage and security of documents. Over and above the normal office tools, planning, drawing and collaboration tools may be required. Chapter 5 should be referred to in planning the tools and infrastructure support.

Where the programme or project is large and would potentially benefit from a tools-based approach, consider the need for purchasing tools or developing your own and the associated timescales. It may be more efficient to use hosted solutions rather than purchase and install tools. The hosted solution may provide the same capability quickly and cost-effectively (because infrastructure, configuration and connectivity are provided by the supplier).

As part of the programme or project start-up, the COE may supply processes, templates and tools, and may assist in the setting up of information portals, collaboration and web-based tools etc. Where processes and templates are provided through a COE, consider whether they should be tailored to meet the needs of the particular programme or project being supported.

The COE should also be seen as a source of recorded lessons at the start of a new programme or project, and delivery support staff should take advice from the COE on the best way to tailor processes, tools etc. to meet the needs of the programme or project, on the basis of organizational experience.

A temporary programme or project office may be simply a single person (multi-role, multitasking programme or project officer) or may be resourced with a team of generic and/or functional-based roles (see Appendix A for typical roles and responsibilities).

Establishing a clear understanding of the stakeholders, the business environment the office will be delivering within, the scope it will be delivering and its timescales will indicate what type of skills may be required. If the programme or project has multiple stakeholders with complex communications and reporting requirements, the programme or project could benefit by having a specialist stakeholder and communications role. In the case of complex finance arrangements, it may need to invest in a full- or part-time programme or project accountant to perform the finance role. Where there are complex supplier contracts or relationships, there would be a commercial role that would focus on supplier relationships or procurement. Appendix A outlines both generic and specialist functional roles and these should be used to build job descriptions for specific resources within the programme or project office.

The members of the programme or project office may be permanent members of staff drawn from the organization portfolio office or hub portfolio office or from the business unit itself. Resources for the functional roles can be drawn from the finance, commercial or communications/PR departments and embedded in the programme or project office. They may well bring with them specialist processes and templates as well as expertise. These functional-based roles may be full- or part-time. Where they are part-time, careful negotiation should be undertaken to ensure their time in the programme or project office is used to best effect and with the full understanding and commitment of their line manager.

The members of the programme or project office may also be temporary or contract resources, brought in specifically for the programme or project. Do not underestimate or neglect the need to induct these resources both into the organization and into the standards and templates that the COE will provide. Where there are no organization standards, external resources often bring their own from previous assignments; although in the short term this will enable the team to get started quickly, it also leads to inconsistency of approach and a lack of organizational learning.

The temporary office will also benefit from an injection of time, expertise and standard approaches from a COE. Internal consultants, tools experts or assurance staff can work with the temporary office to run workshops, establish consistent and tested working practices and collaborative tools, and coach any business or external resources in the organization's standard programme and project methods.

Wherever resources are drawn from, and whatever their backgrounds, there will be a requirement for a focused programme or project induction and team building. If a COE exists, it can provide an induction into organization standards and the programme or project manager can deliver a briefing on the scope, timescales etc. of the programme or project.

A common mistake for the temporary programme or project office is not to consider the planned scale and long-term requirements of the programme or project that it will support. Some programmes or

Case study

A multi-year programme to implement improved practices through process optimization and the rationalization of hundreds of legacy systems and interfaces started its lifecycle as a team of five people, identifying the programme and developing outline business requirements. The programme office function was undertaken by one person on a part-time basis, using an individual scheduling application and manual spreadsheets to track finances.

Within a year the team had grown to more than 100 across seven work streams using the same scheduling methods. Processes no longer represented what was really occurring in the programme, providing senior management with poor decision support on progress. Further, it was taking the equivalent of five full-time equivalents to manage the schedule, and the lead time for the report meant that it was out of date by the time it was produced. This impacted on implementation timeframes and the cost of the overall programme, as the planning and control processes were never proactively designed to deal with the scale of the programme.

projects start small in terms of resources and over time increase in scale to large numbers. In the early stages, establishing the temporary office with minimal resourcing can significantly impact the programme or project as it struggles to provide support, quality-decision-support information and other services. A programme or project office that is properly resourced at an early stage is a key success factor in the start-up and delivery of programmes and projects.

A common approach is to use the investment in a temporary programme or project office as a trial or proof of concept for a permanent P3O by subsequently expanding its scope on programme or project completion. This can be a useful way to demonstrate the value of the P3O concept and prove approaches. However, it is important to ensure that the subsequent activity to realize this is planned and managed.

4.3.3 Running a temporary office through to delivery

The requirements for information flows and processes will have been developed and agreed in governance strategy documents, and the structure and functions of the temporary programme or project office will be determined in the programme or project initiation documents for which approval is being sought.

These requirements will drive the temporary programme or project office model and the processes it uses. However, as a guide, Figure 4.5 displays the key areas of focus.

Throughout delivery, the temporary office should revisit its processes and ways of working to ensure they remain the best approaches and are scalable to current information needs.

The resourcing levels and type of resources should also be challenged at regular intervals to ensure the support roles or any functional roles are still adding value. For example, at the beginning of a large programme there may be a need for functional commercial roles, but once the contracts are agreed and suppliers engaged, this need will diminish.

It is recommended that process reviews and resource reviews take place between the programme manager and head of programme office at the end of each stage or tranche to ensure the resource mix continues to add value and processes continue to be scalable and relevant.

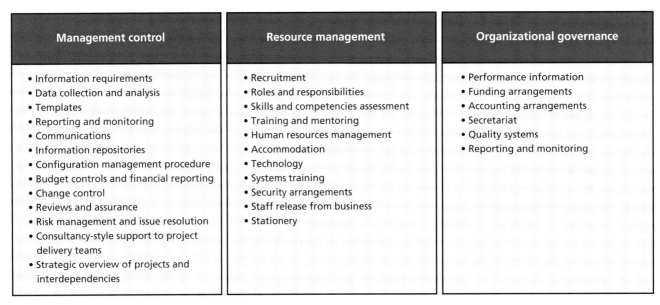

Management control	Resource management	Organizational governance
• Information requirements • Data collection and analysis • Templates • Reporting and monitoring • Communications • Information repositories • Configuration management procedure • Budget controls and financial reporting • Change control • Reviews and assurance • Risk management and issue resolution • Consultancy-style support to project delivery teams • Strategic overview of projects and interdependencies	• Recruitment • Roles and responsibilities • Skills and competencies assessment • Training and mentoring • Human resources management • Accommodation • Technology • Systems training • Security arrangements • Staff release from business • Stationery	• Performance information • Funding arrangements • Accounting arrangements • Secretariat • Quality systems • Reporting and monitoring

Figure 4.5 Key areas of focus for a temporary programme or project office

Appendix F should be revisited during delivery, as the chosen functions and services at start-up will evolve as the programme or project moves into its delivery stages or tranches.

Any lessons identified during delivery should be fed back to the COE at the point the lesson is learned, rather than waiting until the end of the stage, tranche, project or programme.

Another consideration during delivery will be the coordination of assurance and review activities. These may simply be regular health checks, formal gateway reviews or external audits. Whatever their source, the programme or project office should coordinate all reviews, ensuring all team members are aware of them, providing support to external assessors and, on large programmes, providing health checks to the component projects.

4.3.4 Treatment of internal resources within a temporary project office

When resourcing a temporary programme or project office, more careful consideration needs to be given to building internal competencies and career development for individuals seconded to the programme or project, rather than buying in experienced people. A key issue can be a person's temporary elevation in career as a result of a programme or project and a reluctance to return to a lower operational role once the temporary programme or project lifecycle is complete.

Anybody seconded to work on a programme or project, including delivery support staff, should have clear objectives for their role, and these should be assessed in the same way their 'day job' is assessed. It is important to feed back performance information to their line manager and, at the end of their temporary assignment, to ensure their line manager is made aware of any additional skills, knowledge or expertise gained.

A temporary secondment to a programme or project office can sometimes provide a good opportunity for a career change. Managers should look for talented individuals and consider ways of developing their careers for the overall good of the organization.

4.3.5 Closing down a temporary programme or project office

Unlike an organization portfolio office, the temporary programme or project office has a finite lifecycle aligned to the programme or project lifecycle itself. Ensure that a proactive and disciplined approach is undertaken, with transfer to operational areas for documentation, contracts, resources and physical accommodation. Ensure that the benefits management process is transferred to an operational area (if required).

4.3.6 Recycling

A programme or project may have been previously undertaken within an organization and have left a legacy of methods, tools, templates and skills from retained staff as part of a temporary office.

As this capability will have been invested in by the organization for the purposes of supporting the programme or project, it may be possible to recycle rather than reinvent it. This may sound obvious, but there are many instances where there is little or no corporate memory and usable approaches lie dormant, buried deep within an archived project's or programme's documentation.

Provide lessons and reusable elements for subsequent temporary offices to draw from. These should be fed back into a COE, where one exists, to ensure a learning organization. Reusable elements may include processes, templates, tools or best-practice approaches.

Hints and tips

Always assess the lessons from the programme or project, or talk to relevant stakeholders when taking advantage of temporary programme or project office recycling to determine how well the office supported the programme or project.

How to operate a P3O

5

5 How to operate a P3O

Purpose of this chapter

This chapter looks at the operation of P3Os following implementation or re-energizing. It examines the key activities of maintaining a successful permanent P3O and the range of tools and techniques that can be used to support consistent delivery of functions and services across the organization.

5.1 INTRODUCTION

Developing the right P3O model with the correct mix of functions and services will take time and the programme to implement or re-energize it may take up to two years. Even after they have been established, P3Os reorganize on a regular basis, some because of a change of P3O sponsor, others as a result of changing business priorities as well as evolving PPM maturity.

As the organization or individual divisions/departments within it increase their PPM maturity, so the functions and services of the P3O will need to evolve to ensure it continues to add value. Further programmes or projects may be required to continually improve and refine service provision to match or drive the improvement in PPM maturity of the organization over time. This can be undertaken using either a continual improvement approach or as a step-change programme to improve already operating functions or services (see Chapter 4).

The head of P3O must be careful to maintain a stable environment of incremental improvements with periodic change, rather than constantly changing the scope or approach to the functions and services provided.

The first P3O functions and services introduced into an organization with low PPM maturity will often be local administrative functions and services, such as data gathering, reflecting one or more of the following factors:

- Lack of senior management sponsor/support for the P3O model
- Limited funding available

Hints and tips

Scaling

Use the pool of programme and project managers as members of your extended team to develop new services and tools. One organization had a small hub portfolio office with a team of four permanent staff members. The manager of the hub portfolio office agreed with the head of programme and project management that each programme and project manager in a team of 25 would provide 25 hours of their time per year to support the hub portfolio office. This time was recorded and contributed towards their bonus entitlement at the end of the year. The hub portfolio office manager found herself very popular at year end, with project managers volunteering time to develop tools or run workshops to enable them to hit their personal targets. The project managers also found that the time spent with the hub portfolio office helped them to address their own development needs, keep up to date with best practice and improve their skills.

- Lack of competency of P3O team members
- Lack of competency of programme or project managers or business change managers
- Lack of commitment of business owners or senior management to the need for project, programme or portfolio management discipline
- Low level of understanding of the senior management role in sponsoring business change
- Lack of appetite on the part of senior managers for decision-support information.

In an organization with an established P3O, where the organization has increased PPM maturity, P3O resources will possess the competencies to offer a wider range of functions/services and will be capable of challenging and using the data gathered to inform decision-making. Functions and services will standardize information to aid roll-up and consolidation, enabling portfolio reporting, analysis and decision-making.

The evolution is often linked to the business planning cycle, as evolution may require more resources in the form of people or facilities, with a subsequent increase in budget. Any increase in budget has to be matched with a similar uplift in the benefits delivered due to the increased PPM maturity.

As the P3O evolves from administrative support to developing standards, methods and competent staff, through a tracking and assurance role to an oversight, scrutiny and challenge role, care must be taken that the services the P3O offers and the people within the P3O don't become 'process and templates focused'.

P3Os should provide services to help programme and project communities grow and improve, rather than tracking failure by looking for things going wrong and criticizing the programme and project managers for completing templates incorrectly. P3O staff should be reviewing and challenging the content of documents and templates and offering help where data quality is low.

More mature P3Os experience a higher success rate and are more likely to develop into true enterprise service offices, serving the whole organization and all staff involved in change.

P3Os need to be allowed to evolve and mature if they are to add real value to an organization's programme and project management capability and improve returns on investment.

As P3Os mature they are significantly better at promoting effective sponsorship, improving accountability, developing competent staff and demonstrating value. They also gain more acceptance among their stakeholder communities and are able to access more appropriate funding, ensuring their ongoing survival and the subsequent improvement in organizational portfolio, programme and project performance.

5.2 OVERVIEW OF TOOLS AND TECHNIQUES

Within this context:

- A **tool** is a data manipulation system that is used to present information to inform and improve decision-making. Tools can be as simple as a spreadsheet, a system that has been developed in house or a proprietary product.

- A **technique** is a procedure to accomplish a specific activity or task. Techniques will often use tools to collect, manipulate and present the inputs and outputs of the technique.

When selecting which tools and techniques to deploy within the P3O, a key deciding factor should always be the PPM maturity of the organization. Although 'do-it-all' off-the-shelf software packages are tempting as they provide a final built solution with a host of functionality, it can be more successful to implement something much simpler which suits the core basic need of the organization. Some organizations may already have sophisticated enterprise tools that are no longer fit for purpose. Difficult decisions may have to be made, e.g. the tool is decommissioned for a simpler tool, or a number of the functions are disabled until such time as the PPM maturity of the organization 'catches up'.

It may be easier to change the tool than change the process, behaviours and culture of an organization, so where the organization has bespoke requirements, it may be appropriate to implement a tool that has been specifically designed and built for the organization. However, proprietary products are often built around best-practice processes and with careful implementation may help the introduction of this best practice into the organization and help develop adherence to process and PPM maturity.

Case study

A projects department within a large retail organization acquired an enterprise portfolio management solution that the organization portfolio office had decided to implement across the organization. Their lack of understanding of the wider aspects of the tool meant they continued to maintain the data in a local, easier tool for local reporting. The information was being captured twice and used once.

After an assessment, it was decided that the enterprise solution was too sophisticated for the PPM capability within the department and a simple web-style interface was built to replace it.

Tools and techniques may be delivered by a single office or distributed across the organization in a standard way via the P3O.

Tools may be used in the following ways:

■ **Individual** Where only one person (generally the project manager) uses the tool. There may be multiple installations or instances of the tool across the organization but the relationship is generally one business change initiative to one user. Desktop applications such as project planning software, word processing software or spreadsheets are examples.

■ **Collaborative** Where multiple people access a single set of information through a tool. There may be multiple installations or instances of the tool across the organization; however, the relationship is one business change initiative to multiple users. Collaboration tools such as web-based portals and applications that share information and processes through a centralized server are examples.

■ **Integrated** Where multiple people access multiple sets of information that are integrated in some manner through a tool. There will generally be a single installation or instance of the tool across the organization, with partitions for business change initiatives and the ability to link information in a hierarchical manner. The relationship is multiple business change initiatives to multiple users. Enterprise PPM software, which is distributed across an entire organization, is an example (see section 5.5.1).

Hints and tips

Collaborative and integrated tools can be purchased and implemented by an organization or 'rented' by the organization through hosted services. A critical consideration before implementing such a tool should be the maturity of the P3O. If the P3O is not mature, the software may complicate the situation. It is critical that the software meets the needs of P3O business processes and not vice versa.

Standard techniques for the P3O can be found in a number of places within the organization, such as:

■ Within corporate or P3O standards and policies

■ As examples of good practice in knowledge repositories

■ With programme and project resources through skills transfer or coaching by the P3O

■ Within guides for the use of PPM templates and standard deliverables

■ Through the communication of approaches at PPM communities of practice or forums.

5.3 BENEFITS OF USING STANDARD TOOLS AND TECHNIQUES

The benefits of embedding standard tools and techniques in an organization will vary according to the type of tool used and the PPM maturity of the organization or department that is engaging with or using the tool or technique.

The introduction of tools to support an organization's business processes can ensure a minimum standard is attained. In addition, the tools can help guide inexperienced stakeholders through the processes and procedures of an organization, reducing the need to trawl through documents or guides.

Generally, key strategic benefits will include:

■ Automation of business processes:
  ● Reducing staff requirements to operate P3O functions and services
  ● Reducing the overhead on project delivery teams for P3O business process requirements
  ● Eliminating or reducing the need for manual data collection, amalgamation, printing and distribution
■ Improved compliance with business processes:
  ● Through the automation of workflows, approvals and governance mechanisms
  ● Through the integration of business processes with organization components and information flows for the P3O business model
■ Improved timeliness of decision-support information:
  ● Reducing cycle times for the collection of decision-support information
  ● Improving the response time to potential barriers to successful delivery
  ● Providing the opportunity for higher project throughput
  ● Providing a structured way to gather information
■ Improved quality of decision-support information:
  ● Allowing validation of information automatically against embedded corporate or P3O standards
  ● Providing audited business rules around the information compared with manual unaudited processes
  ● Enabling the reallocation of manual processing time to assessing and improving information quality

- Providing a structured way to gather information and setting expectations for decision-support information requirements
- Introducing automated ways of assessing the health of decision-support information for centrally stored information
- Improved decision-making:
  - Through the integration of many data elements into central repositories, providing higher visibility and analysis of cross-project or cross-programme information
  - Through the ability to automate highlight and exception views of information and the hierarchical structuring of information
  - By using structured ways to assess information and make more objective decisions
  - Through improved capability to undertake scenario or 'what if' analysis on the decision-support information
- Improved management across geography:
  - Through connectivity that allows for improvements to collaboration between programme or project team members
- Improved staff competence:
  - Through skills transfer of structured ways of gathering, analysing and reporting information or undertaking elements of an organization's business change framework
  - Reduction in reliance on conventional wisdom, and a transfer of knowledge to known facts based on historical information
- Rationalization of legacy systems:
  - Tools for the P3O that are of an integrated nature may make it possible to rationalize a number of disparate systems.

5.4 CRITICAL SUCCESS FACTORS WHEN INTRODUCING TOOLS AND TECHNIQUES INTO THE P3O

Although many significant benefits may be achieved by the introduction of standard tools and techniques into the P3O, there are also a number of critical success factors. The most significant are as follows:

- Focus on adding value to the organization rather than the features of the tool:
  - Marketing materials for tools to support the P3O are predominately focused on features of the tools, integration across these features

and level of sophistication, rather than the benefits to the organization or the problems they may solve.
  - Research services that provide comparisons of tool providers in the market generally focus on features, ease of implementation, and the quality and credibility of the organization behind the tool.
  - The introduction of any tool to support the functions or services that a P3O provides needs to be carefully considered as part of the overall P3O blueprint. Be clear about the value that the tool will provide and then match the tools available with the features required.

Hints and tips

Be careful to avoid focusing on 'How can we use this tool feature in our organization?' rather than 'Does our organization need the service or function that this feature supports?'

The implementation of an integrated tool is an expensive investment that will require significant effort and training. It should therefore be run as a project where the requirements are fully defined, the business case is justified and the implementation is planned in detail.

- Match the sophistication of the tools and techniques to the PPM maturity of the organization:
  - With the move to higher levels of integration and innovation in the features offered by many tools on the market, some of the tools available to the P3O can be quite sophisticated in their functions and usability. Equally, a number of best-practice techniques may be dependent on having basic practices in place or require a high level of competency to be undertaken successfully.
  - Because tools and techniques need to integrate with the business processes and information flows and the competencies of resources using them, ensure that the sophistication of the tools and techniques matches the PPM maturity of the organization. For example, there is little value in implementing a tool with features that support robust benefits management and resource competency management (P3M3 Level 3) when the organization is not properly defining projects consistently (P3M3 Level 1).

Using the tool itself will not drive the organizational capability if more basic PPM maturity 'building blocks' are not in place.

Hints and tips

Tools are available to support all levels of PPM maturity. However, if the tool does not match the PPM maturity of the organization, there will be a detrimental effect on PPM effectiveness, the morale of the PPM community and the credibility of the P3O.

■ There is a need for programme and project standardization and data quality:
  ● Introducing tools or techniques with features that prioritize multiple projects based on information provided in costs, benefits, risks, timeframes or strategic alignment is of little value if confidence in the project's data quality is low, which will be the case if a project lifecycle is not in place.
  ● Ensure that the governance for programme and project delivery is in place to enable decision-making, and align the software with this decision-making structure.

Hints and tips

When moving from manual processes to a higher level of process automation through an integrated tool, do not underestimate the challenges of configuring the system. The quality of existing P3O processes and programme and project information will be the number-one critical success factor in the implementation of the enterprise PPM software, so an early activity should be to improve data quality before introducing the tool. Organizations may struggle to derive all the benefits from collaborative or integrated tools prior to achieving Level 3 P3M3 maturity.

■ Understand the intent of the tool or technique:
  ● Although different industries may have different forms of P3O, they will generally be aiming for similar value from their respective P3O models. However, a number of the tools and techniques available have been developed to meet a specific requirement for an industry or a large client, or are based on assumptions that may hold for one industry but not for others. This can create significant issues with adoption when the tool or technique is then offered to the wider market

for implementation. For example, a tool that has been developed with construction projects in mind, using construction industry language and standards, may not be easily adapted to an IT or marketing portfolio environment.
  ● Understand the portfolio, programme or project management methods from which the tool or technique was derived or for which it was developed.
  ● Understand the history of the tool or technique and how it can add value before focusing on required features, detailed requirements and adoption. For example, some tools are focused on the provision of sophisticated earned value analysis, which is derived from complex resource-usage modelling when planning or measuring activity. For organizations where there may be regular changes to the baseline, there may be little value to be gained by adopting earned value analysis as a tool or technique.

Hints and tips

Undertake a request for information (RFI) to obtain the history, key clients and system functions when investigating tools for the P3O.

■ Implement tools as part of an organizational change effort:
  ● Tool suppliers generally focus on accelerated approaches to tool implementation and accordingly provide standard project approaches, frameworks or transition plans for implementing tools.
  ● Additionally, some integrated tools do not have the same basic project management assumptions that individual tools may provide (generally due to lower sophistication) and it can take time for staff to learn new ways of working.
  ● As a minimum, it is critical to consider and plan the enabling projects and subsequent projects around the tool implementation project. Ideally, the implementation of tools should be considered as part of an organizational change programme, but it can be successfully run as a stand-alone project. (Refer to Chapter 4 for further information.)
  ● Manage the tool implementation as a business change project and not a technology implementation project. The tool selection

and implementation is only a part of the activities required for successful implementation and adoption.

- With any tool, clear guidance and training should be developed and delivered as part of the implementation activities.
- When selecting a tool, an assessment of the time and effort required to administer the tool should be undertaken to understand whether any new skills are required within the P3O and whether the PPM community will need any additional time to use the new tool.

Hints and tips

The timeframe for an organization to become proficient with integrated tools and fully realize the benefits to be achieved can be between 12 and 18 months. The timescale will depend on many factors, including size of organization, skill set of existing staff etc. It may be an appropriate strategy to use appropriately skilled external resources to expedite the tools implementation and then transfer skills to internal staff.

- Maximize successful programme and project delivery through incremental implementation:
  - Concentrate the efforts of the programme and project delivery teams by considering how implementation may be adopted incrementally.
  - Use pilot projects and early adopters – make sure a communications plan is developed to communicate success to the rest of the programme and project management community.
  - The disadvantages and problems associated with a 'big bang' project implementation apply equally to integrated tool implementation.

Hints and tips

Consider a proof-of-concept/pilot approach or parallel running of current and new ways of working in those teams impacted by the tool implementation, to provide confidence before 'readiness for service'. Other incremental options include implementing on a feature-by-feature basis or adopting the tool for new programmes and projects only.

- Agree tool ownership within the organization:
  - For integrated tools being used across a P3O with hub portfolio offices, it is particularly important that the ownership of and accountability for tool operations and improvements is clear (single point of accountability), with agreed processes for tool users to provide feedback and request enhancements.

Hints and tips

Where the P3O is operating at an organization level, the portfolio office or centre of excellence (COE) is generally the most appropriate owner of an integrated tool, because of the need for project standardization across the organization. Where the P3O is temporary, the programme or project office supporting it will generally be the appropriate owner.

5.5 P3O TOOLS

The tools that support the P3O business processes and information flows may be as simple as individual documents, forms, spreadsheets and databases, or much more sophisticated. Some of the high-level types of collaborative and integrated tools that may be employed within the P3O are:

- **Strategic mapping software** Systems that map programmes and projects to benefits, outcomes and strategy
- **EPM solutions** Enterprise PPM systems, specifically designed for portfolio, programme and project management environments. These solutions can capture such information as plans, resources, costs, risks, issues, and documentation supporting the project
- **Enterprise architecture systems** Systems that model the organization's structure, systems and processes, and allow mapping of projects to demonstrate the journey from the as-is landscape to the desired future state
- **Knowledge management systems** Systems that are used to disseminate and share learning, such as FAQs, wikis, intranets etc.
- **Performance management systems** Tools that align expected performance with strategic aims and track actual performance

■ **Risk management systems** Systems that support a common, integrated approach to risk management by supporting the identification, analysis and monitoring of risks, issues and associated mitigation actions

■ **Requirements management systems** Systems that are used to manage the detailed scope of projects by analysing, tracing and prioritizing project requirements.

These high-level types of tools can have a multitude of features and functions that support the value of the P3O, and there is significant duplication among them. Tools can often span more than one PPM perspective.

Hints and tips

Develop a solution architecture for the tools used to support the P3O business model that addresses features required now and features required in the future.

5.5.1 Enterprise PPM (EPM) solutions

The most common integrated tools used in the P3O are enterprise PPM solutions. These provide a single systems solution for programme and project data collection, maintenance and reporting, allowing for roll-up of information from a single source of data (one version of the truth) to programme and portfolio levels. Core functions are generally provided across portfolio, programme and project management, from strategic planning through to programme or project workflow or delivery support (see Table 5.1). A key benefit of these tools is the ability to produce integrated reports for multiple audiences from a single set of data.

Many tools may already exist within operational functions and could be adopted and developed for P3O use. A wide range of EPM solutions are available on the market, but not all organizations have the PPM maturity to fully utilize the functionality available. The tool selection must not be based on 'What is the best tool on the market?' but on 'What is the right tool that matches the PPM maturity of the organization?'

Table 5.1 Core functions of enterprise PPM tools

Portfolio management	Resource management	Programme and project management
Strategic planning	Skills matching	Workflow and delivery support
Organizational budgeting	Capacity/forward planning	Demand management and project collaboration
Portfolio identification	Resource assignment	Governance processes
Portfolio analysis	Scheduling, tracking and measurement	Benefits management
Strategic resource planning	Timesheets	Lifecycle and stage-gated review process
Strategic risk management		Programme and project guides and support
Strategic issue management		Information and document management
Portfolio schedule and planning		Risk management and issue management
Portfolio categorization		Change control
Portfolio prioritization		Information portals
Portfolio tracking		Dependency management
Portfolio review		Progress reporting
Portfolio optimization		
Asset management		

Hints and tips

When selecting the appropriate tool, consider the expected level of PPM maturity at the end of the implementation or re-energizing programme or project, not just at the start.

5.5.2 Selecting and implementing an enterprise PPM solution

Table 5.2 provides a checklist of key questions that should be considered when developing a requirements document for the selection and implementation of a PPM solution.

5.6 P3O TECHNIQUES

The techniques that support the P3O business processes and information flows can be extremely complex in a mature PPM environment. In contrast, in an environment that has a lower PPM maturity, they may be at a basic, yet effective, level. Techniques may also be used under licence or provided as part of a professional service from a supplier.

The number and focus of techniques that a P3O may use to achieve its blueprint are evolving and refining even faster than the tools available.

The following sections describe some of the key P3O techniques in further detail.

Table 5.2 Key questions for developing a requirements document for a PPM solution

Function	Questions
Strategic	How will the PPM tool(s) support the proposed P3O model?
	What is the key objective of the PPM tool(s)? Has the vendor designed the features around managing mature project product breakdown structures (PBS) or work packages, measuring earned value, for a particular environment or around a key client? Does this align with the organization's requirements?
	Is the organization planning to use the PPM solution to support strategic or business planning cycles?
	What features are required now and what features may be required in the future as the PPM maturity of the organization increases?
	Is the current PPM maturity of the organization appropriate for a move from individual tools to collaborative or integrated tools?
	Is it possible to do a staged roll-out of the features of the PPM solution as the PPM maturity of the organization increases? Is it easy to hide the visibility of these features in the interim?
	What is the track record of PPM tools within the organization?
	Does the organization need to purchase and implement the PPM tool(s) as part of a permanent P3O model or use a hosted or outsourced solution as part of a temporary P3O model (if the requirement will not exist once the programme or project completes)?
	How will senior management respond to new ways of working as a result of the PPM solution?
	What are the organizational change management implications of moving to a PPM solution? Will the delivery staff need to work in a new way or will they continue to use familiar interfaces?
	Will there be an impact on the successful delivery of the portfolio, programmes and projects as a result of implementing PPM tool(s)?
	Is the organization's investment in multiple individual tools and software less efficient and effective than implementing a PPM solution at an enterprise level?
	What are the risks associated with the implementation of the PPM solution and how will they be managed?
Process	What processes will the PPM solution be aligned with? Can it support the current processes and evolve as the new or revised processes are introduced?

Function	Questions
Process *continued*	What processes can be done more efficiently using the PPM solution than they could by using a manual solution?
	What benefits can be realized through implementing additional features of the PPM solution?
	What processes are the highest priority to implement to realize early benefits?
	How will the PPM solution integrate with the wider organizational processes?
	Will the PPM solution require the delivery staff to spend more or less time doing administration and to comply with governance processes and procedures?
Organization	What roles and responsibilities are required to support the PPM solution?
	What skills and competencies are required to implement, maintain and improve the PPM solution?
	Will the PPM maturity of the organization positively or negatively impact the PPM solution implementation and take-up, and the realization of benefits from its use?
	Are suitably skilled resources available to operate the PPM solution in production?
	If the organization invests in competency development for current staff in the PPM solution, how will that impact on programme or project delivery and what ramp-up time will be required?
Tools and technologies	Will the architecture support project delivery?
	What licence requirements best suit the organization's approach?
	Is there a solution architecture roadmap to be followed that can align with portfolio, programme and project management capability implementation over time (e.g. module based)?
	Should the tool be purchased outright, outsourced or used via a hosted solution? Is it possible to transfer to an alternative option at a later point?
	Is (Are) the PPM tool(s) easily configurable? Do the tools within the PPM solution integrate?
	What costs are associated with customization of the tool? Is the PPM tool(s) provider the only route through which the tool can be customized or can changes be made by third parties?
	What integration requirements will there be to legacy or line-of-business systems?
	What are the minimum data requirements? How much effort is required to ensure all aspects of information assurance (IA)?
Information flows	What key questions are being asked by senior management about the portfolio?
	What information is required from the programmes and projects to achieve this?
	What information does the organization need to monitor to achieve better programme and project outcomes?
	Do project delivery staff have to feed information into multiple systems for PPM information requirements, or will the information automatically be rolled up?
	Can data be migrated easily from current systems/approaches into the PPM solution? Is the data of suitable quality?
	Can data be easily validated after migration to maintain data quality?
	What capability is there to provide metrics on the health of the information within the PPM solution?

5.6.1 Portfolio prioritization and optimization

The objective of a portfolio prioritization and optimization technique is to categorize or force-rank the programmes and projects within a portfolio based on one or more agreed measures. The most common measures are financial (e.g. cost, business benefits etc.) and/or some form of multi-criteria analysis (MCA) such as strategic alignment, risk, complexity etc.

Prioritizing the portfolio is critically important in order to determine where investment should be directed as the portfolio is delivered. Failure to prioritize at board level will usually result in every project trying to deliver at the same time, using the same resources, which will result in initial chaos and significantly increase the risk of non-delivery. Optimizing the portfolio may involve increasing capacity or reducing commitments.

Its key benefit is in supporting senior management investment decisions using an objective alignment technique to determine how a programme or project supports and aligns with strategic objectives in relation to other programmes and projects.

Portfolio prioritization and optimization is covered in more detail in the Best Management Practice publication *Management of Portfolios* (MoP) (Office of Government Commerce, 2011).

This technique can be undertaken periodically (e.g. quarterly) to optimize the portfolio against overall risk and the agreed strategic objectives, and to refine the weighting of investment.

Key inputs are information on planned or current programmes and projects in the portfolio and an agreed framework for prioritization.

Table 5.3 Components of a simple prioritization framework

Note: column numbers refer to those in the prioritization model shown in Table 5.4.

Risk level (columns 3, 4, 5 and 6)	
Assessment	*Score*
High	3
Medium	2
Low	1
Project length (column 12)	
High (>3 months)	3
Medium (>1 month but <3 months)	2
Low(<1 month)	1
Investment (columns 8 and 9)	
Driver	*Weighting*
Service delivery Investment is directly linked to improving service delivery to the organization's customers	9
Compliance Investment is required to ensure compliance	10
Revenue growth Investment benefit is predominantly an increase in revenue or the capacity to increase revenue	7
Operational risk treatment Investment benefit is predominantly in the treatment of risk to the organization's operations	5
Productivity Investment benefit is predominantly derived from an increase in productivity	5

An example of components of a simple prioritization framework is shown in Table 5.3. In this example, the organization has chosen to prioritize the portfolio on the basis of risk, effort required and strategic alignment (based on the investment driver). The weightings for each of the investment drivers have been determined through discussions with senior and strategy management, facilitated by the P3O.

An example of key portfolio information applied to a prioritization model is shown in Table 5.4.

Each project (A, B, C, D and E) is assessed against the components of the prioritization framework to determine its relative priority and create a force-ranked list. It is common to find a mismatch between the priority of strategic objectives and the current investment in programmes and projects. This provides an opportunity for optimization of the portfolio by redirecting investment against the investment drivers more appropriately.

In the example shown in Figure 5.1, it can be quickly determined, on a highlighted basis, which of the projects represent high risk and low strategic value. The size of the bubbles reflects the cost of the project, so senior managers can assess where the investment is being spent. The strategic-value and risk-level numbers relate to the score of each project against a predefined prioritization-model scoring system to determine relative worth.

It is important to note that the portfolio prioritization and optimization technique should be validated by the portfolio direction group (see MoP) or senior management team to ensure that it makes sense.

A number of enterprise PPM solutions with capability at the strategic analysis level will provide more automated ways of determining portfolio prioritization and make recommendations on portfolio optimization opportunities using sophisticated calculations.

5.6.2 Complexity modelling

The purpose of complexity modelling is to determine the appropriate lifecycle and governance for the programme or project based on its complexity. The key benefit is in providing a structured approach to the tailoring of the standard lifecycle and governance structures for a programme or project, thus providing flexibility but maintaining standardization for portfolio management requirements, such as the roll-up of information for governance, escalation and reporting purposes.

Programmes or projects can range from the familiar repeatable-type projects (clarity of objectives, done it before, know how to do it and understand the risks) to highly complex undertakings.

Each programme or project going through business-case approval should be assessed against a range of criteria to give an overall business criticality or risk rating. Criteria may include budget, timescale, innovation, number of suppliers, type of customer (size, new), brand awareness, size of team, number of business functions involved etc. Organizations may develop their own risk ratings based on the organizational risk process.

An example of a tool used to inform the tailoring of approaches for UK government is the risk potential assessment (RPA) provided in OGC Gateway reviews. This assessment is a technique provided via a single spreadsheet that rates the degree of complexity for acquisition-based programmes and projects.

An example of a project complexity model is displayed in Table 5.5.

In the example provided in Table 5.5, the organization has assessed what constitutes complexity for projects and has determined 12 key criteria. Analysis has been undertaken to determine the drivers for each of these criteria and their parameters. Weightings have been applied to create an algorithm that provides an overall complexity score.

The complexity score (representing business criticality or risk rating) is then used to determine the recommended governance structures and tailored lifecycle for the project, as shown in Table 5.6.

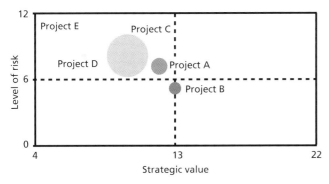

Figure 5.1 An example of a strategic alignment and risk level diagram

Table 5.4 An example of a prioritization model

1	2	3	4	5	6	7 (sum of columns 3–6)	8	9	10	11	12	13 (sum of columns 9 and 12)
Unique ID	Project title	Technology risk level	Complexity risk level	Benefits risk level	Delivery risk level	Total risk level	Investment driver	Investment driver weighting	Payback <1 yr	Positive ROI Y/N?	Project length >3 months = 3; 1–3 months = 2; <1 month = 1	Strategic value
A	Project A	1	2	2	2	7	Service delivery	9	Y	Y	3	12
B	Project B	1	1	1	2	5	Compliance	10	Y	Y	3	13
C	Project C	2	1	3	2	8	Revenue growth	7	N	Y	3	10
D	Project D	2	1	3	2	8	Operational risk treatment	6	N	N	1	7
E	Project E	2	2	3	3	10	Productivity	5	Y	Y	1	6

Note that this is only the recommended governance structure and lifecycle. The final decision on governance and lifecycle should be made by the project sponsor, with justification if it varies from that recommended.

It is important to note that this technique will require refinement and ongoing review to ensure that the weightings are appropriate to the governance applied and the project outcome.

5.6.3 Management dashboards

A management dashboard should support highlight and exception-based reporting, providing the reader (usually senior management) with the ability to quickly determine whether an organization's investment is on track in terms of progress and outcomes, or where attention should be focused. A management dashboard can be presented as a covering document to the more detailed status reports of a portfolio or programme or can be delivered electronically to provide the ability to drill down to lower levels of detailed information using fit-for-purpose software such as PPM tools.

The objective of the management dashboard technique is to provide key decision-support information across a portfolio using highlight and exception-based reporting, thus providing a rolled-up view of more detailed information. It is generally provided as a top-tier report (exception-based) with links to programme and project information to enable the members of the relevant governance board to drill down to detailed information if required. Appropriate information assurance (IA) must be applied to the data to ensure that the information provided is trusted to be the one version of the truth. Where traffic lights are applied to aspects of the data, it is essential that there are agreed values for red, amber and green to ensure consistent and objective reporting.

The key benefit of the technique is to supplement larger volumes of detailed reporting, allowing the decision-makers to more effectively determine progress and understand where attention and management intervention may be required.

The key input into the management dashboard is information and progress reporting from the programmes and projects within the portfolio. It should be highlighted that this technique will only be valuable if there is confidence in the information,

and this is directly related to the quality of the programme and project information, the P3O processes and skills, and the level and quality of the challenge and scrutiny role within the P3O.

With any dashboard, the focus should not be on how to create the information, but on the outcome the information will drive – what decisions or action is the information asking the reviewer to take?

In some larger organizations, there may be a requirement to have multi-level dashboards presenting various depths of information dependent on the decision-making authority at that level. The dashboards should be aligned to the governance structures within the organization.

When re-energizing or setting up a P3O from scratch, management dashboard report templates should be flexible, as the requirements are likely to evolve. An example of a management dashboard is shown in Figure 5.2.

Figure 5.2 is an example of a board-level management dashboard. A range of sample metrics and graphs have been used to demonstrate key values.

The management dashboard shows an overview of the total portfolio and a breakdown by divisional sub-portfolio. The metrics show that the portfolio has a very high weighting in 'cost reduction' projects (more than half of the portfolio, and representing the entire division sub-portfolio of Division E). This may enable a discussion on whether this is appropriate or whether the portfolio needs to be optimized.

The management dashboard also shows rolled-up data for the constituent projects. When accessing an online version of the dashboard, board members can click on various sections to drill down to more detail, e.g. to investigate which six projects are currently at red status. Figure 5.3 is an example of a management dashboard representing an individual project.

You will notice that this looks very much like a status report. In essence, that is what it is. Most projects and programmes now provide status updates via a dashboard and supply additional information only when requested. When the details are provided as a dashboard, the project board can quickly see the key information and identify where they need to provide direction and support.

Table 5.5 An example of a project complexity model for Project A

Description	A–0	B–10	C–20	D–40	Select column	Complexity scoring
Customer Assess how the solution will impact customers. The impact could be an awareness or it could imply change in the behaviour of the customer	No customer impact	Awareness from customers	Minor behaviour change from customers	Major behaviour change from customers	C	20
Risk exposure Assess the organization's exposure to risk and the downstream system/process impacts if errors were found in the solution	No impact	Minor impacts to organization's reputation and downstream processes	Minor impact to organization's reputation but major impact to downstream processes	Major impacts to organization's reputation and downstream processes	C	20
Internal Assess how the solution may affect the work process of the business area and any ripple effects on work processes of other business areas	Within business team	Minor impact to business areas	Medium impact to business areas	Major impact to business areas	B	10
External Assess how the solution may affect the work processes of suppliers, partners or other external stakeholders	No impact to external stakeholders	Requires awareness from external stakeholders	Minor behaviour change from external stakeholders	Major behaviour change from external stakeholders	C	20
Number of stakeholders Each stakeholder may represent a group of people either internal or external to the organization. More stakeholders in the project would imply increased complexity for the project manager	1 key stakeholder	2–4 key stakeholders	5–10 key stakeholders	11+ key stakeholders	B	10
Knowledge of technology If knowledge of the technology is limited, especially if not in house and not easily available, this means greater risks to the project and requires greater planning	Well established in the organization	Knowledge is with a number of people in the organization	Knowledge can be sought from the market	Marketplace knowledge is limited, i.e. is only with the vendor	C	20
Knowledge of application/ business processes If knowledge of the process is limited, with lack of documentation, this means greater risks to the project and requires more detailed work	Well established and documented in the organization	Knowledge is with a few people but well documented in the organization	Knowledge is with a few people but there is a lack of documentation	Knowledge is very limited and there is a lack of documentation	A	0

Description	A–0	B–10	C–20	D–40	Select column	Complexity scoring
Number of IT platforms Platform refers to the infrastructure, e.g. middleware, operating systems, systems software. The more platforms, the more risky and complex the solution will be	1 key platform	2 key platforms	3 key platforms	≥4 key platforms	C	20
Application systems, interfaces and types of data Assess how the solution may need to integrate with internal systems in the organization and if the data exchange is with external sources	1 key system and no data interface with external groups	2 key systems and no data interface with external groups	3 key systems; or, with one interface with external groups; or, if the data is of minor sensitive nature	≥4 key systems; or, with more than one interface with external groups; or, if the data is of major sensitive nature	D	40
Number of service providers The number of service providers who would be working together to provide a solution	1 service provider	2 service providers	3 service providers	≥4 service providers	A	0
Total project costs Total internal and external costs for labour, materials, training, travel etc. charged to the project for the entire project lifecycle	Up to £100,000	>£100,000 up to £500,000	>£500,000 up to £2m	>£2m	D	40
Project completion time The expected elapsed time before project completion	Up to 1 month	>1 month up to 6 months	>6 months up to 12 months	>12 months	C	20
Overall complexity score						220

Table 5.6 Governance and lifecycle requirements determined by project complexity scoring

Complexity score	Sponsor	Project board required	Level of project manager required	Reporting	Project lifecycle*
360–480	Board level	Y	Senior project manager	Fortnightly using detailed highlight report template	Complex
210–350	Divisional level	Optional	Project manager	Monthly using summary highlight report template	Standard
0–200	Department level	N	Junior project manager	Ad hoc using summary highlight report template	Simple

*The content of these lifecycle variations will be detailed elsewhere.

Portfolio management dashboard sample organization

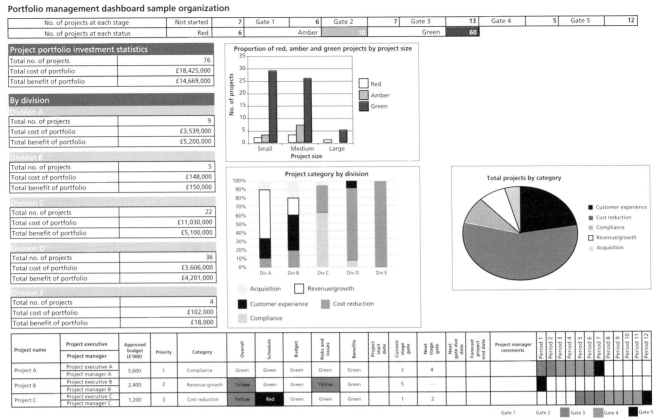

Figure 5.2 *An example of a portfolio management dashboard*

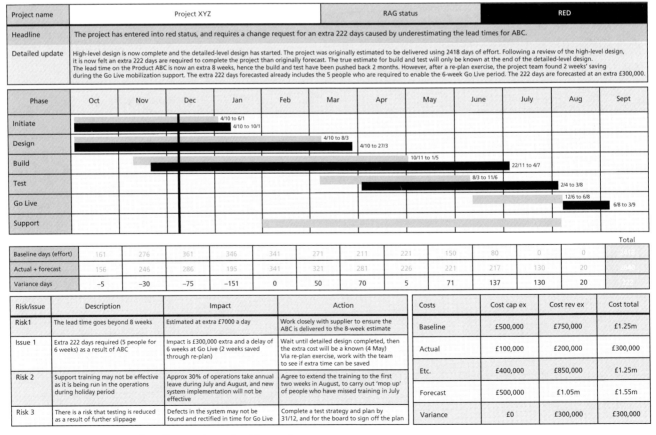

Figure 5.3 *An example of a project dashboard*

The key output is a populated management dashboard that is updated periodically and is provided to the relevant governance group (such as the portfolio progress group) as amalgamated decision-support information.

The design and content of the management dashboard must be fit for purpose for the relevant decision-making body. Fitness for purpose should be confirmed by each of the decision-making bodies to ensure all individual requirements are satisfied.

A number of PPM solutions with capability at the strategic analysis level offer more automated ways of providing amalgamated reporting through management dashboards or balanced scorecards, or ways of reporting using information drawn directly from programmes and projects through a centralized repository.

5.6.4 Knowledge management

Knowledge management means creating an environment and providing tools and processes that support the creation of new knowledge and sharing of what people and organizations know. Effective knowledge management means that ideas, experience and insights are used within and between portfolios, programmes and projects to improve performance.

Knowledge management is often confused with information management. The difference is that knowledge management includes ideas, insights and experience. Because this kind of knowledge is difficult to document, knowledge management involves connecting people to other people. Information management is concerned with material that has been documented.

Different organizations have different ideas about what knowledge actually is. Often these views are not articulated. Some organizations value documented knowledge that has been reviewed and checked by experts. At the other extreme, some organizations value ideas and insights in any form and from any source. Both views have their merits and pitfalls, and both influence the kind of knowledge management practices that are valued. The P3O's approach to knowledge management should be sensitive to the organization's view of knowledge, but the P3O can also change the organization's view by introducing new knowledge management practices that tap into previously undervalued knowledge.

Knowledge management also overlaps with organizational learning. In knowledge management the focus is usually on knowledge as a strategic resource, whereas in organizational learning the focus is usually on how organizations learn.

Hints and tips

Don't put all your knowledge management efforts into documenting what people know. Make sure you connect people to other people as well – otherwise you will end up managing information and missing out on sharing valuable ideas, insights and experience.

5.6.4.1 Creating an environment for knowledge to flow

Creating an environment where people share ideas, insights and experience is just as important as providing knowledge management tools and processes. People don't share their knowledge because they are told to. Neither do they learn because it is mandated.

If the organization already has a knowledge management team, resources from the P3O should work with the knowledge management team to make sure that the PPM environment is conducive to knowledge sharing.

The environment needed to support knowledge activities depends on the nature of the project work and the specific circumstances, as well as the organization's business and its view of knowledge. In creative projects, for example, people are more likely to share their ideas and develop new knowledge if they work in self-managed teams. If the specific circumstances are such that project team members are from different professional backgrounds or have never worked together before, allow time for them to get to know one another. Similar allowances should be made at the commencement of a new 'buddying' or mentoring relationship.

Make it clear that sharing knowledge is important, and encourage project executives to lead by example. Include knowledge sharing in a structured induction process and competency frameworks, and make it part of appraisal systems and performance reviews.

Perhaps the most important factor in creating an environment where knowledge can flow is time. Make it clear that spending time on knowledge sharing and learning is a valued activity and encourage time to be scheduled within the programme and project plans to do so.

5.6.4.2 Knowledge management tools and techniques

There are hundreds of knowledge management techniques (and supporting tools). Most are variations on two themes: connecting people to information (or documented knowledge) and connecting people to other people. Many techniques include both.

The choice of tools and techniques (and their implementation) depends on what the organization and the P3O want to achieve and on the specific programme or project circumstances. What works in one project or organization can be an unmitigated disaster in another. For this reason, it is sensible to introduce several techniques – then continue to support the ones that work best. The techniques that work best are the ones that people use and say they find the most useful. It is extremely difficult to establish direct cause-and-effect relationships between knowledge management practices and performance, especially over short timescales.

General guidance and advice

- Give people a choice of knowledge-sharing tools and techniques. Remember that knowledge sharing and learning are voluntary, so don't restrict what people do by trying to force them to use a single method or a single technology platform.
- Support tools and techniques that connect people to information and to other people. Where knowledge is documented, include the author's contact details so that people can follow up with a conversation. This can go a long way towards avoiding misinterpretation or ill-advised application of written guidance.
- Build on existing knowledge sharing practices. Ask people what is already working.
- Fill gaps. Ask people what is missing, or for examples of situations in which they needed knowledge or advice and didn't know how to get it.
- Remember that people don't know what they don't know. Often they can't search for relevant information and knowledge because they don't know which search terms to use or what

questions to ask. Create mechanisms for people to ask open questions, such as 'What does anyone know about…?'

- Remember that knowledge needs don't necessarily coincide with knowledge production. Just because one project team has learned something, it doesn't mean it is now relevant to other project teams.
- Knowledge sharing is often informal, so give people opportunities to interact socially. If people can't easily meet face to face, encourage them to use software that makes it easy to share information about themselves and to hold online conversations.
- The P3O has a unique overview of the organization's project activities and is well placed to make connections between ideas, insights and experience developed in different places and at different times. Organize seminars, workshops, online forums and other opportunities for people from different programmes and projects to meet and share their knowledge. Allow plenty of time for discussion – don't fill the time with formal presentations. P3O specialists can also broker conversations between different programme and project teams.
- Build an external knowledge network. Build relationships with P3Os in other organizations or divisions, attend external events, join online communities and take part in activities organized by professional associations. Encourage programme and project team members to build their own external knowledge networks.

The following sections give an overview of a few of the most common knowledge management techniques.

Communities of practice

Communities of practice are groups of people who share a common interest and are willing to work and learn together over a period of time to develop and share their knowledge. This can be done through online or face-to-face activities such as programme management/project management forums. These provide a 'home' and stewardship for knowledge about a particular domain. Communities of practice cut across organizational hierarchies and functions, and operate as knowledge networks.

Thinking about communities of practice has changed significantly in the past decade. Much of the early guidance describes communities as emergent and independent from the organizational hierarchy. Current thinking is that communities work better if they are structured, integrated into the organization, and supported by senior management. Communities of practice can take many different forms and are also known by other names, such as communities of interest, knowledge networks, human networks or technical networks.

Lessons

Systems containing detailed case studies of shared lessons are synonymous with knowledge management to many project professionals, despite being implemented ineffectively in many organizations. An effective lessons-recording system has two components: learning reviews in which key learning is identified, with feedback to the P3O including suggested action plans, then some action (e.g. a new process or a change to an existing process) initiated by the P3O to make sure that what went wrong doesn't go wrong again and what went well is repeated.

Simply logging lessons in a database and requiring people to search it doesn't work. Either the database won't be populated, or it won't be populated with anything useful, or no one will look at it.

Learning reviews

The two most common types of review are ad hoc (often called after-action reviews) and planned reviews (e.g. the post-implementation review).

Ad hoc reviews are brief meetings held at short notice, usually after something has gone wrong, with the purpose of stopping the same thing going wrong again. The participants typically consider five questions:

1 What was supposed to happen?

2 What actually happened?

3 Why were there differences?

4 What did we learn?

5 What are we going to do about it?

Ad hoc reviews usually result in learning and actions for the project team. If the team think the learning is relevant to other projects, they should share the learning with the relevant office within the P3O so that it can take further action.

Planned reviews are structured, facilitated meetings held at agreed points in the programme or project, such as at the end of key stages or an agreed period after implementation (where the primary purpose will be to focus on benefits realization). The members of the programme or project team gather to review the project objectives, ask what went well (and find out why) and ask what could have gone better (and how). The learning from a post-project review should be passed to the relevant office within the P3O with suggested action plans.

A third type of learning review is the pre-project review (also known as a peer review or peer assist). A pre-project review is a meeting or workshop, called by a team just starting out on a project or activity, to seek knowledge and insights from potential collaborators and others with experience of similar situations. The purpose is to learn from good and bad experiences on other projects. This can be facilitated by an individual who performs the consultant/performance management role within the COE, as part of a fast-track mobilization.

All three types of learning review can be supported and facilitated by the P3O, which should make sure that the meetings are used to learn from experience rather than to attribute blame when things have gone wrong.

Archiving of portfolio, programme and project good practice

At the end of a programme or project, the team will have amassed a great deal of material that may be beneficial to future programmes and projects. This should be archived with the P3O for future use, as it can provide hints to assist future change initiatives.

5.6.4.3 Tracking knowledge management maturity

Although it is difficult to establish direct cause-and-effect relationships between knowledge management practices and performance, P3Os can track knowledge management maturity at the project, programme and portfolio level, and (if there is no organization-wide knowledge management function) at the organizational level. Various knowledge management maturity frameworks have been published to help with this, e.g. K3M (© WisdomSource Technologies), which provides an eight-level maturity model.

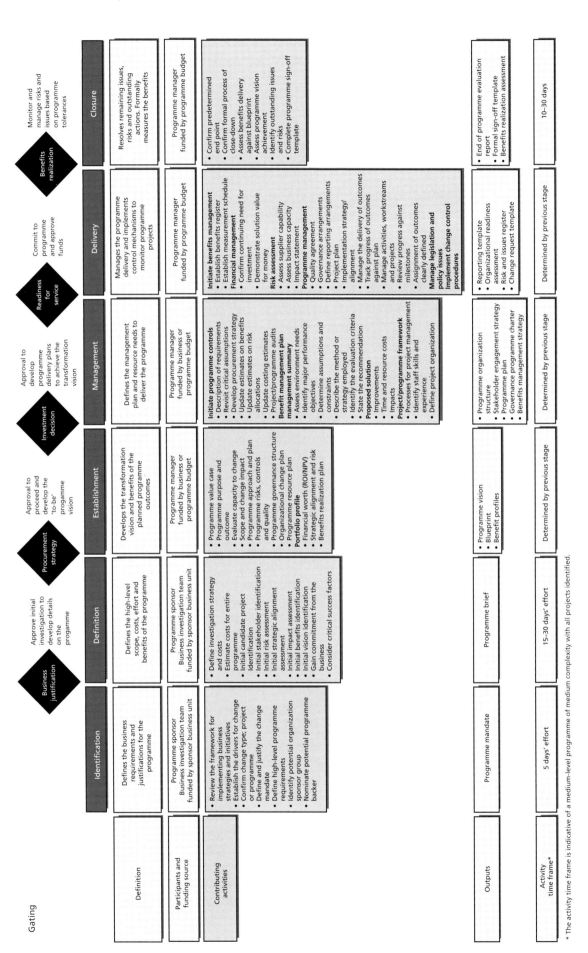

Figure 5.4 An example of an information portal

* The activity time frame is indicative of a medium-level programme of medium complexity with all projects identified.

Table 5.7 Typical facilitated workshops

Name	Purpose/stage
Business solution	Held during the initiation stage to brainstorm options and consider options for the programme or project solution.
Portfolio priorities	Held during the portfolio prioritization process. Identify the strategic drivers or investment objectives and then force-rank each objective by asking the question 'Is strategic objective A more important or less important than objective B?' Repeat against all strategic objectives until a prioritized order is achieved.
Programme/project start-up	Held at any time during the start-up stage or in the early part of the initiation or definition to brainstorm the programme or project objectives, scope, timescales, dependencies, risks etc. Should be attended by board members, the programme or project manager, and prospective team members.
Benefits identification and modelling	Held when determining the key benefits for a programme in the definition stage. Involves identifying the planned benefits and then determining the dependency network for the identified benefits.
	Can also collect input for benefit profile information.
Stakeholder identification and communications planning	Held at any time throughout the programme or project, but particularly valuable in the start-up and initiation stages of a project or the definition stage of a programme or tranche. Used to identify key stakeholders and understand their influence and impact upon and by the programme or project. The initial stakeholder identification stage may be followed by planning key communications.
Risk identification and risk assessment	Held at any time throughout the programme or project, but particularly valuable in the start-up and initiation stages of a project or the definition stage of a programme or tranche. Used to identify threats and opportunities to the objectives of the activities, assess those risks in open session, assign owners and actionees, and monitor activities.
Planning	Held at any time throughout the lifetime of a programme or project. Particularly useful during the initiation stage of a project or the definition stage of a programme or tranche as the solution is clarified and detailed plans are sought. May also be useful during a long implementation stage that has been split into management stages, each of which requires a next stage plan.
Problem solving	May be held at any time to resolve issues and generate solutions, or to consider options for assessing change requests or exceptions.
Lesson sharing	May be held as a workshop to brainstorm all lessons from a programme or project at closure, ends of stages or start-up.
Training	May be held periodically throughout the lifecycle to maintain the appropriate level of skills required to achieve outputs and outcomes.
Blueprinting	Held at the definition stage of a programme and periodically throughout the lifecycle in line with tranches or significant change control. Involves translating the vision into how it will impact the organization's business model in terms of its processes, organization, tools, information and managing a view as a programme progresses.
MoV study workshops	Various workshop types that are held throughout the lifecycle to identify and improve value.
Dependency workshops	Held at regular intervals by the portfolio to identify dependencies between programmes and projects.

5.6.5 P3O information portal

The objective of an information portal for the P3O is to provide easy access to components of the portfolio, programme and/or project delivery framework for the internal PPM community.

The key benefit is easier access to key information by all levels of the organization, compared with traditional approaches of detailed policy guides and PPM handbooks. An example of the lifecycle within an information portal is displayed in Figure 5.4.

In this example, the key stages and gating requirements for an organization in relation to programme management are provided in relation to taxonomy of definition, participants and funding source, contributing activities, templates, outputs and recommended activity timeframe.

Other examples of information-portal taxonomies may include detailed policies, requirements by programme governance theme or project management principle, samples of good organizational practice or education packs.

This technique is ideally delivered by means of an intranet site with links to the required templates or more detailed guidance.

5.6.6 Facilitation – workshop techniques

To be successful, programmes and projects require a shared understanding of their objectives, teamwork and effective decision-making. Programme and project decisions by their nature are contributed to by groups of people in meetings or workshops. However, the ineffective management of workshops can lead to wasted management time and effort, and the demotivation of the participants. Therefore, managing workshops is a key skill in the programme and project environment and the P3O is ideally placed to provide an independent facilitation role.

Table 5.7 shows a list of typical workshops held during the programme and project lifecycles, which may be independently facilitated by a P3O specialist or consultant.

Managing workshops

The effective facilitation of groups of programme, project and non-project staff is a key skill for P3O specialists or consultants.

Example

Planning workshop

A planning workshop is useful when developing a programme, project or stage plan. Attendees should be key stakeholders in the programme or project, or individuals who have been involved in similar initiatives in the past and have an understanding of what needs to be delivered. The workshop should be held during the start-up or initiation stages of a project. It should be facilitated by the P3O where possible and the programme or project manager should be an attendee. Key props include a large piece of brown paper, sticky notes and marker pens. The session should start with an understanding of the scope and objectives of the programme or project as understood to date. Where the planning workshop is being undertaken as part of a programme or project start-up workshop or definition workshop, the programme or project brief should already have been developed before the planning session. Where a stand-alone planning workshop is held, the audience should be given a copy of the brief before the workshop, to set the scene.

The group will then be facilitated to brainstorm the key deliverables and write each one on a sticky note. The sticky notes are then placed on the brown paper/flip charts in a logical time and dependency sequence. Where possible, the group should identify teams/work streams within the project and place the sticky notes in 'swimlanes'. When the sequence has been established and gaps identified and resolved, the diagram should be completed by drawing lines to show dependencies between work streams (swimlanes). The next step is to identify key decision or management review points and identify them by marking red 'milestones'.

By examining the flow diagram, the project team should be able to identify when meetings should be held, both with the project team and with the project board, and these can be marked on the plan.

If the 'right' participants are attending the workshop, it may be possible to assign owners to deliverables.

The final output should be a deliverable flow diagram, which can be converted to an electronic format (such as Visio or PowerPoint) for communication to the programme or project team and board. A simple sticky note would just identify the deliverable name, a reference number and an owner (see Figure 5.5). An agenda for a planning workshop should be developed as a standard template.

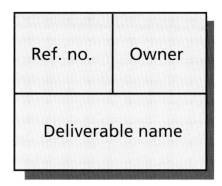

Figure 5.5 An example of a sticky note from a planning workshop

5.6.7 Skills development and maintenance

The objective of skills development and maintenance is to ensure that the appropriate competencies are available across the organization to match against portfolio, programme or project, or requirements.

The key benefit of this is to ensure resources are allocated to PPM roles with the appropriate level of skill. It also allows individuals to understand what their current skills are and what development opportunities they may require.

For the P3O, the benefits include providing an input into training needs analysis and assisting forward planning of resources against skills and competencies as well as capacity. The key inputs are a skills assessment framework (to assess against) and a skills assessment and accreditation process for relevant staff (either self-assessed or facilitated).

Skills development involves identifying the key skill categories and skills for multiple roles in the organization, setting targets for skill level by role and then determining recommendations to close the gaps where they exist.

This information can then be rolled up into an amalgamated resource view and presented as part of a management dashboard or status report.

The skills assessment should then recommend training or capability development opportunities aligned with P3O services or functions (e.g. training, mentoring, coaching, computer-based training etc.). The key output of the skills assessment is decision-support information for the P3O to determine options for professional development and personal support information for individuals to complete personal development plans.

Each organization will have its own set of skills and targets. There are a number of frameworks available that can be used or tailored for use by an organization, such as the International Project Management Association (IPMA) competence baseline (ICB) and the Association for Project Management (APM) competence framework.

Case study
Tailored skills assessment framework

In this example, the key skill areas were developed around generic skills, understanding of the business environment, contractual relationships, programme and project delivery, technical skills and the legal environment. This may be appropriate for a senior responsible owner (SRO)/P3O sponsor role.

The skills assessment involved determining the level of skills, ranging from 0 to 3 (see Table 5.8).

A number of enterprise PPM solutions with capability at the resource management level will provide more automated ways of monitoring and managing skills for PPM resources and matching competencies to programme or project requirements.

5.6.8 Business-process swimlanes

The objective of developing business-process swimlanes is to document standard and repeatable business processes with appropriate linkages (often across multiple divisions or business units within an organization) and agreed accountabilities.

The key benefit of this technique is to clearly document repeatable processes; these can be baselined and continually updated as the process evolves in response to lesson sharing and PPM maturity increases.

Table 5.8 An example of a skills assessment

Competencies	Assessment	Required level	Competency development
Generic skills			
Leadership	3	2	Mentor candidate
Teamwork	2	2	Skill level matched
Interpersonal skills	3	3	Skill level matched
Risk management	1	2	Assurance to provide lessons
Communication	3	3	Skill level matched
Influencing	1	2	Mentoring required
Desktop skills	1	1	Skill level matched
Facilitation	2	3	Mentoring required
The business environment			
Financial management	1	1	Skill level matched
Business-case development	3	2	Mentor candidate
Commercial business	2	2	Skill level matched
Asset disposal	0	2	Training requirement
Service delivery	0	1	Training requirement
Relationship management	3	3	Skill level matched
Commercial negotiation	3	3	Skill level matched
Programme and project delivery			
Programme management	2	3	Development through programme value or complexity increase
Project management	1	2	Mentoring or development required
Business change management	2	2	Skill level matched
Benefits management	1	2	Mentoring required
Team management	3	3	Skill level matched
Technical skills			
Procurement	3	2	Mentor candidate
Agile development	0	2	Training requirement
Information assurance	2	3	Mentoring required
Testing management	0	0	Skill level matched

Skill levels: 0 = No awareness; 1 = An awareness; 2 = In possession of knowledge; 3 = Expert.

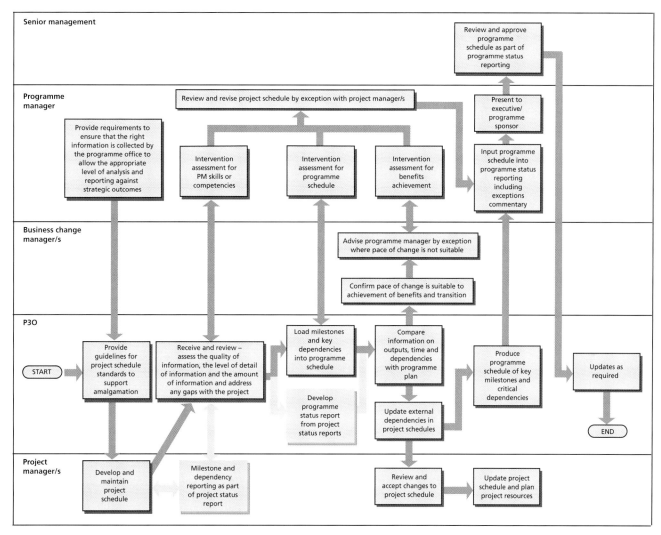

Figure 5.6 An example of a swimlane for schedule management

An example of a swimlane for schedule management in relation to a programme is displayed in Figure 5.6.

In Figure 5.6, the P3O is a temporary structure that has a key role in providing guidelines, receiving and amalgamating schedule information into a programme schedule, undertaking analysis and then updating the projects dossier as required.

5.6.9 Capacity planning for resource management

The objective of capacity planning for resource management at the portfolio level is to understand the resource capacity and competency supply-and-demand levels and take action to match these appropriately to meet delivery requirements.

Its key benefit is to reduce any barriers to successful delivery of programmes and projects that are due to a lack of resource capacity or competencies across the organization (or division/department).

The key inputs are an assessment of the resources available to the PPM environment (these may be full-time resources or those that contribute to projects on a part-time basis in addition to operational roles), skills assessments, and programme and project resource plans.

An example of a resource capacity view is provided in Table 5.9 and Figure 5.7, in both numerical and graphical form.

In the example shown in Figure 5.7, actions will need to be taken to:

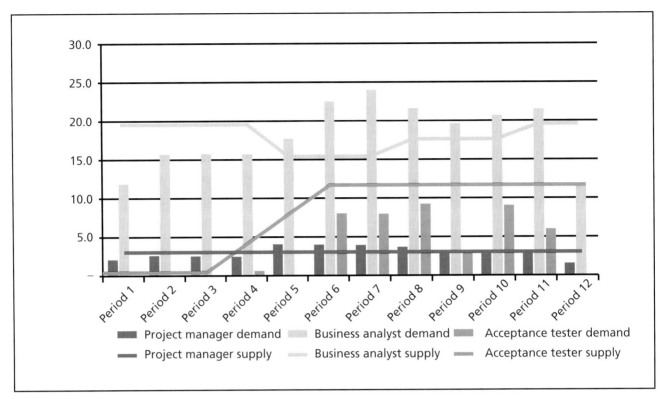

Figure 5.7 An example of a resource capacity view (graphical)

- Increase the number of project managers (in Periods 5 to 8) or delay Project E until Period 9, to smooth out the demand for project managers
- Investigate actions to deal with the oversupply of acceptance testers
- Investigate actions to match supply and demand for business analysts from Periods 5 through to 11.

Depending on the level of PPM maturity in the organization and the capacity of the P3O to undertake the process, capacity planning may simply be an annual baseline for the planned portfolio. This would inform project portfolio phasing to reduce gaps between resource supply and demand for the business year.

Capacity planning may only address the capacity of key known resource points of failure, or it may also include competencies.

As P3O capacity increases and the organization becomes proficient at programme and project planning and control, then capacity planning may involve more frequent assessments based on actual resource experience.

A number of enterprise PPM solutions with resource management functionality will provide more automated ways of monitoring and managing

resource capacity and competencies against the actual set of PPM resources, the tasks required across the portfolio, and known constraints (such as time spent by staff on operational work).

5.6.10 Assurance, gated reviews and health checks

The aim of assurance, gated reviews and health checks is to provide an independent assessment of how well the portfolio, programme or project is performing relative to its objectives and any relevant process or standards.

The key benefit is in providing objective assurance of the quality of decision-support information being provided to the P3O and the ability to highlight any issues requiring remedial action to get the programme or project back on track.

PRINCE2, MSP and MoP provide checklists for health checks. Guidance on gated reviews (OGC Gateway in the UK government) can be adapted to most organizations. The OGC Gateway guidelines also provide an understanding of delivery confidence assessments, which assess the confidence in the ability of the programme or project to deliver its aims and objectives.

Table 5.9 An example of a resource capacity view (numerical)

Project	Resource type	Period											
		1	2	3	4	5	6	7	8	9	10	11	12
A	Project manager					1.0	1.0	1.0	1.0	1.0	1.0	1.0	0.5
	Business analyst					3.0	3.0	3.0	2.0	2.0	3.0	4.0	
	Acceptance tester								1.0	1.0	4.0	1.0	
B	Project manager	1.0	1.0	1.0	1.0	1.0	1.0	1.0	1.0	1.0	1.0	1.0	1.0
	Business analyst	12.0	12.0	12.0	12.0	12.0	12.0	12.0	12.0	12.0	12.0	12.0	12.0
	Acceptance tester						5.0	5.0	5.0				
C	Project manager		0.5	0.5	0.5								
	Business analyst		1.0	1.0	1.0								
	Acceptance tester				0.5								
D	Project manager	1.0	1.0	1.0	1.0	1.0	1.0	1.0	0.5				
	Business analyst		3.0	3.0	3.0	3.0	5.0	5.0	3.0				
	Acceptance tester						3.0	3.0	3.0				
E	Project manager					1.0	1.0	1.0	1.0	1.0	1.0	1.0	
	Business analyst						3.0	4.0	5.0	6.0	6.0	6.0	
	Acceptance tester									2.0	5.0	5.0	
	Project manager demand	2.0	2.5	2.5	2.5	4.0	4.0	4.0	3.5	3.0	3.0	3.0	1.5
	Business analyst demand	12.0	16.0	16.0	16.0	18.0	23.0	24.0	22.0	20.0	21.0	22.0	12.0
	Acceptance tester demand				0.5		8.0	8.0	9.0	3.0	9.0	6.0	
	Project manager supply	3.0	3.0	3.0	3.0	3.0	3.0	3.0	3.0	3.0	3.0	3.0	3.0
	Business analyst supply	20.0	20.0	20.0	20.0	15.0	15.0	15.0	18.0	18.0	18.0	20.0	20.0
	Acceptance tester supply				4.0	8.0	12.0	12.0	12.0	12.0	12.0	12.0	12.0

Appendix A: Roles and responsibilities

A

Appendix A: Roles and responsibilities

When designing the P3O model and deciding on the right model, job descriptions should be identified that are specific to an individual. The job descriptions may focus on a management or generic role (e.g. head of programme office) or on a specific function (e.g. finance officer) or a combination of different functions.

This appendix outlines a set of management or generic roles and functional roles. The functional roles may, in a larger or permanent office, be allocated to a single person or multiple people; in a smaller or temporary office, however, these roles will often be combined in a single person's job description.

The following role descriptions should be treated as a 'pick and mix' set to create custom job descriptions tailored to the organization's business and customer requirements. This may include addition of the qualifications required to undertake the role, years of experience, skills, key performance indicators (KPIs) and refinement of the responsibilities to align with the organization.

Where a role is aligned with a particular function or service, the reader should also refer to the relevant heading in Table F.1 in Appendix F for a more detailed breakdown of services.

The following roles are described in more detail in the rest of this appendix:

- Management roles:
  - P3O sponsor
  - Head of P3O (permanent office)
  - Head of programme or project office (temporary office)
- Generic roles:
  - Portfolio analyst
  - Programme or project specialist (programme or project consultant)
  - Programme or project officer (programme or project coordinator or administrator)
- Functional roles:
  - Benefits and value
  - Commercial
  - Communications and stakeholder engagement
  - Information management

- Consultancy and performance management
- Finance
- Issue
- Change control
- Planning and estimating
- Quality assurance
- Resource management
- Risk
- Reporting
- Secretariat/administrator
- Tools expert.

A.1 MANAGEMENT ROLES

A.1.1 P3O sponsor

A.1.1.1 Purpose

The purpose of the P3O sponsor is to champion and direct the establishment and evolving operation of the P3O. The P3O sponsor will ideally be a member of the main board and may also take the role of portfolio director.

The role requires strong leadership and management skills, coupled with authority to champion the P3O set-up and continual improvement. The individual will need to develop and maintain robust relationships with all parts of the business, as well as with the programmes and projects, to ensure that the P3O meets the requirements of the main board.

The individual will need to understand the wider objectives of the portfolio, have credibility within the environment and be able to influence others. They must be able to develop and maintain effective working relationships with senior managers, the programme and project teams, and any third-party service providers.

A.1.1.2 Responsibilities

- Provide leadership by articulating outcomes and energizing people through change
- Develop and maintain a viable business case to secure the investment required to set up or re-energize the P3O
- Work in partnership with senior managers in business areas to identify how the P3O could assist in the delivery of their change portfolio

- Provide strategic challenge, overview and scrutiny, ensuring alignment with wider policy and strategic initiatives
- Manage the key strategic risks
- Ensure evolving business needs and issues are addressed effectively.

A.1.2 Head of P3O (permanent office)

A.1.2.1 Purpose

The purpose of the head of P3O (also called head of portfolio office, centre of excellence (COE) or hub portfolio office) is to establish and run the permanent office. The head of P3O may also take the role of portfolio manager.

The role requires strong leadership and management skills, coupled with strong PPM or strategy/business-planning skills, to ensure the integrity of the portfolio or programmes and projects. The incumbent will need to develop and maintain robust relationships with all parts of the business, as well as with the programmes and projects, to ensure that all initiatives meet the requirements of the portfolio or programme board. They will also need to work with business areas to identify any gaps in initiatives and to understand what activities are planned to fill those gaps.

The individual will need to understand the wider objectives of the portfolio and programme, have credibility within the environment and be able to influence others. They must be able to develop and maintain effective working relationships with senior managers, the programme and project teams, and any third-party service providers.

The role will also provide strategic challenge, overview and scrutiny, ensuring alignment with wider policy and strategic initiatives.

In some organizations the head of P3O may be a strategic or business-planning manager or director.

A.1.2.2 Responsibilities

- Develop and implement the terms of reference for the COE, portfolio office or hub portfolio office
- Ensure that the portfolio delivers the organization or departmental strategy
- Ensure the portfolio activities contribute to the bottom-line value of the organization and delivery of benefits from all programmes and projects

- Recruit, develop and retain the portfolio office, programme office or COE team
- Work with the senior business managers/directors, senior responsible owners (SROs) and programme managers to define and implement the portfolio or programme(s) management framework
- In conjunction with business owners and programme managers, create strategies for the effective planning, monitoring and delivery of the portfolio
- Assure the overall integrity and coherence of the portfolio
- Support the portfolio director (senior business manager/director) in sanctioning programmes and projects for inclusion in the portfolio/programmes
- Maintain close relationships with other key business initiatives that are currently under way, as well as other bodies, to ensure that there are no overlaps in responsibilities
- Provide an ongoing health check of the portfolio/programme(s) by reassessing whether the programmes/projects continue to meet the overall strategic objectives
- Design, challenge and agree management dashboards
- Establish access to policy and strategic information for all programmes and projects
- Scan the horizon for potential policy changes or initiatives and inform the programme(s) and project(s) when policy or strategy changes
- When strategic initiatives are not as successful as expected and fail to deliver the expected benefits, help to analyse why, particularly to differentiate between a poor strategic idea and the poor implementation of a good strategic idea
- Provide strategic oversight support for the portfolio board
- Establish framework agreements for the purchase, roll-out and maintenance of organization-wide PPM tools, training and consulting
- Act as owner of programme and project frameworks, templates and procedures; be responsible for ensuring they are fit for purpose and continue to be best practice
- Advise on tailoring the templates and procedures to achieve an appropriate project structure
- Keep abreast of and evaluate the effectiveness of new project management tools and techniques.

A.1.3 Head of programme or project office (temporary office)

A.1.3.1 Purpose

The purpose of the head of programme or project office is to establish and run the temporary programme or project office.

The role requires strong leadership and management skills, coupled with strong PPM skills, to ensure the integrity of the programme or project. The individual will need to develop and maintain robust relationships with all parts of the business, as well as with the projects, to ensure that all initiatives meet the requirements of the programme or project board. The individual will also need to work with business areas to identify any gaps in initiatives and to understand what activities are planned to fill those gaps.

The individual will need to understand the wider objectives of the programme or project, have credibility within the environment and be able to influence others. They must be able to develop and maintain effective working relationships with senior managers, the programme and project teams, and any third-party service providers.

They must have the ability to deputize for the programme manager.

The role will also provide strategic challenge, overview and scrutiny, ensuring alignment with wider policy and strategic initiatives.

A.1.3.2 Responsibilities

- Develop and implement the terms of reference for the programme or project office
- Work with the business lead/SRO and programme manager to define and implement the programme or project governance framework
- In conjunction with business owners and programme, project or team managers, create strategies for the effective planning, monitoring and delivery of the programme or project
- Support the overall integrity and coherence of the programme or project
- Support the programme manager in sanctioning projects for inclusion in the programme
- Support the programme or project manager in ensuring that existing initiatives and projects are effectively adopted into the programme
- Support the programme or project manager in agreeing project closure

- Maintain close relationships with other key programmes that are currently under way, as well as other bodies, to ensure that there are no overlaps in responsibilities
- Identify dependencies among the programme, its projects and other programmes/business change initiatives
- On behalf of the programme or project board, provide an ongoing health check of the programme or project by reassessing whether it will continue to meet the overall objectives
- Report progress to the programme or project manager and programme or project board via management dashboards
- Facilitate end-of-tranche reviews and benefits reviews on behalf of the programme manager
- Set up access to policy and strategic information
- When strategic initiatives are not as successful as expected, help to analyse why, particularly to differentiate between a poor strategic idea and the poor implementation of a good strategic idea
- Provide strategic oversight to the SRO, informing the programme or project when policy or strategy changes
- Be responsible for team objectives, one-to-one reviews and evaluation, and continual improvement of the P3O service
- Be responsible for workload management of the team and the prioritization of ad hoc work requests versus core team deliverables.

A.2 GENERIC ROLES

A.2.1 Portfolio analyst

A.2.1.1 Purpose

The purpose of the portfolio analyst role is to facilitate the development and ongoing management of an optimized portfolio, ensuring senior management decisions lead to the fulfilment of strategic objectives through the delivery of programmes and projects (aligned with business-as-usual objectives).

A.2.1.2 Responsibilities

- Provide a strategic overview of all programmes, projects and interdependencies, reporting anomalies or areas of concern to senior management

- Analyse the portfolio and make recommendations on the programme/project mix to the decision-makers
- Balance/optimize the portfolio in terms of strategic goal attainment vs. delivery capacity/ capability and business-as-usual priorities
- Evaluate and help to implement process improvements to improve project workflow and more effective delivery
- Develop and manage the prioritization model
- Develop, maintain and provide expert assistance to the commissioning process whereby programmes and projects are added to/deleted from the portfolio
- Facilitate governance/portfolio meetings
- Develop and maintain the management dashboard
- Initiate reviews of post-programme and post-project evaluation reports and benefits to ensure the strategic goals have been enabled/met
- Develop and maintain the portfolio delivery plan
- Provide support/information to business planning
- Develop and maintain a portfolio resource schedule, mapping available resources against programmes and projects
- Develop and maintain the portfolio risk register
- Develop and maintain a portfolio dependencies register
- Assess benefits management across a number of programmes or projects to identify gaps, overlaps and conflicts, and eliminate double counting in the benefits management plans of individual programmes and projects
- Develop and maintain KPIs for the portfolio
- Scan the horizon for impending strategy or policy changes that may impact on the composition of the portfolio, and communicate an impact analysis to the strategy board
- Provide an aggregated analysis of gated reviews to the strategy board
- Examine post-stage-gated review/gateway improvement plans to ensure key strategic portfolio actions are delivered
- Develop portfolio stakeholder strategy and ensure communications are timely and effective
- Liaise with the finance team regarding monitoring of financial spending and timing/ support for audits
- Provide decision and governance support:

- Regularly review the appropriateness and deliverability of the portfolio
- Review the relative business priorities and risk profiles
- Escalate issues to the strategy board.

A.2.2 Programme or project specialist

A.2.2.1 Purpose

The purpose of the programme or project specialist is to provide specialist hands-on support for programme and project managers. They play a proactive role in knowledge management to promote programme and project management methods and standards, and the implementation of best programme and project management practice.

Post holders provide a consultancy service to programme and project managers or programme and project boards across the organization or department. This consultancy may take the form of advice and guidance or may be of a specific nature in the form of facilitated workshops. At the beginning of a programme or project, the specialist would work with the programme or project manager and the business managers to help define an appropriate level of governance and structured programme/project management and to decide on the level of support and the types of services required.

They may provide a tailored series of workshops, which may include elements of start-up advice, risk analysis, scoping, planning, tailoring of methods etc.

A.2.2.2 Responsibilities

- Provide a centre of expertise and develop consistent standards and procedures, including templates, and guidance in their tailoring across a range of programme or project sizes, to include:
  - Programme/project initiation
  - Risk analysis
  - Issue and change control analysis
  - Information/configuration management
  - Activity- and product-based planning techniques
  - Methods and tools
  - Quality assurance
  - Programme/project organization structures.
- Provide a focal point to promote the use and benefits of the programme or project management method, giving a consistent and common approach – develop and lead collaborative learning forums

- Coordinate information about how programmes and projects run the standard programme or project management method, their progress and problems
- Provide briefings to programme/project board members and programme/project assurance staff on their roles and responsibilities
- Provide a fast-track programme/project mobilization support service through collaborative working, facilitated workshops and tailoring of standard approaches and templates
- Review completed programmes and projects to distil good practice and note any factors that unnecessarily adversely affect the duration or outcome of a programme/project, so that they can be avoided in the future
- Set up 'buddy relationships' for new/inexperienced staff
- Design and support governance/reporting for programmes or projects
- Build and maintain a register of approved training courses in change, programme and project management, and associated disciplines. This register will include details of the courses, the level of person they are aimed at, and the dates when they will be held throughout the year
- Build and maintain a register of PPM events – exhibitions, forums, seminars etc. – and publicize them to the PPM community
- Provide a central coordination point for change management training, both internal and external. Provide an administrative service in the form of booking and organizing courses, both internal and external. This will include the booking of venues and refreshments, liaison with tutors and external organizations, the issuing of delegate lists and course joining instructions, and the management of course fees due
- Build and maintain a repository of good examples of programme and project documentation, e.g. project initiation documentation (PID), blueprints, product descriptions, end stage/tranche assessments, programme/project closure reports, benefit profiles, stakeholder maps, quality management strategy, risk management strategy
- Build and maintain a library of resources – training aids, DVDs, reference material, manuals etc.

A.2.3 Programme or project officer

A.2.3.1 Purpose

The purpose of the programme or project officer (who may also be known as the coordinator or administrator) is to improve the planning and delivery process by collecting and maintaining data in a consistent form.

A.2.3.2 Responsibilities

- Implement guidelines, procedures and templates to collect and maintain consistent data and provide hands-on delivery support to a programme or project
- Facilitate the creation and update of programme or project plans as required by the programme/project manager. Identify where cross-project dependencies exist and track/monitor these in support of the programme/project manager
- Implement agreed regular progress-reporting mechanisms for all projects and thereby monitor the routine progress of projects, and assist the programme/project manager in the preparation of the programme status/project highlight reports
- Establish and maintain an information management system, and manage both electronic and hard-copy configuration libraries. Provide basic training in configuration management techniques
- Establish risk, issue and change-control processes and templates, and assist the programme and project team in their delivery
- Manage or facilitate the quality review process for programmes or projects
- Provide a coordination/administration service to a programme or project.

A.3 FUNCTIONAL ROLES

A.3.1 Benefits and value

A.3.1.1 Purpose

The purpose of the benefits and value role is to ensure that a consistent 'fit for purpose' approach to benefits and value management is applied across the portfolio or programme and that benefits realization is optimized from the organization's investment in change. The role may be undertaken by the portfolio benefits manager or report to the portfolio benefits manager.

The finance department plays a key role in determining the approach, methods and standards to be applied.

A.3.1.2 Responsibilities

■ Develop and maintain the P3O's benefits management framework and ensure alignment of MoV activities

■ Establish the infrastructure required to implement the benefits management framework

■ Provide training and awareness-building sessions on the application of the benefits management framework

■ Participate in investment appraisals, ensuring that business-case benefits forecasts are consistent with the organization's benefits eligibility rules

■ Work with business change managers and their teams to promote more effective benefits management practices

■ Provide advice and support to PPM and business-as-usual colleagues on the development of initiative-level benefits forecasts and benefits management strategies

■ Provide assurance on the effectiveness of benefits management

■ On behalf of portfolio or programme management:
  ● Facilitate agreement of the benefits management strategy
  ● Lead benefits and dis-benefits identification activities
  ● Lead and facilitate MoV studies
  ● Facilitate benefits-mapping workshops and develop and maintain a benefits map
  ● Facilitate agreement of the benefit profiles
  ● Apply MoV techniques to enhance the expected benefits and to add more value
  ● Facilitate agreement of the benefits realization plan
  ● Maintain the benefits forecast
  ● Assess the impact of change requests for their potential effect on benefits realization
  ● Track and report benefits realization progress for the dashboard
  ● Escalate issues with benefits realization as appropriate

■ Set the standards for, and monitor, post-implementation reviews to compare benefits realized with benefits forecast to capture lessons in relation to benefits management for wider dissemination

■ Work with the business managers or business change managers and their teams to identify additional opportunities for benefits management

■ Work with the business managers or business change managers and their teams to minimize any dis-benefits

■ Regularly review and improve the effectiveness of benefits management arrangements

■ Assess benefits management across a number of programmes or projects to identify gaps, overlaps and conflicts, and eliminate double counting in the benefits plans of individual programmes and projects.

A.3.2 Commercial

A.3.2.1 Purpose

The purpose of the commercial role is to ensure that the organization carries out the role of 'informed customer', and that all commercial/procurement practices and decisions meet designated standards and offer the organization value for money. It may also take on the role of supplier relationship manager, developing efficient and effective relationships with suppliers, outsourcers and partners.

The role may be a P3O role, but it is more likely to be embedded in the P3O, with formal line management from the commercial, procurement or purchasing function. It may also exist within a virtual P3O.

A.3.2.2 Responsibilities

■ Early engagement with commercial, procurement or purchasing teams to scope the commercial element of the portfolio, programme or project

■ Provide ongoing liaison with commercial, procurement or purchasing teams

■ Provide liaison with relevant statutory procurement functions (e.g. Government Procurement Service in the UK government)

■ Develop and execute the portfolio, programme or project procurement strategy

- Undertake contracts management, including tracking deliverables against existing contracts and managing any third-party or subcontractor contracts
- Ensure all contracts remain up to date and exit strategies are in place
- Provide analysis of any requests for change that may have a contractual impact
- Coordinate purchase order activity
- Ensure compliance with any applicable organizational, national and international standards and legislation
- Provide commercial expertise/advice to the portfolio and programme teams and constituent projects
- Facilitate relationships between the organization's senior management community, SROs and senior managers within the supplier community
- Take on supplier relationship manager responsibilities (in partnership with the commercial, procurement or purchasing department/function), which may include:
  - Facilitating the management of supplier and contractual risk and measuring all aspects of supplier performance, instigating remedial actions whenever and wherever necessary
  - Conducting contractual reviews with all major suppliers to the programme or project on a regular basis
  - Managing all aspects and stages of the contract lifecycle on behalf of the programme or project manager
  - Maintaining a catalogue of suppliers, services, products and contracts within the programme or project
  - Providing a single liaison and contact point for all supplier and contractual issues
  - Developing a full understanding of supplier strategies, plans, business needs and objectives
  - Ensuring that the programme or project is working in partnership with suppliers, building on long-term relationships
  - Facilitating the development and negotiation of appropriate, achievable and realistic contracts and contractual targets with suppliers
  - Facilitating the negotiation of 'value-for-money' services and products with all suppliers.

A.3.3 Communications and stakeholder engagement

A.3.3.1 Purpose

The purpose of the communications and stakeholder engagement role is to ensure the effective management of the portfolio, programme or project's stakeholders.

A.3.3.2 Responsibilities

- Maintain the list of stakeholders and their interests
- Lead the work to identify and document the programme stakeholders (internal and external), their interests and their potential impact on the programme, recording the information in stakeholder profiles
- Facilitate the formulation of a stakeholder engagement strategy and the associated portfolio, programme or project communications plan to ensure:
  - Awareness among all stakeholders of the benefits and impact of the portfolio or programme
  - That expectations do not drift out of line with the planned delivery
  - Commitment from stakeholders to the changes being introduced – thus ensuring the long-term success of the portfolio, programme or project
  - That all stakeholders are informed of progress before, during and after the implementation or delivery of project outputs and programme outcomes
  - The promotion of key messages from the portfolio, programme or project
  - A demonstration of the commitment to meeting the requirements of the portfolio, programme or project sponsors
  - Truly two-way communication exists by actively encouraging stakeholders to provide feedback and ensuring they are informed about the use of their feedback to influence the portfolio, programme or project
- Promote opportunities to maximize the benefits obtained from the portfolio or programme
- Coordinate stakeholder engagement and communication, ensuring effective timing and interdependency management of communications
- Coordinate internal portfolio and programme communications

- Monitor the effectiveness of communications
- Handle press enquiries (providing the point of contact between portfolio, programme or project and the press office)
- Establish and maintain any portfolio, programme or project intranet site or information portal.

A.3.4 Information management

A.3.4.1 Purpose

The purpose of the information management role (also known as configuration librarian) is to act as the custodian and guardian of all master copies of the portfolio, programme or project's information. The role may also take on asset management.

The role should work closely with the security function or department in an organization in order to ensure full information and physical security is considered within a portfolio, programme or project.

A.3.4.2 Responsibilities

- Ensure key information assets are under configuration management and change control, sharing information within the project, programme or portfolio as required
- Create and operate libraries or other storage areas to store products and keep reference materials (such as induction packs) up to date
- Develop and manage document control procedures to cover baseline management, controlled issue of master documents, version control, document history and distribution lists
- Create an identification scheme for all products and assist in the identification of products – naming and filing conventions
- Establish and administer baselines
- Control the receipt, storage and issue of all portfolio, programme or project products
- Maintain a record of all issued copies of products and notify holders of any changes to their copies
- Undertake configuration audits and maintain status information on all products
- Ensure supplier configuration items (documentation and assets) are under control by providing a single point of entry to and exit from the programme for such items (working with commercial staff as appropriate)

- Seek out knowledge about how to access relevant information outside the programme office, other systems in the organization, internet resources etc.
- Ensure processes are in place to handle the security and confidentiality of programme/project documentation or other assets (see section 3.3.6).

A.3.5 Consultancy and performance management

A.3.5.1 Purpose

The purpose of the consultancy and performance management role is to provide internal consultancy and expertise in PPM and organization processes, and the monitoring of certain programmes and projects. The services provided are focused on maintaining minimum standards and achieving target performance.

Post holders seek to continually improve the performance of the portfolio, programme and projects within an organization. They create, maintain and disseminate good practice.

A.3.5.2 Responsibilities

- Own PPM standards and methods, ensuring processes and templates are maintained in line with industry best practice
- Set up and maintain a performance (process) improvement plan (fed by previous lessons)
- Set up and track portfolio, programme or project metrics to monitor and control performance
- Own the process for sharing lessons and devising action plans, disseminating lessons
- Provide specialist high-level planning skills for programmes and projects
- Provide project assurance services to project and programme boards, either directly or through the engagement of third parties
- Run facilitated workshops, e.g. start-up, risk, planning, requirements, lesson sharing, benefits mapping
- Undertake mentoring or coaching of portfolio, programme or project staff, including programme and project sponsors/SROs; set up 'buddy relationships' for new/inexperienced staff
- Undertake portfolio, programme or project induction (to purpose, roles, processes etc.)
- Develop case-study material and feed back to COE

- Perform programme and project fast-track start-up and closure assistance (through facilitated workshops)
- Support programme and project 'rescues' through hands-on development and delivery of action plans
- Act as trainer in PPM for internal courses/workshops
- Act as method specialist/expert in PPM – provide help, advice and guidance on tailoring
- As tools expert (enterprise project tools, risk tool, collaboration tool etc.), provide technical leadership, coaching and mentoring in all PPM tool utilization
- Provide consultancy-style services to programme and project delivery teams at mobilization and throughout the lifecycle of a programme or project, ensuring a common approach is adopted and tailored, and good practice is distilled and shared
- Carry out health checks on programmes and projects at any time during the lifecycle, when requested by the programme/project manager or board
- Provide business performance monitoring and reporting
- Keep abreast of and evaluate the effectiveness of new programme and project management tools and techniques that support the development and change management approach
- Provide performance deviation escalation management.

A.3.6 Finance

A.3.6.1 Purpose

The purpose of the finance role is to establish a professional finance function within the portfolio, programme or project to ensure the timely provision of portfolio, programme or project funding and effective financial control.

The role may be a P3O role, but it is more likely to be embedded in the P3O, with formal line management from the finance function. Post holders may also assist the portfolio, programme or project manager with budget control.

A.3.6.2 Responsibilities

- Work with the central finance function to ensure the availability of appropriately profiled funding across financial period(s)

- Administer budget allocations and estimates of future spending
- Develop and maintain the portfolio, programme or project financial controls, paying particular attention to audit requirements
- Review and track portfolio, programme or project costs and, where applicable, revenues (using earned value analysis techniques where applicable)
- Analyse and collect portfolio, programme and project financial information, review and track programme or project costs and (where applicable) revenues; calculate and analyse cost variance
- Support benefits profiling
- Manage invoicing and collection activities
- Prepare monthly financial reports for the portfolio, programme or project manager and for inclusion in status reports
- Create and maintain financial models for the depreciation and amortization of programme and project costs
- Provide programme accountancy assistance with:
  - Developing and refining programme and project business cases
  - Creating and distributing financial reports
  - Development and maintenance of the resource management plan
  - Advice on cost control and opportunities for savings
  - Adherence to accounting procedures
  - Capitalization of capital assets.

A.3.7 Issue

A.3.7.1 Purpose

The purpose of the issue role is to take the lead in ensuring that the portfolio, programme or project has effective processes in place to identify, monitor and resolve issues.

A.3.7.2 Responsibilities

- Develop and implement the issue management strategy, ensuring that the commercial function leads on contractual issues
- Clearly communicate the issue management strategy, and the benefits of following it, to all personnel involved with the portfolio, programme or project
- Establish and maintain the portfolio, programme or project issue register

- Register issues for subsequent investigation and resolution, monitoring items identified as requiring action, prompting timely actions and reporting on whether required actions have been carried out
- Ensure that all issues have a nominated owner and actionee
- Ensure that the agreed responses to issues are planned, resourced and implemented
- Communicate with stakeholders, particularly those who are directly affected either by the issue itself or by the response to the issue
- Assess how effective any issue response has been
- Facilitate the regular monitoring and review of all issues
- Proactively examine issue registers across the portfolio or programme (within projects) to look for common themes and establish consistent resolution strategies
- Establish and maintain an efficient two-way flow of information between the portfolio, programmes and their projects, regarding issues and their handling
- Facilitate cross-programme/cross-project impact analysis
- Escalate issues to higher authority, e.g. business area management, when necessary
- Liaise with the information role on configuration management.

A.3.8 Change control

A.3.8.1 Purpose

The purpose of the change control role is to take the lead in ensuring that the portfolio, programme or project has effective processes in place to identify, monitor and resolve changes.

A.3.8.2 Responsibilities

- Develop and implement the change control process, ensuring that commercial functions lead on contractual changes
- Clearly communicate the change control process, and the benefits of following it, to all personnel involved with the portfolio, programme or project
- Establish and maintain the portfolio, programme or project change register

- Register changes for subsequent investigation and resolution, monitoring items identified as requiring action, prompting timely actions and reporting on whether required actions have been carried out
- Ensure that all changes have a nominated owner and actionee
- Ensure that all changes have appropriate impact analysis and are planned, resourced and implemented through formal configuration management
- Communicate with stakeholders, particularly those who are directly affected either by the change itself or by the response to the change
- Facilitate the regular monitoring and review of all changes
- Proactively examine change registers across the portfolio or programme (within projects) to look for common themes and establish consistent resolution strategies
- Establish and maintain an efficient two-way flow of information between the portfolio, programmes and their projects, regarding changes and their handling
- Facilitate cross-programme/cross-project impact analysis
- Escalate changes to higher authority, e.g. business area management
- Liaise with the information role on configuration management.

A.3.9 Planning and estimating

A.3.9.1 Purpose

The purpose of the planning and estimating role is to take responsibility for facilitating the development and maintenance of the portfolio, programme or project plan and dependency logs.

A.3.9.2 Responsibilities

- Define planning standards for portfolio, programmes or projects to enable ease of roll-up of milestone data and dependencies
- Facilitate the design, development and ownership of the portfolio, programme or project plan, ensuring that all milestones and internal and external dependencies are identified, logged and monitored
- Maintain and update plans, advising on missed forecasted milestones, missed dependencies and impact assessment

- Maintain and update resource plans, advising on resource clashes and shortcomings
- Ensure all product-based plans include activities, time and resource estimates for risk mitigation
- Ensure quality review activities and associated time have been allocated realistically
- Analyse interfaces and dependencies between projects and recommend appropriate actions where anomalies exist or there are areas of concern
- Undertake tracking and maintenance of dependencies
- Establish and operate mechanisms to track portfolio, programme or project delivery against the plan; update progress against the plan
- Identify and report deviations and trigger exception reports when appropriate
- Review plans against business-as-usual plans to ensure change can be adopted effectively
- Provide estimating support to the portfolio, programme(s) or projects
- Define and manage time-recording processes; use systems/tools to capture actual progress data
- Ensure impending policy or strategy changes are assessed for their impact on the portfolio, programme or project plans or dependencies.

A.3.10 Quality assurance

A.3.10.1 Purpose

The purpose of the quality assurance role is to lead the work to ensure that any new products or services delivered by the portfolio, programme or project are fit for purpose and are capable of delivering the benefits required by the organization board.

A.3.10.2 Responsibilities

- Ensure compliance with any applicable organizational, national and international standards and legislation
- Bring together portfolio, programme or project staff of different disciplines and drive the group to plan, formulate and agree a comprehensive quality management strategy and quality management plan
- Establish consistent quality practices and standards, adhering to governance arrangements; monitor performance by gathering relevant data and producing statistical reports

- Ensure tests and procedures are properly understood, carried out and evaluated, and product modifications are investigated if necessary
- Work with the finance manager/analyst to ensure the portfolio, programme or project complies with audit requirements
- Develop bespoke processes, standards and templates (tailored approach) for quality management
- Coordinate quality reviews of portfolio, programme or project documents and deliverables (this could be independent, reporting directly to the board or SRO)
- Provide health checks
- Provide guidance on quality criteria, reviewers and sign-off authority to ensure cross-portfolio or cross-programme(s) consistency
- Work with commercial/purchasing staff to ensure an effective interface with suppliers' quality systems and oversee the quality review process for contractual supplier deliverables
- Liaise with COE or other bodies to arrange stage-gated reviews (OGC Gateway reviews in UK government programmes and projects), health checks and audits, as required
- Coordinate gated reviews and stage reviews, and ensure all information is available in a timely manner and a quality format.

A.3.11 Resource management

A.3.11.1 Purpose

The purpose of the resource management role is to ensure that current and future programmes and projects are equipped with enough human resources of the right skills, at the time they are needed, and that those human resources are used as efficiently as possible.

A.3.11.2 Responsibilities

- Provide a capacity planning and resource tracking service across a portfolio or programme(s)
- Capture the resource requirements of the portfolio, programme or project and the P3O itself
- Forecast future resource needs, based on portfolio/programme/project plans, close liaison with the relevant managers and (where appropriate) wider business plans and business-unit objectives (demand management)

- Provide a view of commitments (of portfolio, programme or project staff) on other programmes/projects and/or on business-as-usual activities that will impact the ability of a portfolio, programme or project to deliver
- In consultation with human resources and others, decide on the best source for the required resources, depending on the long-term requirement for a particular skill and its likely availability
- Plan and initiate the acquisition of the necessary staff, in terms of both skill content and quantity, ensuring they are in place at the time needed
- Actively monitor the deployment of staff, arranging new postings (where possible) in advance of assignments ending, to meet staff development needs and to maintain a good match of skill to role – both delivery and P3O staff
- Work with human resources (HR) and line management to facilitate succession planning, including knowledge management and leavers' process as required
- Maintain a database of resources, for people and their skills/attributes, location, availability, contact details and lead responsibility for the resource
- Take an active role in the training and development of portfolio, programme or project staff to increase the available skills capability and capacity within the business
- Review the provision of skills audits (delivered through the COE or hub portfolio office) to determine whether the proposed programme/project staff have the required skills to deliver their role on the programme or project
- Establish formal mentoring and coaching guidelines and mechanisms
- Provide 'help squads' – supplementary skills to fill shortfalls within the portfolio, programme or project; assist in engaging 'just in time' resources where new requirements surface at short notice
- Manage consultants' and interims' contractual status, closely monitoring use of externals to ensure ongoing value for money and that the requirement still exists
- Where a flexible PPM resource pool is in place, manage resource planning, data collection and PPM skills development.

A.3.12 Risk

A.3.12.1 Purpose

The purpose of the risk role is to take the lead in ensuring that the portfolio, programme or project has effective processes in place to identify and monitor risks, has access to reliable and up-to-date information about risks, and uses the appropriate controls and actions to deal with risks. This role should also ensure that these processes are aligned with corporate risk management policy.

A.3.12.2 Responsibilities

- Develop a risk management strategy for the P3O in accordance with the corporate risk management policy; clearly communicate the strategy, and the benefits of following it, to all personnel involved with the portfolio, programme or project
- Establish and maintain the portfolio, programme or project risk register
- Assist in the identification and ongoing management of risks by running risk workshops and risk-review workshops
- Ensure that all risks have a nominated owner and actionee; ensure that risks are proactively managed
- Ensure that the agreed risk responses are planned, resourced and implemented; give advice on appropriate risk responses and contingency planning
- Ensure risks are prioritized and dealt with at an appropriate level of management
- Ensure all project risks that have wider programme implications are escalated and dealt with at programme level, and that any programme risks that have wider strategic implications are escalated to either corporate risk management or the senior management board, and facilitate this escalation process
- Provide cost estimates for all outstanding risks and ensure that risk mitigation costs do not exceed risk occurrence costs
- Communicate with stakeholders, particularly those who are directly affected either by the risk itself or by the risk responses
- Assess how effective any response actions have been and whether the risks identified have actually materialized, including the realization of opportunities
- Actively monitor and regularly review all risks on a constructive, 'no blame' basis

- Establish and maintain an efficient two-way flow of information between the portfolio, programmes and their projects, regarding risk handling
- Proactively examine risk registers across the portfolio or programme (within projects) to evaluate the net effects of common threats and opportunities using modelling or simulation techniques
- Establish consistent mitigation and contingency plans for risks that should be tackled across the portfolio or programme
- Support the sharing of risk registers with the supplier community
- Assess and monitor the effectiveness of risk processes and refine as necessary.

A.3.13 Reporting

A.3.13.1 Purpose

The purpose of the reporting role is to provide a reporting service to the portfolio, programme or project. It also collates base data and generates reports to multiple audiences through aggregated data.

A.3.13.2 Responsibilities

- Provide regular reports to boards, including a commentary on performance, coordinating upward aggregation of data/information and reports – highlight reports, programme status reports, management dashboards etc.
- Ensure integrity of reports through consistent traffic lights; define and challenge traffic-light status
- Identify and report deviations and trigger exception reports when appropriate
- Develop processes to fulfil the internal reporting needs of the programme, including the development and production of any contractual reports
- Ensure that reporting deadlines are achieved
- Ensure the reporting process is robust, exception-based and flexible enough to meet the changing needs of the programme or project
- Develop a weekly/monthly reporting calendar with reminders to information contributors
- Implement and manage the weekly and monthly reporting cycle, chasing information as required and challenging the quality of the component data

- Build and maintain an information base of trend data for the programme or project reporting, e.g. rolling traffic lights to ensure 'glitches' are seen as such and not exaggerated out of context.

A.3.14 Secretariat/administrator

A.3.14.1 Purpose

The purpose of the secretariat/administrator role is to provide portfolio, programme or project administrative support and a secretariat function for the relevant boards.

A.3.14.2 Responsibilities

- Maintain knowledge/reference library/repository in relation to governance boards, using the approaches set by the information librarian
- Support facilities requirements (accommodation, IT support, office equipment), as far as possible matching supply to demand, switching and releasing facilities as necessary
- Support the resource management role with the acquisition of resources by maintaining relationships with external organizations that can supply resources: contract agencies for staff, organizations that rent plant and equipment, agencies that rent/let building space (work with the commercial team) etc.
- Support the quality assurance role by liaising with the COE or other bodies to arrange health checks, audits, third-party reviews and stage-gated/gateway reviews, as required
- Provide a help desk facility for enquiries/issues/problems; record requests for assistance, assign them to members of the P3O team and track the requests to resolution
- Provide administrative support to the P3O, including workshop/meeting administration and the establishment and maintenance of the filing system (in conjunction with the information/configuration management function)
- Provide logistical support for training courses (booking rooms, trainers and refreshments, and liaising with attendees)
- Provide administrative support for other non-PPM activities, e.g. travel and hotel bookings.

A.3.15 Tools expert

A.3.15.1 Purpose

The purpose of the tools expert role is to provide expertise in software tools to support the change environment. The role may provide support to the PPM community to configure software, or to provide training and coaching in its use. Examples of tools may include enterprise programme and project software, and planning, risk, document management or collaboration tools.

A.3.15.2 Responsibilities

- Examine the market to source tools
- Liaise with tools vendors regarding requirements specifications
- Liaise with tools vendors regarding implementation plans and training
- Carry out internal mentoring/coaching in tools
- Advise new programmes and projects on the appropriate use of tools.

Appendix B:
Business case example

B

Appendix B: Business case example

This appendix describes a business case for a programme or project to develop or enhance a P3O model or office.

B.1 AIMS

By [*specify date*] the organization will have a mature [*define desired level of P3M3 maturity*] P3O that will improve the development of a prioritized portfolio and improve capabilities across the organization to deliver and realize the business change associated with programmes and projects across the portfolio.

The P3O will improve return on investment across the portfolio by a minimum of x [*specify amount*] %.

The organization will be a learning organization with established PPM standards, using highly visible work practices and processes, accountabilities, governance and reporting, coupled with appropriately skilled staff and fit-for-purpose technology.

B.2 BACKGROUND/REASONS

- Lack of visibility of all change leading to inappropriate investment decisions
- Strategic objectives not being met
- Lack of information to make investment decisions and prioritize funds and resources effectively
- Lack of effective capacity planning leading to top-heavy programme and project resourcing and inappropriate use of scarce technical and business resources
- Lack of consistency in programme and project approaches and methods
- Adverse impact on organization's reputation
- Inconsistent delivery of programmes and projects against time, cost and quality targets – late, over budget, failure to deliver capability or outcomes
- Actual benefits not being realized as specified in business cases.

B.3 OBJECTIVES

To achieve the stated aims, the P3O will achieve the following high-level objectives for the organization.

B.3.1 Portfolio level

- Compile the current business-change portfolio and details of potential additional programmes and projects
- Integrate the current business-change portfolio and organizational strategy, identifying opportunities for optimization
- Establish and maintain the capability to deliver a balanced, prioritized portfolio of change, clearly aligned with organizational strategy
- Establish and maintain a capacity planning and resource management service
- Establish and maintain a decision-support service through management dashboards
- Coordinate programme and project activity across the portfolio to minimize bottlenecks (e.g. decision-making bodies) and constraints
- Establish benefits management and strategy realization links to performance measurement.

B.3.2 Programme level

- Facilitate progress towards the achievement of strategic outcomes for each of the programmes by maintaining a programme management methodology and ensure that it is consistently applied and continuously improved
- Act as the information hub to support effective governance, prioritization and performance management towards required strategic outcomes
- Support strategic governance and senior stakeholder engagement through management reporting at a highlight level or by exception (where required)
- Support the assurance of the delivery of each programme through gated reviews and health checks on behalf of relevant boards
- Improve cost management approaches across programmes.

B.3.3 Project level

- Support more effective project delivery through the maintenance of a project management methodology, processes and supporting systems, skills management and the provision of advisory services

- Support more efficient project management through the centralized management of key components of the project management process across projects
- Assure the quality of project management outputs through a flexible governance structure to monitor all projects, project health checks and ad hoc assurance of key project management components
- Enable higher-quality results with more realistic project plans
- Improve cost management approaches for projects.

B.4 COST–BENEFIT ANALYSIS

B.4.1 Typical costs

For each cost type, consider both initial or set-up cost and ongoing cost (per year or per programme/project (in a temporary office)) – see section 2.4.5 on running costs. Table B.1 gives examples of different cost types.

B.4.2 Expected benefits

Benefits may be those derived from setting up and operating the P3O model from scratch, or those derived from expanding the services of an existing P3O model.

This section may also take into account any cost savings (e.g. staff costs) or income generated (through selling services) to provide a balanced cost–benefit analysis.

Some typical benefits may be:

- **Supporting programme and project management standards** Projects following a standard lifecycle are more often completed on time, on budget, to the required quality and within scope. We have:
  - Estimated savings = no. of projects × no. of people × average hourly rate × hours per week x weeks
  - Example: 20 projects × 10 people × £30/hour × 40 hours/week × 4 weeks = £960,000

This example assumes time to market will be reduced by 4 weeks for 20 projects. Of course, the additional revenue that can come from new products delivered to market more quickly can make these benefits pale by comparison.

- **Identify programme and project risk and resource constraints** A P3O will require project managers to improve risk mitigation, dependencies, constraints and subsequent impacts on the business. We have:
  - Estimated savings = no. of projects × no. of people × hourly rate × hours per week x weeks
  - Example: 6 projects × 10 people × £30/hour × 40 hours/week × 11 weeks = £792,000

Proper risk identification can result in the cancellation of 20% of projects before the execution phase. In the example above, savings assume six projects will be cancelled before execution begins. The time savings are the average for the execution and subsequent phases.

Table B.1 Cost elements

Cost type	Description
Staff	The people employed within the P3O. Consider salaries, contract rates and other costs of employment (employer costs).
	Consider also recruitment and retention costs (training etc.)
	There may be a mix of permanent and temporary (contract or consultant) staff. What are optimum levels?
Infrastructure	Office space, desks, equipment, collaboration zones (for facilitated workshops, meetings etc.)
Tools	PPM software, resource management, collaboration, intranet etc.
Training/development	Include the training and development of P3O staff and those who use their services.
	Include any team-building activity costs.
Consultancy	Initial costs to set up the office or model and ongoing support costs for interim assignments, e.g. workshop facilitation, independent gated reviews etc.
Communications and marketing	Costs incurred in engaging key stakeholders, marketing the P3O services and communicating effectively.

■ **Development cost improvement** Tracking and monitoring progress on projects will provide better information to make decisions on the deployment and use of resources and capital. In addition, the significant increase in visibility, cross-functional management support and tracking of these projects will enable the portfolio of projects to accelerate their delivery. We have:

● Estimated savings: average aggregated budget of 60 active projects in portfolio, annualized = £75 million

● A 5% annual delivery improvement in time and budget for the projects in the portfolio = £3.75 million.

■ **Programme and project prioritization** Delivering unnecessary or inappropriate programmes and projects inhibits the organization's ability to maximize profit, increase its market share and deliver its strategy whilst using scarce resources. Prioritization of a portfolio of programmes and projects should lead to the elimination of these unnecessary or inappropriate programmes or projects, with a subsequent cost saving. Thus we have:

● Example: Elimination of 10 projects at an average cost of £600,000, annualized, for total expected savings of £6 million

● This assumes that the project prioritization process assists management in making the decision not to implement a specific project based on the strategic objectives of a programme.

■ **Reduction in programme or project start-up timescales** Evidence from organizations has shown that providing a focused programme or project start-up service through facilitated workshops can reduce start-up times by more than 50%. Additional benefits are that a programme or project is better scoped and more realistically planned, and stakeholder engagement improves measurably. We have:

● Estimated savings = no. of projects × no. of people × hourly rate × hours per week × weeks

● Example: 10 projects × 2 people × £30/hour × 40 hours/week × 6 weeks = £144,000.

■ **More effective use of resource pool** Evidence has shown that programmes and projects hang on to resources for longer than their natural 'value add' period, e.g. a planner can add value at the beginning of a project but is often retained throughout the lifecycle of the project. Use of a flexible resource pool through a hub portfolio office means that resources can be deployed and their usefulness/'value add' monitored so that they are only deployed for a minimum time period.

■ Similarly, where scarce resources exist within an organization, such as technical architects, testers and others, the portfolio can be designed around their availability and optimal usage, thereby reducing overall delivery costs. A side benefit usually occurs as programmes and projects are less likely to be held up while awaiting the availability of scarce resources or are able to use less expensive internal experts rather than going to the contractor market.

B.4.3 Key performance indicators

See Table B.2 for examples of KPIs and how they are measured.

Table B.2 Key performance indicators

KPI	How the KPI will be measured
10% improvement in benefits delivered per year	% of business-case benefits delivered
Programme management office (PMO) provides value five times greater than its cost	Satisfaction of IT governance board
10% faster project completions per year	Average total elapsed project time
10% lower capital spend per year	Average project cost (normalized for size)
10% lower support costs per year	Average ongoing support costs

B.5 HIGH RISKS

As mentioned in Chapter 2, a number of common barriers may need to be overcome in order for the establishment of a P3O model to be successful. Table B.3 outlines a selection of risk events and possible treatments to counteract some of these common barriers.

B.6 INVESTMENT APPRAISAL (TO INCLUDE OPTIONS)

The format for an investment appraisal will vary according to the organization, and advice should be sought as to the appropriate format in the organization. Any investment appraisal should include costed options for developing the approach being suggested, so that a balanced decision on the return on investment may be made. The organization's finance department will generally advise on internal standards and policies on investment appraisals, and will provide support for the process to be followed to develop the appraisal and obtain agreement.

A sample investment appraisal form is shown in Table B.4.

Table B.3 Risk events and possible responses

Risk event	Risk response
P3O may be seen as bureaucratic and adding to paperwork burden on delivery resources	Ensure all standards and templates are tailored to the organization, with additional flexing guidelines. Include project teams in the development of the standards
P3O may become a dumping ground for non-portfolio, programme and project activities, or people, that don't have a 'home'	Develop a P3O blueprint clearly defining its role and responsibilities
P3O staff are seen as administrators with a lack of experience to carry out a meaningful oversight, challenge and scrutiny role	Define roles/responsibilities for P3O staff, ensure they are appropriately graded by independent human resources (HR) assessment and obtain commitment to the seniority of the roles by a senior management champion
May have problems recruiting the right mix of people in the organization and on the open market (or obtaining appropriate funding for credible staff)	Define roles/responsibilities for P3O staff; grade appropriately to attract the best staff. As part of mobilization, consider recruiting consultants or interims to establish best practice and engineer a skills transfer to internal or newly recruited staff
Lack of commitment from senior management to the benefits of P3O	Engage a senior management champion and sell them the benefits and impact on the bottom line. Use the champion to engage the rest of the senior team
P3O may be seen as a resource bottleneck	Ensure processes are seen as fair and workable. Involve current project teams in their development
Lack of career path for P3O staff, or programme and project community, resulting in loss of key resources and replacement costs	Ensure that career development is included in the P3O functions and services
P3O may be seen as getting in the way of decision-making and delivery	Engage a senior management champion and ensure all P3O processes are clearly aligned with organization governance processes and decision-making bodies
Lack of senior management ownership of portfolio of programmes and projects (similarly, lack of enterprise-level strategy for alignment)	Ensure main board owns the full portfolio of change – hold stakeholder workshops to ensure common understanding of the strategy, the portfolio of change required and the plan to successfully implement the strategy

Table B.4 An example of an investment appraisal form

	Including redundancy costs	Excluding redundancy costs
Benefits/annual savings/income		
One-off costs		
Annual costs		
Payback period		
Net present value		
Return on investment		
Author		
Business sponsor	Suggested approver should be main board director	

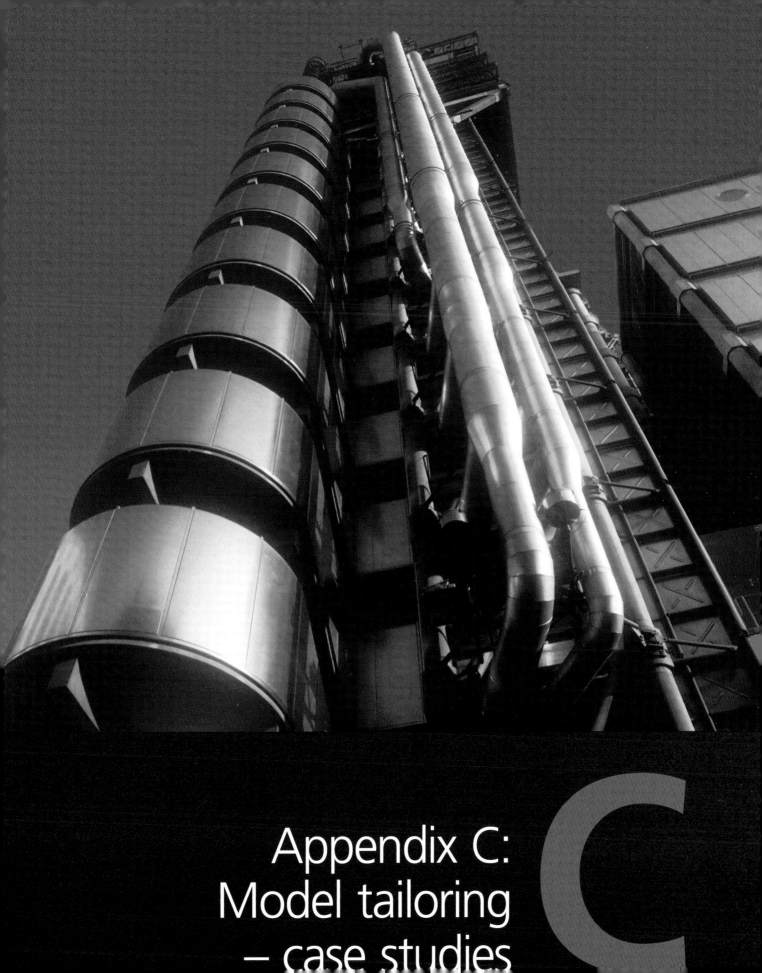

Appendix C:
Model tailoring
– case studies

Appendix C: Model tailoring – case studies

This appendix describes a series of case studies for different P3O models across a variety of organization types (see Table C.1). Each model has been developed to meet a specific business need and some have evolved over several years as the organization's PPM has evolved or the business drivers and organization structure have changed.

In developing a P3O model, consider the organizational context of these case studies and be aware of the success factors in their evolution.

As has been said before, there is no 'one size fits all' solution, but these case studies may provide some ideas to implement in similar organizations.

CASE STUDY 1 – OLYMPICS 2012 PROGRAMME OFFICE

The Olympics 2012 programme office (see Figure C.1) was established to provide assurance and oversight to the high-level governance bodies. It provided an oversight role for the four key objectives of the 2012 Olympics and their programme and project management delivery organizations. Its key role was to provide a 'critical friend' through scrutiny and challenge, reviewing and reporting performance across the programme, monitoring and measuring progress against delivery plans and

an integrated programme plan, and proactively challenging risks, issues and changes across the programme.

It was set up with a small team of programme specialists, all of whom were experts – senior professionals who were able to challenge through experience and knowledge. It did not impose standards on the constituent programmes/projects that delivered the four key objectives but used common standards for reporting of performance through progress reports, enabling the creation of management dashboards for the governance bodies. Reporting to the programme's senior responsible owner (SRO), it was empowered to challenge at the highest levels and encountered a receptiveness and willingness to work together across the programme. Its key driver was putting in the right framework rather than imposing rigid standards.

The secretariat and office administration, finance and strategic communications functions were all provided through separate but linked teams. This allowed the central programme office to provide a true 'critical friend' role, unencumbered by day-to-day operational functions.

Table C.1 Sample P3O models across a variety of sectors

Number	Organization type	Key features
1	International sporting event	Temporary; oversight, scrutiny and challenge; assurance; collaborative
2	Government agency	Organization portfolio office; hub portfolio office; functional roles; standards; assurance; delivery support; scrutiny and challenge
3	Food manufacturing	Permanent centre of excellence (COE); generic roles; standards; delivery support
4	Retail organization	Organization portfolio office; governance; assurance; standards; business-focused programmes; outsourced project office through work packages
5	Services organization	Permanent COE + delivery support office; flexible resourcing model
6	Telecommunications	Permanent strategic office + COE; hub-and-spoke model with small generic teams focused on business divisions; flexible resource model
7	Pharmaceutical wholesale and retail	Organization portfolio office; move from delivery support services to strategic planning/portfolio support; organizational context and evolution

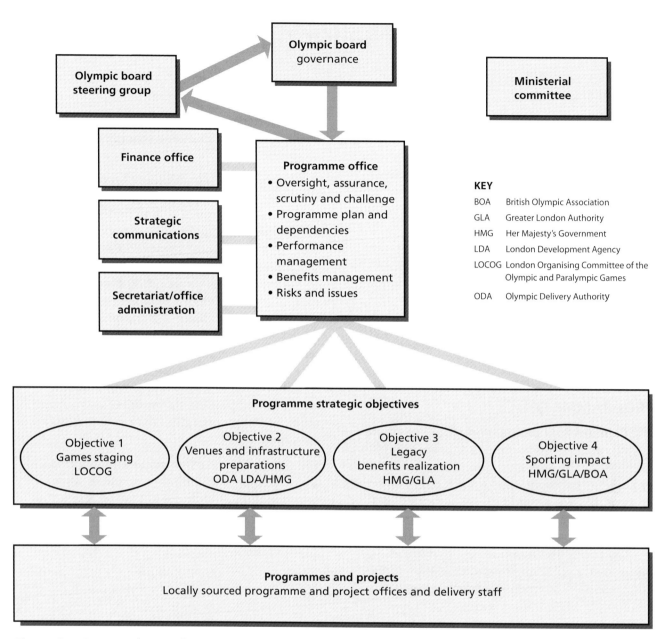

Figure C.1 Case Study 1 – Olympics 2012 programme office

Hints and tips: Case Study 1

A key challenge on a programme of this nature is to ensure good communications across the various delivery strands. The programme office does this through a facilitated programme managers' network, which all the programme offices attend. A key role of the network is to raise the profile of PPM across the programme and provide the linchpin for good practice and the building of relationships.

A key success was in providing ownership and scoping for cross-partner issues and the definition of boundaries of responsibility around issues, providing a central point for the escalation and resolution of aspects of risk. The programme office also provided a professional facilitation service for issue workshops to ensure speedy resolution.

As the programme progressed, it also owned the process for sharing lessons and the database, capturing overall programme delivery issues to inform future Olympic delivery programmes around the world.

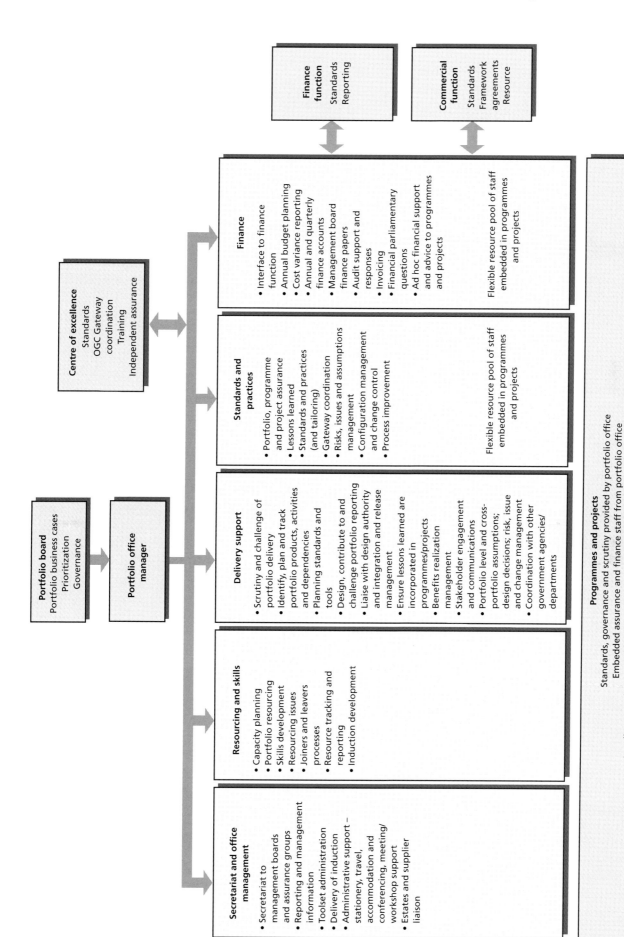

Figure C.2 Case Study 2 – Government agency

CASE STUDY 2 – GOVERNMENT AGENCY

This portfolio office services a business division within a larger government department (see Figure C.2). The government department has a COE with standards and methods, assurance and good-practice teams, and gateway coordinators. The division operates a portfolio of change to meet its strategic objectives and goals, governed through a portfolio board aligned with the business and operational functions. The portfolio office provides governance support, tracks alignment with other government department initiatives, provides tailoring of COE standards and assurance against the standards, and provides a delivery support and scrutiny/challenge function. It also provides financial tracking and consolidated progress reporting.

Some staff from the portfolio office, i.e. for the finance and assurance roles, are assigned or embedded in individual programme and project teams. However, individual temporary programmes and projects design and build their own teams, including programme and project staff. Programme and project office staff carry out planning, risk, issue, change management, information management and administration roles. They may be permanent or contract staff and the central resourcing function considers their utilization as part of an overall resource planning approach. However, in practice the programme and project office teams tend to be too large, as they are taken on for a specific role and not redeployed once their original function has been delivered.

Hints and tips: Case Study 2

This model demonstrates two key issues: (1) a lack of centralized capacity planning and (2) individual programmes and projects creating their own teams, which grow over time and can be overstaffed. A strong assurance function is important to ensure that standards and methods are adhered to and tailored appropriately, otherwise the roll-up of plans, milestones and progress reports becomes difficult, unwieldy and time-consuming. The portfolio team of functional experts need to be empowered to ensure central standards are followed. Wherever possible, a proper capacity-planning function should be in place, with a flexible pool of embedded resources, rather than allowing temporary programme/project managers to employ the support staff they want.

CASE STUDY 3 – FOOD MANUFACTURING COMPANY

This organization's programme office is a typical single office with a focus on 'doing things right', providing a COE, reporting and practical hands-on help across all change in the organization (see Figure C.3). Its stated aim is to drive lower costs, reduce uncertainty and increase the predictability and success of outcomes. It improves project capability across the organization by developing a standard approach to running projects (based on PRINCE2), working in partnership with project managers to ensure the successful delivery of key corporate projects (advice/guidance or practical hands-on support) and adding value by communicating effectively, providing leadership and training in best-practice PPM. It does not perform the role of a portfolio office, in that it focuses on programme and project delivery support rather than enabling or supporting business planning, prioritization or overall capacity/capability planning.

Hints and tips: Case Study 3

This type of programme office has to have a P3O sponsor who believes in the value it can provide, which may sometimes be intangible. It can be the target for cost cutting as it is sometimes viewed as a 'nice to have' overhead. Ensure performance metrics are built that illustrate the value the office brings and the impact on the bottom line.

The head of programme office and key staff in this scenario should be senior trusted individuals who are good communicators, coaches and mentors – they need to 'sell' successful project approaches and overall must have practical experience of running projects. The best programme offices of this kind are staffed by former programme or project managers with a flair for stakeholder engagement and the right level of experience. They must have credibility: all too often, programme offices are staffed with junior staff who add little value to the project managers they seek to serve and help.

CASE STUDY 4 – RETAIL ORGANIZATION

The programme management office (PMO) has a number of linked teams that provide a virtual portfolio office, including COE functions (see Figure C.4):

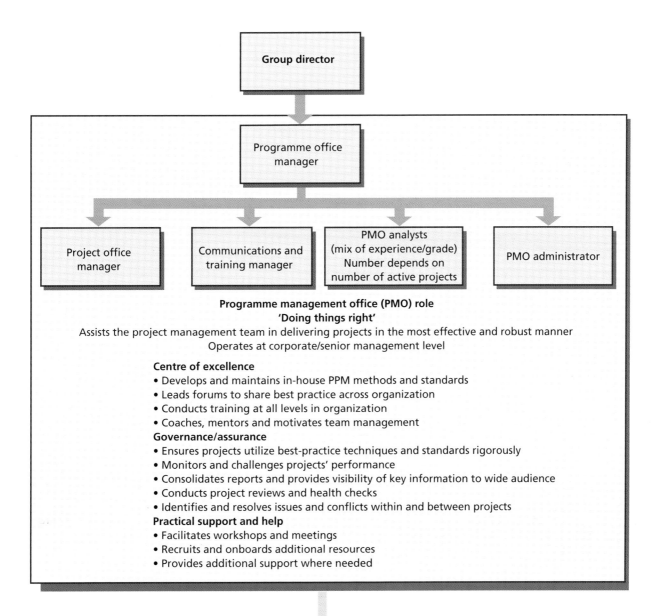

Figure C.3 Case Study 3 – Food manufacturing company

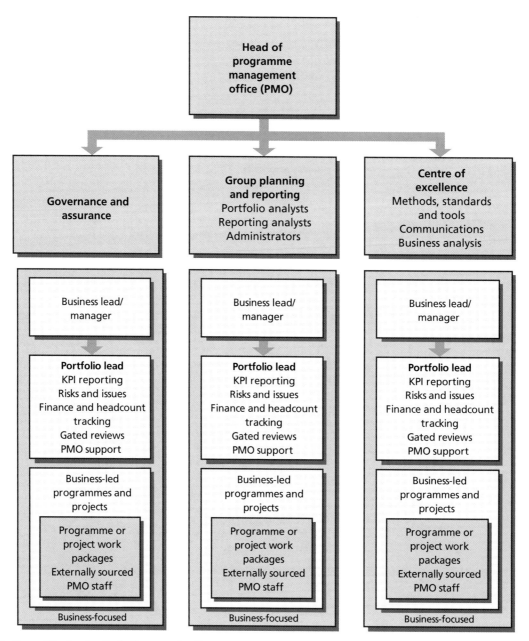

Figure C.4 Case Study 4 – Retail organization

■ **Governance and assurance** Defining governance arrangements for major programmes and projects, and assuring that they continue to meet strategic objectives and have effective governance and plans in place to deliver benefits

■ **Group planning and reporting** Portfolio functions of planning, prioritization, alignment with strategy, finance tracking and consolidated reporting

■ **Centre of excellence** Standards/methods, communications and business change.

Each business function has a portfolio lead, a permanent member of staff reporting into the business line, who provides a delivery support and challenge function to the business lead. Many of the new programmes or projects are outsourced via work packages to external PPM consultancies via framework agreements. In these instances a temporary programme or project function consisting of programme/project managers and programme/project support staff, including planners and risk, issue and change analysts, is bought in. The work package is closely monitored and support staff are retained only for specific tasks, with bottom-line 'value add' being a key driver.

Hints and tips: Case Study 4

This model requires good relationships with external suppliers who understand the business and its PPM standards. The work packages need to be focused on outputs rather than roles, so that the onus is on the supplier to provide the most effective set of resources to ensure delivery. Independent assurance from the core PMO team is essential to ensure that programmes and project work packages provide good value for money and that external resources use internal methods and standards effectively.

CASE STUDY 5 – SERVICES ORGANIZATION

This services company had a very strong group IT function that provided programme and project management for all key initiatives across the group (see Figure C.5). Each year, as part of the business-planning cycle, individual business divisions agreed their portfolios of change and these were prioritized centrally by the strategic development team (led by the group strategy director) and ratified by the group board. Once the full portfolio of change was agreed, the programme and project management group provided a programme manager per business division, supported by a team of project managers

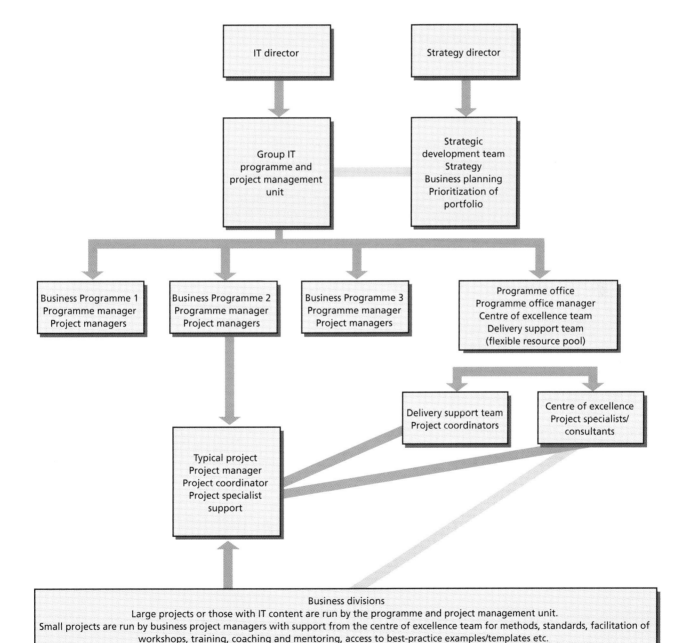

Figure C.5 Case Study 5 – Services organization

and project support staff from a central pool. Where possible, these were permanent staff, supplemented by contract staff where demand exceeded internal supply or authorized headcount.

The programme office consisted of two teams. The COE team provided methods and standards, help, advice and guidance, facilitated workshops, knowledge management and training. Individual consultants within the COE team were assigned to projects to provide start-up assistance, support collaborative workshops and assist in the development of plans where required. The delivery support team provided project coordinators who were assigned to projects to work with project managers, providing secretariat and administrative support, risk register, issue log and change log maintenance, plan and report maintenance, and acting as configuration librarian.

Hints and tips: Case Study 5

In this model, responsibility for consolidated progress reporting, resource management across the programme, and prioritization of delivery into the business environment lay with business programme boards consisting of the programme manager, business information manager and senior business managers/directors. Overall optimization of programme and project capacity was done through team meetings between the head of programme and project management and the programme managers.

The business divisions also ran portfolios of small/medium business-based projects or initiatives. These were often serviced through satellite programme offices consisting of project managers and project coordinator roles. The standards adopted by these satellite teams were those from the IT COE and training in their use was provided across the group.

CASE STUDY 6 – TELECOMMUNICATIONS

This organization has divisions responsible for different threads of the group strategy (see Figure C.6). Each division has evolved its own programme and project delivery model, with different gated

lifecycles in existence to suit the local business drivers. The technology division has a strategic office that manages strategic alignment, approval of business cases and prioritization of delivery. Once programmes and projects are approved, the business teams/departments manage their own programmes/projects using staff from the central programme office and a programme/project management team. The central programme office provides COE functions, capacity planning of programme/project staff, and centralized consolidated planning and reporting.

Each business team or department (a variable number) is assigned a PMO lead (line-managed by the central PMO), who is responsible for ensuring central standards are adhered to and tailored, providing the link to the central programme office for milestone and dependency tracking and reporting, and acting as the point of escalation for risks, issues and changes. The PMO lead has a flexible pool of resources at three levels of competency, consisting of specialists (PPM experts, planning, workshops, knowledge management etc.), support analysts and administrators (reporting, risk, issue and change, quality reviews, information management and administration). The PMO leads may have line management responsibility for resources in other business teams and meet regularly in a PMO forum to exchange ideas, lessons etc.

The central programme office's flexible pool of specialists, support analysts and administrators is composed of 60% permanent and 40% contract staff.

Hints and tips: Case Study 6

This model is widespread in private organizations, providing centralized control of standards, assurance and reporting while establishing delivery support resources at the point of delivery. It requires strong leadership from the central programme office and continuity of the P3O sponsor. The PMO leads need to be carefully chosen, trained and coached, with a particular emphasis on matrix management techniques. They should also be permanent members of staff wherever possible.

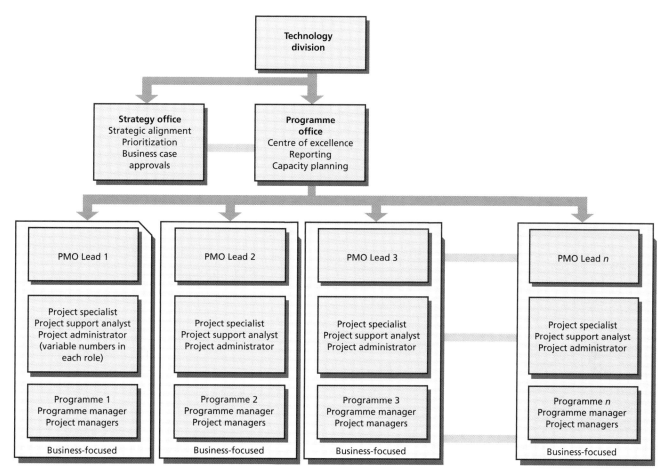

Figure C.6 Case Study 6 – Telecommunications

Key successes for this model have been: adherence to a single consistent gated lifecycle; reductions in the number of contract staff; and centralized capacity planning reducing overall headcount, with more control over what the programme and project teams use support staff for (and for how long). Another noted success has been the roll-out of a collaborative approach to project start-up, which has accelerated progress through gates 0–2 of the standard gated lifecycle from nine months to nine weeks on average. This was achieved by setting up collaboration zones (physical spaces) around the offices and training the core programme office team, PMO leads and specialists in collaborative facilitated workshop techniques.

CASE STUDY 7 – PHARMACEUTICAL WHOLESALE AND RETAIL

This organization (see Figure C.7) has a typical IT function which provides a range of functions and services to the business, including help desk,

operations maintenance and support, changes and project work. The IT function is fully financed by recharging the costs to other business functions through a fixed monthly charge for operations and small changes, together with a time-and-materials charge for project work.

The IT function has an established project delivery method but has historically struggled to balance resource demands across all the business requirements.

Initially, the PMO manager reported to the projects delivery manager and was part of the project delivery team. Functions and services focused on providing delivery support to the project managers. The successful (or otherwise) delivery of projects was often overshadowed by the delivery of low-value/priority projects.

After spending time engaging with the senior team to establish credibility and identify where the PMO could add the most value, the reporting line of the PMO manager was moved to the IT director. Focus moved from providing services to the projects delivery team, to IT senior management and the UK

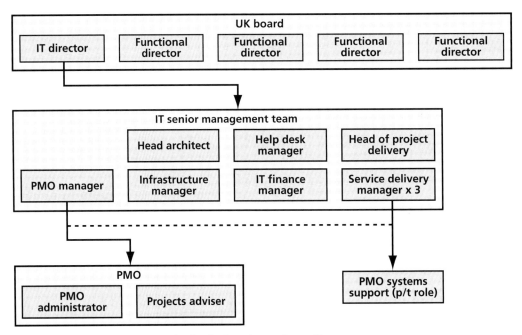

Figure C.7 Case Study 7 – Pharmaceutical wholesale and retail

board. Portfolio management was implemented within the function to provide a more effective use of resources against the strategic programmes. This included the maintenance of registers of project and business-as-usual activity, implementation of appropriate prioritization processes for the various types of work, and information assurance to ensure that the information provided to the IT senior management team and UK board was fit for purpose.

Hints and tips: Case Study 7

This small PMO focuses on the functions and services that add the most value to the organization and are primarily for the benefit of the IT senior management team and the UK board, with only minimum support being provided to the projects or delivery teams.

Input to prioritization can only be established with a PMO manager who has a high level of credibility with their peers and maintained with clear evidence of the improved contribution to the strategic programmes. Information assurance is critical for success.

Appendix D: Examples of tools and techniques

Appendix D: Examples of tools and techniques

To assist with a number of the concepts described in Chapter 5, an online repository of a sample set of generic tools and techniques has been provided. To access this repository go to the following website and follow the links for Knowledge Centre, Best Practice Guidance and P3O:

www.best-management-practice.com

The tools and techniques are provided as a starting point for tailoring and alignment with the organization's requirements.

The site is designed so that samples of good practice can be uploaded for sharing with the wider P3O community. All contributions are welcomed.

Appendix E:
P3M3 summary

Appendix E: P3M3 summary

P3M3 (also known as the Portfolio, Programme and Project Management Maturity Model) provides a very useful input into the development of a P3O blueprint in terms of current and target portfolio, programme and project management capabilities. It is an excellent tool for measuring the success of capability improvement over time, based on three individual models:

■ Portfolio Management Maturity Model (PfM3)
■ Programme Management Maturity Model (PgM3)
■ Project Management Maturity Model (PjM3)

Figure E.1 shows the overarching structure for these three models.

Tables E.1–E.3 provide a summary of the attributes for portfolio, programme and project management (respectively) across each of the process perspectives for five maturity levels.

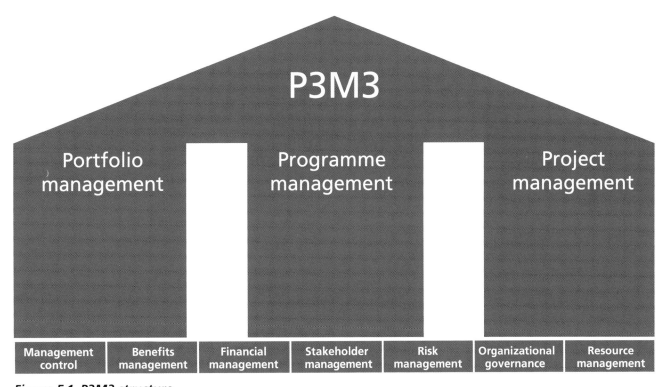

Figure E.1 P3M3 structure

Table E.1 Portfolio level (PfM3)

Level	Process perspective	Comment
1	Management control	The organization recognizes the portfolio, but has little or no documented processes or standards for its management, and a limited directory of programmes and projects.
		The recognition of a corporate or departmental portfolio by the organization is a significant step usually associated with the investment control or business-case approval process. It is an important first step towards PPM maturity because, by articulating the portfolio, the organization sets out its criteria for prioritization and oversight.
	Benefits management	There is a recognition that programmes and projects exist within the corporate portfolio to enable the achievement of benefits for the organization. However, this will not translate into a defined benefits management process.
	Financial management	Portfolio oversight of programmes and projects may be recognized but there is little or no corporate investment control.
		There is some financial control but it is often left to budget centres to approve and control programmes and projects according to their own criteria.
	Stakeholder management	The portfolio may be acknowledged, but there is little or no connection between programme and project output, and business outcome and benefits.
	Risk management	There is a growing recognition that risks need to be managed and that, at least for key business initiatives (e.g. cost saving, major site developments), risks threaten success.
		There is risk identification (probably in different systems, e.g. spreadsheets, text documents, databases etc.) and maybe some quantification of risk, but little actual management of risk.
	Organizational governance	The organization has some inconsistent and informal attempts to align individual programmes and projects with corporate objectives, and there is an ad hoc, inconsistent and ineffective oversight of programmes and projects.
	Resource management	Programme and project resource requirements are recognized but not systematically managed. Resources are planned, developed and allocated on an ad hoc and, usually, project basis.
		The symptoms of not having a portfolio approach to resource identification and allocation are all too obvious, but the organization has yet to fully commit to undertake robust corporate portfolio management.

2		
Management control	There are some pockets of portfolio discipline within individual departments, but this is based on key individuals rather than implemented as a comprehensive and consistent organization-wide approach.	
	The concepts of portfolio management will have been grasped by some and indeed there may be local experts. Work will be ongoing to establish a portfolio management approach across the organization through the recognition of an investment cycle, e.g. proposition, feasibility, design, implementation, review etc.	
	Improved business-case definition is enabling programmes and projects to be tested against the corporate objectives and priorities.	
Benefits management	The development of the investment cycle will be increasing the awareness and importance of identifying benefits and subsequently tracking whether they have been achieved. However, the realization of benefits is still likely to be patchy, inconsistent and not monitored.	
Financial management	There are some pockets of good business-case production and some, usually departmental, structures to oversee investment decisions. However, business cases are often appraised independently of each other, and real corporate priorities have not been established.	
	Reasonable financial control, business-case production, procurement appraisal, and investment control are restricted to individuals and departments.	
Stakeholder management	A portfolio of programmes and projects that serve the corporate objectives and priorities is increasingly seen as the driving force for approval, oversight and performance management.	
	The portfolio is tending to be driven by individual programmes and projects, i.e. bottom up.	
Risk management	The increasing awareness that the organization bears corporate risk tends to lead to a top-down (perhaps 'knee-jerk') approach to identifying portfolio risk (focusing on major corporate initiatives) that is unconnected to the bottom-up identification of risks in programmes and projects. This often leads to duplication of effort, competing teams, non-optimal allocation of funding, inconsistency and, therefore, the ineffective management of corporate risk.	
Organizational governance	Some attempts are made to recognize the portfolio of programmes and projects, but there is still no overall leadership and direction for the process.	
	Programmes and projects may be initiated and run without full regard to the corporate goals, priorities and targets.	
	It is difficult to establish the rationale for which programmes and projects are funded or approved.	
Resource management	The organization has started to develop resource management processes and improve the identification and allocation of resources to specific initiatives. However, this is likely to be reliant on key individuals and does not assess the impact of resource allocation against the wider portfolio.	
	The problems of not managing resources across the portfolio will be better understood and solutions are starting to be developed in isolated programmes or departments.	

Table continues

Table E.1 *continued*

Level	Process perspective	Comment
3	Management control	Standard portfolio management processes, as well as roles and responsibilities for governance and delivery, are defined, documented and understood.
		Corporate portfolio management processes have specified owners and there is evidence of use and effectiveness of a portfolio management office.
		Planning and reporting tools are implemented and used effectively, and portfolio guidelines exist and are actively used.
		Portfolio management is both defined and established across the organization, and defined processes are being used to reduce and manage corporate risk.
	Benefits management	A centrally managed framework is used to define and track the delivery of benefits across the business operations.
	Financial management	There will be established standards for the investment management process and the preparation of business cases. The costs, expenditure and forecasts will be monitored at portfolio level in accordance with organizational guidelines and procedures. There will be defined interfaces with other financial functions within the organization.
		Portfolio financial management is defined and established across the organization, and defined processes are being used to improve investment and procurement decisions, and monitor programme and project budgets.
	Stakeholder management	Stakeholder management in the portfolio and individual programmes and projects is taken seriously and genuine authority is extended to appropriate stakeholders. The investment cycle is fully functioning and drives entry to the portfolio, and the importance of business-process design is recognized.
		The portfolio is tending to drive individual programmes and projects, i.e. top down.
	Risk management	Portfolio risks are identified and quantified, and mitigation plans developed and funded. Risks across the portfolio are continually reviewed and there is reporting to senior management.
		Robust risk management includes: the identification of strategic, delivery and operational risks; the consistent analysis of risk in terms of probability, impact (on project schedule, cost and quality of deliverable) and timing; the production and funding of contingency plans; and the continual review by knowledgeable experts, risk owners and senior managers.
	Organizational governance	The principles of portfolio, programme and project management are widely understood, practised to a consistent standard, and underpin the governance framework.
	Resource management	Programme and project resources are being managed within defined and well-used processes. This allows the organization to increase the targeting and development of resources against corporate objectives.
		The competent identification of the required resources, skills and experience (especially in the business as distinct from the project team) enables the organization to improve the likelihood of committed resources being released in a timely manner to support the work of programmes and projects.

4	Management control	Portfolio management processes are integrated with those of programme and project management, with programme and project performance capability metrics in place and used.
	Benefits management	The benefits management process is well established and is integrated into how the organization manages itself.
	Financial management	The organization has effective and robust financial control of its investment decisions and the approval and monitoring of programmes and projects. There is proactive, evidence-based management of the portfolio. Financial oversight of the portfolio is corporate-centric rather than programme- or project-centric.
	Stakeholder management	The organization, as part of the initial planning, readiness preparation and deployment planning, consistently ascertains the current organizational culture and determines the climate and activities required to improve the effectiveness of business change and the generation of ideas. Business areas fully own the transition to new ways of working and, via the corporate portfolio, see programmes and projects as suitable vehicles to effectively manage that transition.
	Risk management	The organization's appetite for risk, and the balance of risk and benefit across the portfolio, are continually reviewed and managed. Senior managers own and oversee the management of risks across the portfolio. Portfolio risk management is embedded within the corporate reporting and management structures.
	Organizational governance	All programmes and projects are integrated into an achievable portfolio aligned with corporate objectives and strategic targets.
	Resource management	The organization has established effective capacity and capability strategies and processes for obtaining, allocating and adjusting resource levels (including people, funding, estate and tools) in line with medium-term and long-term investment plans.

Table continues

Table E.1 *continued*

Level	Process perspective	Comment
5	Management control	Potential problems in the programme and project management context are identified and prevented from occurring. There is an awareness of the likely potential and impact of new technology being embedded into the standard programme and project management processes.
		Quantitative and qualitative measures, and lessons, are being routinely used to improve the effectiveness of corporate portfolio management.
	Benefits management	Benefits management is integral to the development and maintenance of the business strategy.
	Financial management	Financial control of the portfolio is an integral part of the organization's financial control regime.
		Appropriate financial control is embedded within programmes and projects, and integrated with that for the organization.
	Stakeholder management	Continual business-process improvements are undertaken in a planned manner, aligned with corporate objectives and priorities, with demonstrable benefits and measurement of the efficacy of programmes and projects.
		The portfolio, programmes and projects are viewed as the preferred instruments to achieve continual improvement in the organization's business processes.
	Risk management	The process of portfolio risk management is continually improved, based on analysis of evidence from within the organization and comparison with other organizations.
		The corporate risk management process is continually improved, and the corporate risk model is refined to align with the organizational culture and corporate objectives.
	Organizational governance	The portfolio is proactively managed to ensure that it remains sufficiently dynamic and agile to cater for changes in business direction and priorities. The portfolio is supporting the organization's goals by its use of performance measures, improving quality and productivity, and the effective use of the organization's assets.
		The governance of investment management has moved from a programme- or project-centric process to a corporate-centric process.
	Resource management	The analysis and management of the portfolio drives the planning, development and allocation of programme and project resources to ever improve the effective use of resources in achieving the corporate objectives.

Table E.2 Programme level (PgM3)

Level	Process perspective	Comment
1	Management control	The programme management terminology may be in use but will be used inconsistently. The general approach will be based on project rather than programme level.
	Benefits management	There is recognition of the concept of benefits that can be differentiated from project outputs. Benefits will be developed at a project level with minimal programme control.
	Financial management	There are minimal or no financial controls; those that exist are principally related to projects.
	Stakeholder management	Programme management is principally seen as an area of activity outside the remit of business operations. Managers may see the programme approach as threatening rather than adding value.
	Risk management	There is minimal evidence of risk management being deployed to any beneficial effect; the main focus is on issue management.
	Organizational governance	Informal governance of programmes exists but has undefined linkage to projects and the broader organizational controls. Roles are likely to be notional.
	Resource management	The focus is on the project resources being deployed, with minimal focus on programme management resource requirements.
2	Management control	There is general understanding of the concepts of programme management. There is evidence of good examples of deployment but there will be inconsistency and varying levels of commitment. There is a strategic acknowledgement of the value of programme management.
	Benefits management	Benefits are recognized as a key element and differentiating factor for programmes. The focus is likely to be at the project level but initial evidence exists of tracking at a programme level. There will be more detailed definition of benefits.
	Financial management	Financial approvals for projects are evident but the cost of the programme is not being fully accounted for in all cases.
	Stakeholder management	Operational and business staff are involved with the programme and engaging with the delivery. Engagement is consultative and reactive rather than decision-making.
	Risk management	Risk management is recognized and used on programmes, but there are inconsistencies in approach, commitment and deployment.
	Organizational governance	Programme management is beginning to take shape but with ad hoc controls being applied and no clear strategic control. Roles and responsibilities will be unclear, as will reporting lines.
	Resource management	Resources are being deployed across the organization but there is little evidence of a consistent approach to acquisition, planning or management.

Table continues

Table E.2 *continued*

Level	Process perspective	Comment
3	Management control	There is a consistent approach to programme management controls, with the application of approaches in all programmes. A defined lifecycle exists and there is active management and application of controls to programmes within it.
	Benefits management	A centrally managed framework is used to define and track the delivery of benefits across the business operations.
	Financial management	There are standard approaches to financial management and cost assessments that are tracked through the lifecycle and are deployed consistently across all programmes.
	Stakeholder management	There is organization and business engagement with the programme approach. There is active and regular input into the way programmes are managed, with the major focus on the achievement of business change rather than programme delivery.
	Risk management	Risk management has a clearly defined process that is followed consistently by all programmes. The framework is based on industry standards and is supported by a toolkit.
	Organizational governance	All roles and responsibilities are documented within terms of reference. Strategic controls are applied consistently, with decision-making structures in place.
	Resource management	There is planned deployment and effective utilization of resources across the programme, supported by standard approaches to planning and tracking.
4	Management control	Programme management is seen by the board as a key tool for the delivery of strategic objectives. There is acceptance of a common approach, which is supported by management behaviour. Within the programme environment the focus is on improvement, adoption and measurement.
	Benefits management	Benefits management is embedded within the programme management approach and management of each programme.
	Financial management	Programme lifecycles are being flexed effectively to manage the availability of finance, and effective decision-making is occurring on the basis of financial evidence.
	Stakeholder management	There is extensive engagement with business operations, with an equal focus on business and organization improvement and programme delivery.
	Risk management	Risk management works effectively, with active management and avoidance of risks being evident and embedded behaviours.
	Organizational governance	Clearly aligned decision-making processes adopt and integrate the broader organizational governance and are transparent to those involved. Programme management responsibilities are embedded within broader role descriptions.
	Resource management	There is measurement of resource utilization, proactive engagement to raise and broaden capability, and evidence of a resulting improvement in delivery.

5	Management control	There is integration between a programme approach and the delivery of strategic aims and objectives. Programme management is accepted throughout the organization as the optimal approach to strategic delivery.
	Benefits management	Benefits management is embedded within the organizational approach to change and benefits are assessed as part of the development of corporate strategies.
	Financial management	Financial control is evident throughout the programme lifecycle and a balanced view of risk taking is underpinning the programme governance.
	Stakeholder management	Business operations are integral to the design and delivery of effective programmes. Management methods are integrated within the programme framework. Programme management is seen as the route to business change and improvement.
	Risk management	Risk management is embedded in the organizational culture and underpins all decision-making within the programme.
	Organizational governance	Programme management is embedded at board level, with clear ownership and control responsibilities embedded within individual directors' terms of reference.
	Resource management	Resources are deployed optimally; there is clear evidence of balancing internal and external expertise, and knowledge is being embedded into the business.

Table E.3 Project level (PjM3)

Level	Process perspective	Comment
1	Management control	Project management terminology is being used by some within the organization but not in a consistent manner and indeed without it being understood by all stakeholders. Some projects will be defined, conducted and managed to some extent.
		Where projects have been defined, the scope and objectives may be articulated to a wider audience with the aim of achieving commitment and support.
	Benefits management	There is recognition of the concept of benefits that can be differentiated from project outputs. Benefits may be cited within some project documentation but will tend to be qualitative or intangible. There will be limited, if any, responsibility for benefits planning and realization. The organization will have difficulty in reviewing benefits and attributing them to projects.
	Financial management	There are minimal financial controls at the project level and a general lack of accountability for monitoring project expenditure.
		The lack of formal business cases will present some difficulties for the organization in fully appraising potential projects, making investment decisions and directing such investments.
	Stakeholder management	Project management process improvement will be unplanned. There will be evidence of some 'fire-fighting', with experienced managers perhaps being used to rescue projects in difficulty.
		The project management process is likely to be chaotic and therefore in need of some basic standardization and established baselines on which to consider improvement.
	Risk management	There is minimal evidence of risk management being deployed to any beneficial effect.
		A risk management process will not have been established, although some projects will be cognizant of some of the risks that threaten them and these may be documented in an inconsistent manner within project risk registers. There will be little evidence of these registers being maintained.
	Organizational governance	Informal governance of projects exists but has undefined linkage to the broader organizational controls. Project roles are likely to be notional and terms of reference for the governance structures are unlikely to be fully documented. Planning for business review and governance checkpoints is unlikely to be fully developed.
		Leadership and responsibilities may not be fully attributable.
	Resource management	There is little recognition of the skills and competencies needed to deliver projects successfully.
		As projects are poorly defined, the role of project manager is compromised; project managers are unlikely to have the support and commitment of the organization, or the resources needed to accomplish project objectives in a consistent and planned manner.

2		
Management control	The concepts of project management will have been grasped by some within the organization and indeed there may be local experts, e.g. experienced project managers working within the organization on key projects. Work will be ongoing to establish a project management approach across the organization through the recognition of a project lifecycle, supported by document templates and some tools and techniques. Such initiatives are likely to be championed by the experienced project managers.	
Benefits management	Benefits are recognized within project business cases. There will be some documentation on who is responsible for particular benefits and their realization, but this is unlikely to be followed through. The difference between outputs, outcomes and benefits will be understood by most managers within the organization. The role of senior responsible owner (SRO) in benefits management and realization may be articulated on some projects. Post-implementation reviews (post-project reviews) will be focused on the project activities and deliverables.	
Financial management	Business cases are being produced in various forms and the better or more formal cases will present the project rationale on which to obtain organizational commitment to the project and take an investment decision.	
	Financial management of projects will be variable, depending primarily on the competency of the project manager. There will be little, if any, evidence that cost considerations are used in, for example, contingency planning and risk evaluation.	
Stakeholder management	Project management process development and improvement actions are not necessarily planned across the whole organization. Strengths and weaknesses will be identified by project managers in isolation and action taken to address specific weaknesses.	
	Project management will be assessed at the local level by individual managers, and some improvements will be initiated. There will be little dissemination of good practice between projects and little central control of the improvement agenda.	
Risk management	Risk management is recognized and used on all projects, but there are likely to be inconsistencies in approach, commitment and deployment.	
	Key project managers will understand and articulate the purpose and importance of risk management, but there will not be the same level of commitment and understanding across all projects and throughout the organization generally. There will be inconsistencies in the reporting and escalation of risks from projects to other stakeholders within the organization.	
Organizational governance	Project management from an organizational perspective is beginning to take shape but with ad hoc controls being applied and with no clear strategic control. Roles and responsibilities are sometimes unclear, as are reporting lines and accountabilities.	
	Some projects are perceived as falling outside of the organizational governance arrangements. There is little effective analysis and management of stakeholder groupings or management of their expectations.	
Resource management	Resources are being deployed on projects, but there is little evidence of a consistent approach to acquisition, planning or management of these resources.	
	The organization has started to adopt formal project management methods and perceives the need to familiarize staff with the methods, tools and techniques that are being adopted.	
	Appropriate individuals will be selected for principal project activities based on the project outline or high-level brief. Managers may be recommending some project training.	

Table continues

Table E.3 *continued*

Level	Process perspective	Comment
3	Management control	There is a consistent approach to project management controls across the organization, based on standard processes and methods. This standardization facilitates staff training and development and enables a common set of tools and other support arrangements to be deployed economically and effectively.
		The project lifecycle will not only focus on project initiation and development activities, but will also place equal emphasis on review and verification activities, implementation and handover.
	Benefits management	A centrally managed framework is used to define and track the delivery of benefits from the project outputs and in order to achieve the desired outcomes from delivered projects.
		Measures of success for projects are becoming defined and explicit. Post-project reviews are used to report formally on outcomes, and there may be procedures for periodic reviews of benefits after project closure. There will be a review of all qualitative benefits to ascertain whether these can be made more tangible and how they might be measured.
	Financial management	The organization will have established standards for the preparation of business cases and processes for the management of business cases throughout the project lifecycle. Project managers will monitor costs and expenditure in accordance with organizational guidelines and procedures, and there will be defined interfaces with other financial functions within the organization.
		SROs will have responsibility for each business case.
		Business cases are likely to be developed by iteration throughout the project lifecycle.
	Stakeholder management	The organization will have considered project management process improvement in the wider context of organizational improvement frameworks and approaches. A quality management approach will have been adopted and project improvement initiatives defined and managed as a change programme across the organization.
		Project management processes will be reviewed regularly and information made available to quality management.
	Risk management	Project risk management is conducted as a defined process that is cognizant of the organization's policy for the management of risks.
		Inherent project risks are being minimized effectively through project initiation and planning stages, while acquired risks are identified throughout the project lifecycle and are either being eliminated or mitigated through viable contingency measures. Risks are being escalated to the appropriate levels within the organization, as necessary.
	Organizational governance	Project roles and responsibilities are explicitly documented within terms of reference, including those of governance and control, e.g. the project board. Strategic controls are being applied consistently, with decision-making structures in place.
		The governance arrangements for projects are clearly defined and embedded within the organization, although the value and benefit of these controls is not being fully realized. Stakeholder involvement is both planned and analysed, and the project manager confirms that stakeholder management is in place.
	Resource management	The organization has well-defined projects and project managers who are able to review and assess the resource requirements in relation to project delivery. Project managers will undertake sufficient planning to ascertain their project resource requirements. They will be able to highlight resource shortfalls and indicate individual/team training and development needs.
		The role of project manager will be a recognized skill within the organization, with an associated set of competencies.

4		
Management control	Project management is well aligned with the business plans and objectives. Project management has sufficient strategic importance for the organization to ensure that it is integrated with other business/strategic planning functions. Project management processes are fully embedded within the organization and there is a move towards more quantitative management and performance measurement.	
Benefits management	Benefits management is embedded within the project management approach. Projects can demonstrate strong business focus and strategic alignment. This will be documented in the business case. The organization will ensure that claimed benefits are realistic and that they are endorsed by the SRO.	
	Systems will be in place to capture the measurement of benefits and collect information on benefit types.	
Financial management	The organization is able to prioritize investment opportunities effectively in relation to the availability of funds and other resources. Business cases are evaluated and investment decisions are ratified by the business. Project budgets are managed effectively and project performance against cost is monitored and compared. Cost models are used to demonstrate the efficacy of projects.	
Stakeholder management	The organization has established a continual improvement process by which lessons from previous projects are captured and embedded in new projects. There are quantitative goals for project management improvement across the organization. Improvement actions are tracked and measured across all projects, and necessary changes are planned and implemented.	
Risk management	Risk management is working effectively and the value of risk management can be demonstrated from the organizational perspective.	
	Business stakeholders are comfortable with the management of project risks and their involvement, as appropriate, in that management process. Project managers are able to demonstrate integration between risk management and their planning and control mechanisms.	
Organizational governance	Decision-making processes associated with project performance adopt and adapt the broader organizational performance management and governance arrangements. Projects have explicit governance arrangements and clear channels of communication to ensure that stakeholders are informed and commitment remains high.	
Resource management	Resource management for projects is considered at a more strategic than tactical level within the organization. There is evidence of resource capacity management, through capacity planning. Resource availability and utilization are being measured and actions are taken to ensure the organization has the capacity and capability to meet its project delivery needs.	

Table continues

Table E.3 *continued*

Level	Process perspective	Comment
5	Management control	Project management controls are being optimized to ensure that they are effective and efficient from the organizational perspective. They are regularly evaluated and enhanced so that they remain aligned with business imperatives, strategies and plans.
		Controls are not only used to monitor existing projects; the organization uses information feedback to proactively plan and design better control mechanisms for future projects. The level of control is planned in accordance with the criticality and complexity of the project to be managed.
	Benefits management	Benefits management is embedded within the organizational approach to change, and benefits being achieved are assessed as part of the development of corporate strategies.
		Projected benefits are fully documented in business cases in terms of a benefits management strategy that is fully supported by a benefits realization plan. Benefits network diagrams are likely to be in evidence to analyse dependencies. There is strong evidence that post-project reviews are performed and trends are established. Lessons are fed back into benefits realization planning and other management activities.
	Financial management	Project financial controls are fully integrated with those of the organization. Cost estimation techniques being used at the project level are continually reviewed in terms of actual vs. estimate comparisons to improve estimation throughout the organization.
		The organization will display effective cost analysis systems, in order to improve future project economy, efficiency and effectiveness.
		The organization will be able to demonstrate the value for money that is being achieved through its projects.
	Stakeholder engagement	Continual process improvement to the project management processes is undertaken in a planned manner across all projects, with demonstrable benefits and measurement of the efficacy of project management to the quality of projects.
		There is strong evidence of knowledge management and performance information being used to achieve improvement goals, with quantitative improvements in productivity, project quality and other measures. The organization has an established quality culture and is keen to contribute to best practice.
	Risk management	Risk management is embedded in the organizational culture and underpins all decision-making with respect to projects.
		Risk management will be integrated effectively with project planning and estimation, the project management control mechanisms, and the governance arrangements. There will be strong links with financial management processes, and any risks to project benefits will be highlighted and examined. Project managers will clearly demonstrate the value of risk management in terms of contingency budget savings.
	Organizational governance	The governance arrangements for projects are taken seriously by the organization, with demonstrable reporting lines to board level and with clear ownership, control and rew porting responsibilities embedded within the organization.
		The governance arrangements for all projects will be explicitly stated in relevant project documentation, including the business case. There will be evidence that these arrangements are periodically reviewed for effectiveness, based on lessons from project activity.
	Resource management	Resources are deployed optimally; there is clear evidence of load balancing and the effective use of both internal and external resources in accordance with a resource strategy. Project managers will have an understanding of the business processes and business objectives and will be able to assure senior managers that project resources are sufficiently focused on business needs. Resource managers are proactive in identifying future needs and in anticipating future criticality through, for example, technical time forecasting models. Succession plans are maintained for key positions.

Appendix F:
Functions and services

F

Appendix F: Functions and services

This appendix outlines the most common P3O functions and services. The functions are shown in Figure 3.4.

Tables F.1–F.3 detail:

- Function or service name, e.g. risk or planning
- Portfolio activities (permanent office)
- Centre of excellence (COE) activities (permanent office)
- Programme or project office activities (temporary office)
- Useful tools/techniques relevant to the function or service – may refer or link to other Best Management Practice guidance.

Hints and tips

Where there is only one office in an organization's P3O model, all functions in all columns should be considered when building the P3O blueprint. In reality, heads of P3O designing a P3O model should use Table F.1 as a 'pick and mix' selection of services to meet local business need and PPM maturity.

Keep it simple – it is best to keep the functions and services design simple initially and then build in or add to services and information when their value has been established and the relevant skill sets built up. For example, in relation to resource management and capacity planning, first focus on the skill types where the number of resources is severely constrained.

With regard to the content of the tables, two special features should be mentioned:

- **Portfolio office and COE** In some organizations there is only one organization-wide office providing both portfolio management and COE functions – often referred to by a single name, e.g. portfolio office. In other organizations they are very different offices: the portfolio or strategic change functions may be undertaken by a portfolio office or the strategy department, whereas the COE is an office where standards, training, mentoring, coaching, process improvement and internal consultancy reside. The tables separate out portfolio and COE functions, but the reality may be a combination of both, so remember the 'pick and mix' rule to meet any organization's needs.

- **Hub portfolio office** A hub portfolio office (permanent) is often set up to provide portfolio or COE functions and services to a division/agency/department or business unit or function, tailoring them to local need. The hub portfolio office may also provide a central flexible resource pool for delivery-focused programme and project support staff, enabling improved capacity planning and adherence to standards. The central pool of resources will be allocated to temporary programmes and projects as they launch and may change throughout the programme or project lifecycle. For example, at the start of a programme or project there is a need for a higher level of planning support, but this can be reduced as the programme or project moves into implementation. By creating a central flexible resource pool and resourcing programmes and projects from the central pool, less time will be spent on induction, staff will 'hit the ground running' on standards, and there will be opportunities to share staff and recorded lessons. In terms of the functions and services provided, each hub portfolio office will reflect local need and will be dependent on the size and responsibilities of the organization's portfolio office or COE (where these offices exist). There is no separate column in the tables to identify hub portfolio office activities, as in reality this office may offer a subset of the portfolio and COE activities in addition to providing programme and project activities (through a central flexible resource pool). Again – remember the 'pick and mix' rule.

Table F.1 Planning functions and services

	Function	Potential services of an organization portfolio office or a hub portfolio office	Potential services of a permanent COE	Potential services of a temporary programme office or project office	Useful tools/techniques/references

1	Portfolio build, prioritization, analysis and reporting	Overall – supports the planning and management of the implementation of the organization's strategy via a strategic programme or similar, ensuring that critical programmes and projects are well briefed and started on time, remain aligned with strategy, provide regular feedback to strategy etc. It does this by:
		■ Maintaining a register for current and potential programmes and projects (may be separate registers, subdividing current from potential activity)
		■ Establishing a framework for assessing and comparing programmes and projects against strategic, financial and risk value parameters
		■ Establishing and managing a gated review process, including portfolio entry criteria (elements that must be met or commented on prior to an idea being submitted)
		■ Providing decision support to enable the identification, selection and prioritization of new programmes and projects:
		  ● Facilitating the choice of the right programme and project mix (workshops/information)
		  ● Developing a framework for categorizing programmes and projects
					MoP
					Prioritization framework/model
					Strategy maps
					Categorization guidelines for programmes/projects
					Portfolio baselining/optimization guidelines
					Achievability vs. affordability matrix tool
					Design/enterprise architecture tools – supporting business blueprinting
					SWOT
					PESTLE
					MOSCOW
					Enterprise project management (EPM) tools with a strategic portfolio planning and analysis focus
					Post-implementation review and lesson techniques

- Developing strategy maps
- Facilitating benefits mapping workshops
- Developing scenario modelling – to reduce commitments or increase capacity
- Quantifying current commitments externally with partners/third parties and internally to existing service levels and operations

■ Coordinating feedback to the senior management team responsible for strategy so they can measure the success of strategic initiatives

■ Providing analysis of unsuccessful initiatives to inform future strategic decisions/priorities

■ Providing tools/analysis for business capacity management

■ Enabling the identification of programmes and projects that cannot be justified – advising on pet projects and challenging divergence from strategic intent

Table continues

Table F.1 *continued*

Function	Potential services of an organization portfolio office or a hub portfolio office	Potential services of a permanent COE	Potential services of a temporary programme office or project office	Useful tools/techniques/references
2 Programme and project set-up and closure	On behalf of relevant governance board: ■ Trigger programmes/projects as part of business planning/prioritization ■ Trigger post-programme/project reviews to assess return on investment/benefits for the portfolio	Programme or project fast-track mobilization service – tailoring advice/guidance, templates/processes, facilitated workshops, library set-up Support closure process through independent workshops on lesson sharing Capture good-practice examples for inclusion in good-practice repository Define/advise on programme or project assurance services – delivery, technical, benefits, stakeholders, risk, audit and compliance	Programme or project fast-track mobilization service – tailoring advice/guidance, templates/processes, facilitated workshops, library set-up Scope management – ensure scope is clear and delineated Support closure process through independent workshops on lesson sharing, archiving of libraries, redeployment of resources through flexible resourcing Programme or project accommodation and facilities services	Facilitated workshops Tailoring guidelines Standard processes and templates PRINCE2 MSP

3	Stakeholder engagement and communications	Develop stakeholder profiles Facilitate the formulation of stakeholder engagement strategies Enable the formulation of portfolio communications plans Coordinate stakeholder engagement and communication, ensuring effective timing and interdependency management of communications across the portfolio Coordinate internal portfolio communications Monitor the effectiveness of communications Provide answers and briefings to queries/information requests Support press enquiries (providing the point of contact between programmes and the press office) Establish and maintain portfolio intranet site or information portal	Define stakeholder engagement and communications planning processes and template Facilitate stakeholder identification and communications workshops Advise on key stakeholders and influencing strategies Be aware of stakeholders with an interest in the organization's delivery portfolio; identify gaps, overlaps and potential conflicts of interest Develop stakeholder profiles Facilitate the formulation of stakeholder engagement strategies Enable the formulation of programme and project communications plans Coordinate stakeholder engagement and communication, ensuring effective timing and interdependency management of communications across programmes and projects Coordinate internal programme/project communications Monitor the effectiveness of communications Provide answers and briefings to queries/information requests Support press enquiries (providing the point of contact between programmes/projects and the press office) Establish and maintain programme/project intranet site or information portal	MoP PRINCE2 MSP: ■ Stakeholder maps ■ Stakeholder profiles ■ Stakeholder engagement strategy ■ Programme communications plan ■ RACI matrix Collaboration/portal tools Publishing software Web-authoring tools

Table continues

Table F.1 *continued*

Function	Potential services of an organization portfolio office or a hub portfolio office	Potential services of a permanent COE	Potential services of a temporary programme office or project office	Useful tools/techniques/ references
4 Planning and estimating	Facilitate the development of high-level portfolio/business plan Develop, track and maintain dependencies across programmes within the portfolio and against the strategy Review plans against business-as-usual plans to ensure change can be adopted effectively Develop resource/capacity plans to underpin the portfolio plan	Define planning standards for the portfolio, programme and projects to enable ease of roll-up of milestone data and dependencies Provide planning assistance to projects – templates, resources, planning workshops Provide estimating support through experienced staff or estimating database	Define planning standards for projects to enable ease of roll-up of milestone data and dependencies Facilitate the development of high-level programme/project plan, including the collation of lower-level plans into programme/project-level milestones Develop, track and maintain dependencies Facilitate the review of plans against business-as-usual plans to ensure change can be adopted effectively Provide estimating support to the programme/projects	Enterprise and local planning tools ('what if' scenario planning) Estimating databases Facilitated planning workshops Planning standards – processes and templates PRINCE2 – product-based planning

5	Capacity planning and resource management (may include demand management)	Capture the resource requirements of portfolio, programmes, projects and the portfolio office itself	Assist in the recruitment and evaluation of programme and project manager	Capture the resource requirements of programmes, projects and the programme or project office itself	Resource/capacity planning tools (part of enterprise project tool)
		Forecast future resource needs, based on programme/project plans, close liaison with the relevant managers and (where appropriate) wider business plans and business office objectives	Provide standard role descriptions for PPM staff, including support staff and programme/project delivery staff	Forecast future resource needs, based on programme/project plans, close liaison with the relevant managers and (where appropriate) wider business plans and business office objectives	Flexible resource pools
		In consultation with human resources (HR) and others, decide on the best source for the required resources, depending on the long-term requirement for a particular skill and its likely availability	Maintain a database of resources for people, their skills/ attributes, location, availability, contact details and lead responsibility for the resource	In consultation with HR and others, decide on the best source for the required resources, depending on the long-term requirement for a particular skill and its likely availability	Resources/skills database
		Plan and initiate acquisition of the necessary resources, in terms of both skill content and quantity, ensuring the resources are in place at the time needed	Define a process for selection of key PPM roles	Plan and initiate acquisition of the necessary resources, in terms of both skill content and quantity, ensuring the resources are in place at the time needed	Standard role descriptions/ templates
		Actively monitor the deployment of staff, arranging new postings (where possible) in advance of assignments ending, to meet staff development needs and to maintain a good match of skill to role (as roles vary with programme/project phase)	Define strategy for developing/ acquiring skills/competencies	Actively monitor the deployment of staff, arranging new postings (where possible) in advance of assignments ending, to meet staff development needs and to maintain a good match of skill to role (as roles vary with project phase)	Resource capacity views
		Maintain sufficient management information to enable the above activities and the reporting of resourcing status to senior management	Ensure HR practices and procedures are aligned with successful operation of programme and project management		
		Maintain a database of resources for people, their skills/attributes, location, availability, contact details and lead responsibility for the resource			

Table continues

Table F.1 *continued*

Function	Potential services of an organization portfolio office or a hub portfolio office	Potential services of a permanent COE	Potential services of a temporary programme office or project office	Useful tools/techniques/references
5 Capacity planning and resource management (may include demand management) *continued*	Provide a view of commitments (of programme staff) on other programmes/projects and/or on business-as-usual activities that will impact the ability of the portfolio to deliver		Maintain sufficient management information to enable the above activities and the reporting of resourcing status to senior management	
	Provide a resource-tracking and capacity planning service across the portfolio/programme(s)		Work with HR and line management to facilitate leavers' process, including knowledge management, as required	
	Facilitate the management of consultants' and interims' contracts – acquisition/contract engagement/extensions etc.		Provide a view of commitments (of programme staff) on other programmes/projects and/or on business-as-usual activities that will impact the ability of the programme to deliver	
	Provide 'help squads'– supplementary skills to fill shortfalls within the programmes/projects		Provide a resource-tracking and capacity planning service across a programme	
	Where a flexible PPM resource pool is in place, manage resource planning, data collection and PPM skills development on a wider front, in accordance with a flexible resource deployment model		Facilitate the management of consultants' and interims' contracts – acquisition/contract engagement/extensions etc.	
	Provide a succession planning service for key roles		Assist in the recruitment and evaluation of programme and project managers	

6	Benefits management	On behalf of relevant governance boards: ■ Assess benefits planning and realization across a number of programmes or projects within the portfolio to identify gaps, overlaps and conflicts and to eliminate double counting in the benefits plans of individual programmes and projects ■ Review post-programme/project benefits against strategic investment decisions ■ Establish and implement benefits-variance escalation process	Develop standards for benefits management, including processes, templates and tools Facilitate agreement of the benefits management strategy between the senior responsible owner (SRO), programme manager and business areas Facilitate agreement of the benefit profiles between the SRO, programme manager and business change managers Facilitate agreement of the benefits realization plan between the SRO, programme manager and business area/business change managers Track benefit realization on behalf of the business, collating benefits data for reporting purposes	MoP MoV MSP: ■ Benefits management strategy ■ Benefits realization plan ■ Benefits map ■ Benefit profiles Benefits database/spreadsheet Radar (spider) diagrams for reporting benefits Functional Analysis System Technique (FAST) Value trees
7	Performance monitoring	On behalf of relevant governance board: ■ Set up and track portfolio metrics (key performance indicators – KPIs) ■ Set up and track portfolio office performance metrics – value proposition	Manage portfolio/programme or project performance improvement plan (PIP) template, enabling process and resource (fed by lessons) Recommend ways to reduce or shorten project lifecycle times through effective working practices	MoP Performance improvement plans Department capability review (UK government) Standard KPIs/tracking databases Balanced scorecard Performance management systems

Table F.2 Delivery functions and services

Function	Potential services of an organization portfolio office or a hub portfolio office	Potential services of a permanent COE	Potential services of a temporary programme office or project office	Useful tools/techniques/references
8 Monitor and review	Undertake periodic reviews of progress (outputs/outcomes) against strategy and portfolio plans	Develop standards – processes and templates – for monitoring and review	Undertake periodic reviews of progress (outputs/outcomes) against programme/project plans	Timesheet recording tools (enterprise programme and project tool)
	Identify and report deviations (forecast and actual) – advise and trigger exception reports	Develop time-recording standards and systems	Identify and report deviations (forecast and actual) – advise and trigger exception reports	Earned value analysis
	Provide strategic oversight support for SROs and management boards (horizon scan for impending policy/strategy changes/new business initiatives and assess impact on portfolio)		Horizon scan for impending policy or strategy changes and assessment of their impact on the programme or project	
	Perform ongoing amalgamation of data, analysis of portfolio/project selection and delivery performance:		Constructive challenge, scrutiny and assessment of the overall progress of the programme, rather than the collation of individual project reports	
	■ Provide 'what if' analyses ■ Provide 'forward look' – current commitments and track record of delivery ■ Provide strategic alignment analysis ■ Provide dependency analysis		Give advice and constructive challenge to programme and project management boards	
	Make a constructive challenge, scrutiny and assessment of the overall progress of the portfolio, rather than just the collation of individual reports, through:		Make recommendations on corrective actions and options to management boards	
	■ Advice and constructive challenge to management boards ■ Challenging key decisions concerning 'scale of risk'		Monitor assumptions log	
			Monitor dependency log	
			Implement and monitor timesheet systems to capture actual time spent	

	■ Recommendations on corrective actions and options to management boards Identify over-commitment of resources Identify over-commitment of changes to the business Monitor assumptions log Monitor dependency log			
9	Reporting	Report portfolio status to boards – timely and accurate information focused on decision-making Develop and maintain a single comprehensive picture of the portfolio (portfolio management dashboard, balanced scorecard) Provide a single source of truth for reporting – single report/data feed – consolidated/aggregated reports to different audiences	Provide reporting standards, templates, tools and reporting timetable (checkpoints, highlights, programme and portfolio status reports) Define and monitor traffic-light status to ensure consistency of reporting	Report programme and project(s) status to programme or project boards – timely and accurate information focused on decision-making Develop and maintain a single comprehensive picture of the programme (programme/project management dashboard, balanced scorecard) Provide a single source of truth for reporting – single report/data feed – consolidated/aggregated reports to different audiences	Enterprise project tools Portfolio/programme management dashboard Balanced scorecard Reporting standards – processes and templates Rules for escalation of data/decisions Definition of traffic-light colours for red/amber/green reporting Delivery confidence assessments – traffic-lighted assessments (gateway)

Table continues

Table F.2 *continued*

Function	Potential services of an organization portfolio office or a hub portfolio office	Potential services of a permanent COE	Potential services of a temporary programme office or project office	Useful tools/techniques/references
10 Risk management	Establish and maintain the portfolio risk register	Develop the overall risk management strategy, processes and templates	Establish and maintain the programme/project risk register	Risk tools
	Monitor portfolio risk register to ensure that all risks have a nominated owner and actionee	Develop/source/tailor tools for managing risk and train the organization in their use	Monitor programme/project risk register to ensure that all risks have a nominated owner and actionee	Risk database/spreadsheets
	Monitor portfolio risk register to ensure that the agreed risk mitigations are planned, resourced and implemented	Facilitate independent risk workshops	Monitor programme/project risk register to ensure that the agreed risk mitigations are planned, resourced and implemented	Standard scoring mechanism
	Communicate with stakeholders, particularly those who are directly affected either by the risk itself or by the risk mitigations	Clearly communicate the risk management strategy, and the benefits of following it, to all personnel involved with the portfolio, programme and projects	Communicate with stakeholders, particularly those who are directly affected either by the risk itself or by the risk mitigations	M_o_R
	Assess how effective any mitigation actions have been and whether the risks identified have actually materialized	Advise on risk mitigation and contingency planning	Assess how effective any mitigation actions have been and whether the risks identified have actually materialized	Risk potential assessment (RPA) tool
	Actively monitor and regularly 'check and challenge' all risks		Actively monitor and regularly 'check and challenge' all risks	MSP
	Establish and maintain an efficient two-way flow of information between the portfolio, programmes and their projects, regarding risk handling and escalation		Establish and maintain an efficient two-way flow of information between the portfolio, programmes and their projects, regarding risk handling and escalation	MoP
	Proactively look at risk registers across the portfolio (within programmes and projects) to identify common themes and establish consistent mitigation and contingency plans across the portfolio		Proactively look at risk registers across the programme to identify common themes and establish consistent mitigation and contingency plans	PRINCE2
			Proactively examine project risk registers for common risks that should be tackled programme wide (+ escalation)	PRAM

Table continues

Advise on risk mitigation and
contingency planning

Support sharing of risk registers
with supplier community

Facilitate risk escalation to higher
authority (e.g. portfolio
management)

Proactively examine programme
and project risk registers for
common risks that should be
tackled portfolio wide

Advise on risk mitigation and
contingency planning

Support sharing of risk registers
with supplier community

Facilitate risk escalation to higher
authority (e.g. strategic/business
management)

Facilitate independent risk
workshops

At portfolio level, monitor the
organization's total exposure to risk

Table F.2 *continued*

Function	Potential services of an organization portfolio office or a hub portfolio office	Potential services of a permanent COE	Potential services of a temporary programme office or project office	Useful tools/techniques/ references
11 Issue management	Perform logging and tracking to resolution of portfolio issues	Develop the overall issue management strategy, processes and templates	Perform logging and tracking to resolution of programme or project issues	Issue database/spreadsheet
				Issue tools
	Proactively examine issue logs across the programme(s)/projects for common issues which should be tackled at a portfolio level	Develop/source/tailor tools for managing issues and train the organization in their use	Proactively examine issues for links to existing issues that should be tackled together	Standard scoring/priority mechanisms
				MSP
	Control escalation of issues to higher authority, e.g. strategic or business management	Facilitate independent issue management workshops	Control escalation of issues to higher authority, e.g. portfolio or business management	PRINCE2
				ITIL
		Clearly communicate the issue management strategy, and the benefits of following it, to all personnel involved with the portfolio, programme and projects, including business operations		
		Establish the portfolio, programme or project issue management process, ensuring that procurement/ commercial leads on contractual issues and changes		
		Review the effectiveness of issue identification and resolution processes		
		Facilitate cross-portfolio/programme impact analysis workshops		

12	Change control	Establish and operate the change control process for the portfolio, ensuring that procurement/commercial leads on contractual changes	Establish and operate the change control process for the programme/project, ensuring that procurement/commercial leads on contractual changes	MoP
		Control escalation of changes to higher authority, e.g. business area management	Manage the change control process for business operations whilst the programme is still impacted by subsequent tranches	MSP
		Provide secretariat function to change approvals board (CAB) or change control board (CCB) for the portfolio	Control escalation of changes to higher authority, e.g. portfolio or business area management	PRINCE2
		Develop the overall change control strategy, processes and templates	Provide secretariat function to CAB or CCB for the programme/project	ITIL
		Develop/source/tailor tools for managing change and train the organization in their use		Change logging and tracking tools
		Facilitate independent change impact assessment workshops		
		Clearly communicate the change management strategy, and the benefits of following it, to all personnel involved with the portfolio, programme and projects, including business operations		
		Facilitate cross-programme impact analysis for changes that affect the wider portfolio arena		

Table continues

Table F.2 *continued*

Function	Potential services of an organization portfolio office or a hub portfolio office	Potential services of a permanent COE	Potential services of a temporary programme office or project office	Useful tools/techniques/references
13 Finance (these activities may be provided by the P3O or through finance staff embedded within the P3O)	Monitor and report on portfolio spend	In conjunction with finance, develop and maintain the portfolio, programme or project financial processes, controls and templates, paying particular attention to audit requirements	Monitor and report on programme or project spend	Finance planning and tracking tools
	Calculate and analyse portfolio cost variance	Develop the business-case process and templates	Calculate and analyse programme or project cost variance	Net present value technique
	Estimate future portfolio spend, challenge cash-flow/spend profile and forecast cash-flow/spend profile as appropriate	Provide advice/guidance on developing business cases and going through the approvals process	Estimate future programme/project spend, challenge cash-flow/spend profile and forecast cash-flow/spend profile as appropriate	Discounted cash-flow technique
	Manage invoicing and collection activities of portfolio deliverables and activities		Manage invoicing and collection activities of programme/project deliverables and activities	Cost–benefit analysis technique
	Prepare monthly financial reports for the portfolio, manager/strategic board and for inclusion in management dashboard reports		Prepare monthly financial reports for the programme/project manager or the programme/project board and for inclusion in management dashboard reports	Earned value analysis
	Work with finance/accountancy assistance to:		Work with finance/programme accountancy assistance to:	
	■ Administer and track budget allocations		■ Administer and track budget allocation	
	■ Ensure availability of appropriately profiled funding		■ Ensure availability of appropriately profiled funding	
	■ Develop and refine portfolio business cases		■ Develop and refine programme and project business cases	
	■ Develop and maintain the costed resource management plan for the portfolio		■ Develop and maintain the costed resource management plan	
	■ Advise on cost control and opportunities for savings		■ Advise on cost control and opportunities for savings	
	■ Control adherence to accounting procedures		■ Control adherence to accounting procedures	
	■ Oversee capitalization of capital assets		■ Oversee capitalization of capital assets	

14 Commercial (these activities may be provided by the P3O or through commercial staff embedded within the P3O)	Liaise with procurement/commercial teams on new initiatives to ensure early engagement Support supplier liaison across the portfolio Assist in the development of the procurement strategy Support contracts monitoring and management Place small orders for portfolio equipment and resources	Work with procurement/commercial teams to agree standards for purchasing within a programme/project environment	Liaise with procurement/commercial teams on new initiatives to ensure early engagement Support supplier liaison across the programme Assist in the development of the procurement strategy Support contracts monitoring and management Place small orders for programme/project equipment and resources Ensure all programme/project supplier relationships are effectively embedded in business as usual, with support arrangements and effective handovers of relationships	Framework agreements for interim resources Service and operational level agreements ITIL Best Management Practice policy and standards framework

Table continues

Table F.2 *continued*

Function	Potential services of an organization portfolio office or a hub portfolio office	Potential services of a permanent COE	Potential services of a temporary programme office or project office	Useful tools/techniques/ references
15 Quality assurance	Ensure compliance with standards/ good practice	Provide a stage-gate review or gateway support/coordination service	Work with internal audit and finance to ensure the programme complies with audit requirements	MoP
	Enable quality assurance of portfolio management products	Provide health checks, assurance or audits through a risk-based approach geared to the programmes and projects that need it most	Work with procurement/purchasing staff to ensure effective interface with suppliers' quality systems	MSP
	Coordinate quality reviews of portfolio documents and deliverables	Enable/conduct post-programme/ project reviews	Ensure compliance with COE standards/good practice	PRINCE2
	Oversee the quality review process for contractual supplier deliverables	Develop, implement and promote a comprehensive quality strategy	Coordinate quality reviews of programme/project documents and deliverables	MoV
	Liaise with internal or financial audit functions	Agree standards and establish clearly defined quality methods for staff to apply	Oversee the quality review process for contractual supplier deliverables	Stage-gating framework
		Assure the development of portfolio, programme and project quality plans	Provide quality control for management products	Gateway (including delivery confidence assessments)
		Monitor quality performance		Health checks
		Provide guidance on quality criteria, reviewers and sign-off authority to ensure cross-portfolio/programme(s) consistency		
		Analyse feedback from reviews, including stage-gate reviews/ gateway, health checks, post-programme/project reviews, audits and lessons		

	Function	Portfolio	Programme	Project	Tools
16	Information management (including configuration and asset management)	Hold master copies of all portfolio information (custodians of the information repository)	Develop and implement configuration management standards and processes	Hold master copies of all programme/project information (custodians of the information repository)	Collaboration tools
		Establish and administer portfolio baselines	Develop/source tools for configuration management	Establish and administer programme/project baselines	Document management tools
		Control the issue of portfolio products and deliverables	Develop/source tools for collaborative working	Control the issue of programme/project products and deliverables	Information library/portal
		Establish and maintain the index to an electronic library of portfolio information	Develop information strategy	Establish and maintain the index to an electronic library of programme/project information	Intranet
		Undertake configuration audits	Develop standard information library structures and templates	Undertake configuration audits	PRINCE2
		Ensure supplier configuration items (documentation and assets) are under control by providing a single point of entry to and exit from the portfolio for such items (working with procurement/commercial staff as appropriate)		Ensure supplier configuration items (documentation and assets) are under control by providing a single point of entry to and exit from the programme/project for such items (working with procurement/commercial staff as appropriate)	ITIL
		Manage archives of portfolio documentation		Manage archives of programme/project documentation	MSP
		May own asset management			
17	Transition management	Give assistance to SRO and business change managers with transition management		Give assistance to SRO and business change managers with transition management	MSP
		Support sign-off of capability and acceptance into operational running		Support sign-off of capability and acceptance into operational running	ITIL

Table continues

Table F.2 *continued*

Function	Potential services of an organization portfolio office or a hub portfolio office	Potential services of a permanent COE	Potential services of a temporary programme office or project office	Useful tools/techniques/references
18 Secretariat/other	Provide secretariat service to management boards Plan, forecast and manage non-HR resource requirements for both P3O and portfolio (match supply to demand – switch and release resources as necessary) for: ■ Accommodation ■ IT/tools support ■ Office equipment/stationery	Work with procurement/commercial to establish frameworks for the acquisition of: ■ Contract resources ■ Plant and equipment ■ Facilities/building space	Provide secretariat service to programme or project management boards Plan, forecast and manage non-HR resource requirements for both programme or project office and programme/project delivery team (match supply to demand – switch and release resources as necessary) for: ■ Accommodation ■ IT/tools support ■ Office equipment/stationery	Standard agendas/minutes

Table F.3 Centre of excellence functions and services

Function	Potential services of an organization portfolio office or a hub portfolio office	Potential services of a permanent COE	Potential services of a temporary programme office or project office	Useful tools/techniques/references
19 Standards and methods	Define and implement governance standards – reporting and information requirements, financial management standards (through links to finance), accountability and escalation routes	Develop and implement standard PPM methods and approaches Develop tailoring/flexing guidelines for standards, methods and approaches Provide links to other standards, e.g. ITIL for service management Ensure tools and processes facilitate collaborative working across team, department and organization boundaries Advise on PPM tools/software Reduce project lifecycles through effective methods	Tailor standard processes and templates to the programme or project Set up standards for collaborative working across teams/organizations	Standard PPM processes and templates Intranet Collaborative portal PRINCE2 MSP MoP MoV M_o_R ITIL Stage-gating framework/PPM delivery framework Gateway

Table continues

Table F.3 *continued*

Function	Potential services of an organization portfolio office or a hub portfolio office	Potential services of a permanent COE	Potential services of a temporary programme office or project office	Useful tools/techniques/references
20 Internal consultancy	Provide advice/guidance on impact of programmes/projects on business as usual	Execute specialized tasks for programme and project managers		Facilitated workshops – standard agendas
		Provide a help desk manned by experts in PPM to provide knowledgeable responses		Tailoring guidelines
		Provide a facilitation service (workshops/meetings)		Intranet
		Provide tailoring advice and guidance		Programme/project health
		Provide programme or project rescues (help programmes/projects in trouble with reviews and analysis, hit squads or recovery plans)		
		Promote good PPM within the organization		
		Advise SROs and management boards of appropriate frameworks/ governance models		
		Provide project assurance services to project and programme boards, either directly or through the engagement of third parties		
		Help programmes and projects 'in trouble' – 'broker' problems and potential solutions, including bringing in external good practice/ consultancy		

		Maintain relationships with experts inside and outside the organization to act as a clearing house for demand for analysis expertise with regard to: ■ Business ■ Risk ■ Organization restructuring ■ Change management ■ Advice on the application of best practice		Good-practice repository/database
21	Organizational learning and knowledge management	Undertake trend analysis – through both internal and external monitoring/reporting Collate post-programme/project reviews and analyse lessons for future investment decisions Assess historical perspective of how the organization has implemented change previously, based on appetite for change, culture and capacity for change	Maintain lesson logs on behalf of the programme or project Liaise/share lessons with other programmes/projects Facilitate lessons– process, templates, workshop facilitation, maintenance of information database, dissemination of lessons, action plans Develop and maintain good-practice repository (document examples) Develop case-study material Enable portfolio/programme/project management/SRO forums and sharing of good practice Liaise/share with P3Os in other departments/organizations Perform external networking – attendance at best-practice events, seminars Maintain knowledge/reference library Develop and run end-of-programme/project workshops on lesson sharing Enable post-programme and project reviews Develop relationships with other organizations, including delivery partners, and sustain networks to share lessons and experience	Programme/project management forums Networking/best-practice events Case studies PRINCE2, MSP, MoP, MoV, M_o_R, ITIL, workshops or forums Special interest groups Topic-specific events Subject-matter/topic/technique experts Knowledge management systems

Table continues

Table F.3 *continued*

Function	Potential services of an organization portfolio office or a hub portfolio office	Potential services of a permanent COE	Potential services of a temporary programme office or project office	Useful tools/techniques/ references
22 People and skills	Undertake portfolio induction	Monitor use of corporate guidance and standards to identify weaknesses and take corrective action as necessary	Undertake programme/project induction	Intranet
	Identify skill/competency shortages to deliver the portfolio and recommend suitable development	Define development strategy for organizational learning in PPM – training/development needs, courses/modules available, link to training department or external providers	Identify skill/competency shortages to deliver the programme/project and recommend suitable development	Skills/training databases
				Professional skills government (PSG)
				Online role/skills assessment tools
		Take an active role in the training and development of programme/ project staff to increase the available skills capability and capacity within the business		Training courses
				E-learning modules
		Perform PPM skills assessment and enhancement service:		International Project Management Association (IPMA) competence baseline
		■ Role/skills and competencies matrices		Association for Project Management (APM) competence framework
		■ Independent advice		
		■ Standard development/training plans for roles		
		■ Online skills assessment tools		
		Provide training logistics support – liaise with training providers and internal staff		
		Perform mentoring/coaching:		
		■ Develop guidelines/process/ resources		
		■ Organize/match – buddy relationships, secondments		
		■ Provide mentoring to business process owners		

References and
further information

References and further information

Note: this list includes bibliographic references which show the author at the time of publication. This is why some of the guides still refer to the Office of Government Commerce.

Association for Project Management (2004). *Project Risk Analysis and Management Guide* (2nd edn). APM.

Association for Project Management (2012). *APM Body of Knowledge* (6th edn). APM.

Best Management Practice (2008). *P3M3*. Can be downloaded from www.p3m3-officialsite.com

British Standards Institute. BS 6079-2: *Project Management Vocabulary*. TSO, London.

British Standards Institute. BS 6079-3: *Project Management: Guide to the Management of Business Related Project Risk*. TSO, London.

Cabinet Office (2011). *ITIL Service Strategy*. TSO, London.

Cabinet Office (2011). *ITIL Service Design*. TSO, London.

Cabinet Office (2011). *ITIL Service Transition*. TSO, London.

Cabinet Office (2011). *ITIL Service Operation*. TSO, London.

Cabinet Office (2011). *ITIL Continual Service Improvement*. TSO, London.

Cabinet Office (2011). *Managing Successful Programmes*. TSO, London.

ESI International (2012). *The Global State of the PMO – On the Road to the Next Generation*. Can be downloaded from www.esi-intl.co.uk/2012PMO survey/

Gartner symposium (2007). *Project Portfolio Management Processes: Keep the People In and the Complexity Out*.

Hobbs, B. (2007). *The Multi Project PMO: A Global Analysis of the Current State of Practice*. White Paper prepared for the Project Management Institute.

Kendall, G. and Rollins, S. (2003). *Advanced Project Portfolio Management and the PMO*. J Ross Publishing.

KPMG (2005). *Global IT Project Management Survey*.

KPMG (2002–3). *International Programme Management Survey*.

Office of Government Commerce (2009). *PRINCE2: Managing Successful Projects*. TSO, London.

Office of Government Commerce (2010). *Management of Risk: Guidance for Practitioners*. TSO, London.

Office of Government Commerce (2010). *Management of Value*. TSO, London.

Office of Government Commerce (2011). *Management of Portfolios*. TSO, London.

Office of Government Commerce: set of booklets under the *Achieving Excellence in Construction* banner, various dates. Can be downloaded from the National Archives website: http://webarchive. nationalarchives.gov.uk/20110601212617/http:/www. ogc.gov.uk/ppm_documents_construction.asp

Office of Government Commerce: set of booklets under the *Best Management Practice OGC Gateway* banner, various dates. Can be downloaded from the National Archives website: http://webarchive. nationalarchives.gov.uk/20100503135839/http:/www. ogc.gov.uk/what_is_ogc_gateway_review.asp
See also *Major Projects Authority: assurance toolkit,* which includes guidance for project assurance in the UK government and the link to the OGC Gateway booklets: https://www.gov.uk/government/ publications/major-projects-authority-assurance-toolkit

PMO Executive Council (2006). *A Function in Transition: Emerging Organisational Models for the PMO*.

Project Management Institute (2013). *A Guide to the Project Management Body of Knowledge* (5th edn). PMIC.

Project Management Institute (2013). *The Standard for Portfolio Management*. PMIC.

Thorp, J. (2003). *The Information Paradox*. McGraw-Hill Ryerson.

See also the Office of Cyber Security and Information Assurance at https://www.gov.uk/ government/policy-teams/office-of-cyber-security-and-information-assurance and CESG at www.cesg. gov.uk/Pages/homepage.aspx

Glossary

Glossary

aggregated risk

The overall level of risk to the programme or portfolio when all the risks are viewed as a totality rather than individually. This could include the outputs of particular scenarios or risk combinations.

assurance

All the systematic actions necessary to provide confidence that the target (system, process, organization, programme, project, outcome, benefit, capability, product output, deliverable) is appropriate. Appropriateness might be defined subjectively or objectively in different circumstances. The implication is that assurance will have a level of independence from that which is being assured. *See also* project assurance.

benefit

The measurable improvement resulting from an outcome perceived as an advantage by one or more stakeholders, and which contributes towards one or more organizational objective(s).

business as usual (BAU)

The way the business normally achieves its objectives.

business case

The justification for an organizational activity (strategic, programme, project or operational) which typically contains costs, benefits, risks and timescales, and against which continuing viability is tested.

centre of excellence (COE)

A coordinating function for all or part of PPM ensuring change is delivered consistently and well, through standard processes and competent staff. It may provide standards, consistency of methods and processes, knowledge management, assurance and training. It may also provide strategic oversight, scrutiny and challenge across an organization's portfolio of programmes and projects. It may be a function within a wider scope of P3O or may be the only function of a P3O. This function provides a focal point for driving the implementation of improvements to increase the organization's capability and capacity in programme and project delivery.

chief executive officer (CEO)

Describes the role in a commercial organization with the highest level of authority for the total management of the business.

chief financial officer (CFO)

Describes the role in a commercial organization with the highest level of authority for the management of the financial risks, planning and reporting for a business. This role will generally report to the CEO.

chief information officer (CIO)

Describes the role in a commercial organization with the highest level of authority for the management of information technology for the business. This role will generally report to the CEO but may also report to the CFO in smaller organizations.

chief operating officer (COO)

Describes the role in a commercial organization with the highest level of authority for the development, design, management and improvement of the open systems that create and deliver the organization's products and/or services. This role will generally report to the CEO.

cost centre

An accounting term used to describe a division, business unit or part of an organization that does not directly contribute to achieving profit for a company. It indirectly contributes to the organization by providing a service or support function to profit-making parts of the organization.

cost–benefit analysis

An activity that analyses and compares the costs and the benefits involved in one or more alternative courses of action. *See also* business case; internal rate of return; net present value; return on investment.

dashboard

A technique to represent vast amounts of decision-support information at an amalgamated level using tabular and graphic representation such as graphs and traffic lights. *See also* management dashboard.

design authority

A role or function (permanent, temporary or virtual) that provides expert specialist advice or owns some corporate function, service, standard or strategy that will be affected, or a major programme outcome or change that needs to be controlled. This could be an IT or property infrastructure design, or a major service contract; it could also be a business process model or the programme or corporate blueprint. The design authority provides expertise and guidance on a specific area to ensure there is appropriate alignment and control when changes are being planned and implemented. At a programme level this role may advise or own the business blueprint management on behalf of the programme manager. At the enterprise level, this role may manage the enterprise architecture of the organization.

dis-benefit

Outcomes perceived as negative by one or more stakeholders. Dis-benefits are actual consequences of an activity whereas, by definition, a risk has some uncertainty about whether it will materialize.

earned value analysis

A method for measuring project performance. It indicates how much of the budget should have been spent in view of the amount of work done so far and the task.

end project report

A report given by the project manager to the project board that confirms the handover of all products and provides an updated business case and an assessment of how well the project has performed against its project initiation documentation.

enterprise project (or PPM) management (EPM)

A term usually referred to by software vendors in relation to software (i.e. EPM tools) that assists an organization to manage across multiple projects and programme delivery using a common resource pool through to strategic analysis of investment through portfolio management. This term does not reflect the actual offerings of the tools that they generally can support at portfolio, programme and project (PPM) level.

executive

The single individual with overall responsibility for ensuring that a project meets its objectives and delivers the projected benefits. This individual should ensure that the project maintains its business focus, that it has clear authority and that the work, including risks, is actively managed. The executive is the chair of the project board. He or she represents the customer and is responsible for the business case.

expert reference group

A team of subject-matter experts that can be used in a PPM organization to provide input, advice and challenge to the role accountable for an output or outcome to ensure that it reflects the wider experience rather than an individual's perspective only. It is important to note that the role accountable for the output or outcome maintains the final decision and should not treat an expert reference group as a committee. An expert reference group may be drawn together at points in time or may be fully allocated to a project or programme.

full-time equivalent (FTE)

A technique used to measure human-resource involvement in a project, programme or operational activities. It is generally required where human resources are allocated across multiple roles (e.g. 70% allocated to a project and 30% allocated to business operations). An FTE of 1 means that a person or the sum of all people's effort is 100% allocated to an activity, based on the number of working hours available, treatment of overtime and other parameters.

gated review

A structured review of a project, programme or portfolio as part of formal governance arrangements carried out at key decision points in the lifecycle to ensure that the decision to invest as per agreed business cases and plans remains valid.

gateway reviews

Independent assurance reviews that occur at key decision points within the lifecycle of a programme or project.

governance

Ensures that policies and strategy are actually implemented, and that required processes are correctly followed. Governance includes defining roles and responsibilities, measuring and reporting, and taking actions to resolve any issues identified.

governance (corporate)

The ongoing activity of maintaining a sound system of internal control by which the directors and officers of an organization ensure that effective management systems, including financial monitoring and control systems, have been put in place to protect assets, earning capacity and the reputation of the organization.

governance (portfolio)

Encompasses the structures, accountabilities and policies, standards and processes for decision-making within an organization in order to answer the key strategic questions 'Are we doing the right things?', 'Are we doing them the right way?' and 'Are we realizing the benefits?'

governance (programme)

The functions, responsibilities, processes and procedures that define how a programme is set up, managed and controlled.

governance (project)

Those areas of corporate governance that are specifically related to project activities. Effective governance of project management ensures that an organization's project portfolio is aligned to the organization's objectives, is delivered efficiently and is sustainable.

health check

A health check is a quality tool that provides a snapshot of the status of a project, programme or the portfolio. The purpose of a health check is to gain an objective assessment of how well the project, programme or portfolio is performing relative to its objectives and any relevant processes or standards. A health check differs from a gated review in that it is a tool used for assurance purposes by the P3O to inform specific actions or capability maturity development plans, whereas a gated review is part of formal governance arrangements.

hub and spoke

A term to describe a system of organizational design for P3O where there is a centralized office (the hub) connected (via spokes) to a number of smaller decentralized offices (sub-hubs) each with a subset of the centralized office's business objectives, functions and services. All information and processes (connections) are arranged so that they move along spokes to the hub at the centre. A hub-and-spoke model provides the benefit of scalability for large organizations and supports business ownership by maintaining a level of decentralization.

information hub

The centralized element of the hub-and-spoke model for P3O in terms of information flows. It supports highlight and exception-based reporting for projects, programmes and/or portfolios by amalgamating information with the process and information owned by the central office. *See also* hub and spoke.

informed customer

An individual, team or group with functional responsibility within an organization for ensuring that spend on IT/IS or other procurement is directed to best effect, i.e. that the business is receiving value for money and continues to achieve the most beneficial outcome. The term is often used in relation to the outsourcing of IT/IS. Sometimes also called 'intelligent customer'.

internal rate of return (IRR)

A technique used to help make decisions about capital expenditure. It calculates a figure that allows two or more alternative investments to be compared. A larger internal rate of return indicates a better investment. *See also* net present value; return on investment.

ITIL

A set of best-practice publications for IT service management. Owned by the Cabinet Office (part of HM Government), ITIL gives guidance on the provision of quality IT services and the processes, functions and other capabilities needed to support them. The ITIL framework is based on a service lifecycle and consists of five lifecycle stages (service strategy, service design, service transition, service operation and continual service improvement), each of which has its own supporting publication. There is also a set of complementary ITIL publications providing guidance specific to industry sectors, organization types, operating models and technology architectures. See www.itil-officialsite.com for more information.

key performance indicator (KPI)

A measure of performance that is used to help an organization define and evaluate how successful it is in making progress towards its organizational objectives.

management board

A generic term used to describe either project management boards, programme management boards or portfolio management boards, or any combination based on the P3O context.

management by exception

A technique by which variances from plan that exceed a pre-set control limit are escalated for action – for example, where spends exceed budget by 10%.

management dashboard

A technique to represent vast amounts of decision-support information at an amalgamated level using tabular and graphic representation such as graphs and traffic lights.

Managing Successful Programmes (MSP)

A Best Management Practice publication/method representing proven programme management good practice in successfully delivering transformational change, drawn from the experiences of both public- and private-sector organizations (Cabinet Office, 2011).

mandate

Information created externally to a project or programme that forms the terms of reference and is used to start up a PRINCE2 project or identify an MSP programme. A mandate may be initiated through an unstructured approach, or it may be derived from strategic planning, business planning or portfolio management processes.

matrix management

A type of organizational management in which human resources with similar skills are pooled together for the assignment of work to other parts of an organization. In this approach, there is a separation between line management and line of authority in that a person may report to several project, programme or business managers to undertake multiple work assignments at different times but have a line of authority to a different manager altogether.

net present value (NPV)

A technique used to help make decisions about capital expenditure. It compares cash inflows with cash outflows. Positive net present value indicates that an investment is worthwhile. See also internal rate of return; return on investment.

one version of the truth

A technique whereby each element of portfolio progress reporting (costs, benefits, progress etc.) is derived from an agreed source managed by the portfolio office. Individual initiatives and other organizational functions will provide data inputs in relation to cost, benefit, delivery progress, resource requirements, dependency and risk status – and to an agreed schedule. The resulting consolidated data will be recognized as the authoritative source of information on portfolio progress used for monitoring, reporting and management decision-making.

organization portfolio office

A type of P3O model that is designed to centrally manage the investment process, strategic alignment, prioritization and selection, progress tracking and monitoring, optimization and benefits achieved by an organization's projects and programmes on behalf of its senior management.

P3O sponsor

A senior manager with appropriate authority who champions the establishment and evolving operation of the P3O. They will ideally be a member of the main board. See also Portfolio, Programme and Project Offices (P3O).

peer review

Specific review of a project or any of its products where personnel from within the organization and/or from other organizations carry out an independent assessment of the project. Peer reviews can be done at any point within a project but are often used at stage-end points.

PESTLE

Acronym for 'political, economic, social, technological, legal and environmental'. A technique used generally in organizational change management to undertake an environmental scan at a strategic level.

pet project

A project that is championed by an executive in an organization that may be aligned to an individual goal or goals for a specific part of the business, but not necessarily aligned to the strategic imperatives of the organization as a whole.

Portfolio, Programme and Project Management (PPM)

A collective term used for a series of guides aimed at improving the performance of those involved in portfolio, programme and project management. PPM is the accepted term in the industry and covers portfolio as well as programme and project management.

Portfolio, Programme and Project Management Maturity Model (P3M3)

A framework with which organizations can assess their current performance and put in place improvement plans.

Portfolio, Programme and Project Offices (P3O)

The decision-enabling and support business model for all business change within an organization. This will include single or multiple physical or virtual structures, i.e. offices (permanent and/or temporary), providing a mix of central and localized functions and services, and integration with governance arrangements and the wider business such as other corporate support functions.

PRINCE2

See PRojects IN Controlled Environments (PRINCE2).

programme assurance

Independent assessment and confirmation that the programme as a whole or any one of its aspects is on track, that it is applying relevant practices and procedures, and that the projects, activities and business rationale remain aligned to the programme's objectives. *See also* gated review.

programme brief

A statement that describes the specific objectives, required benefits, potential risks, outline costs, timescales and potential options for delivery for a programme.

project assurance

The project board's responsibilities to assure itself that the project is being conducted correctly. The project board members each have a specific area of focus for project assurance, namely business assurance for the executive, user assurance for the senior user(s), and supplier assurance for the senior supplier(s).

project brief

Statement that describes the purpose, cost, time and performance requirements, and constraints for a project. It is created pre-project during the Starting up a Project process and is used during the Initiating a Project process to create the project initiation documentation and its components. It is superseded by the project initiation documentation and not maintained.

project initiation documentation (PID)

A logical set of documents that brings together the key information needed to start the project on a sound basis and that conveys the information to all concerned with the project.

Project Management Body of Knowledge (PMBOK®)

A project management standard maintained and published by the Project Management Institute. See www.pmi.org for more information. *See also* PRojects IN Controlled Environments (PRINCE2).

PRojects IN Controlled Environments (PRINCE2)

The standard UK government methodology for project management. See www.prince-officialsite.com for more information. *See also* Project Management Body of Knowledge (PMBOK).

RACI

A model used to help define roles and responsibilities. RACI stands for responsible, accountable, consulted and informed.

resource

An organization's physical or virtual entities (human or otherwise) that are of limited availability and can be used to undertake operations or business change.

return on investment (ROI)

A measurement of the expected benefit of an investment. In the simplest sense, it is the net profit of an investment divided by the net worth of the assets invested. *See also* net present value.

risk potential assessment (RPA)

A standard set of high-level criteria against which the intrinsic characteristics and degree of difficulty of a proposed project are assessed. Used in the UK public sector to assess the criticality of projects and so determine the level of OGC Gateway review required.

scale of risk

A standard technique for estimating the probability and impact of a risk across an organization, portfolio, programme or project. This may be provided as part of a risk management standard (external) or a risk management strategy or policy.

senior responsible owner (SRO)

The single individual with overall responsibility for ensuring that a project or programme meets its objectives and delivers the projected benefits.

service catalogue

A database or structured document with information about all live IT services, including those available for deployment. The service catalogue is part of the service portfolio and contains information about two types of IT service: customer-facing services that are visible to the business; and supporting services required by the service provider to deliver customer-facing services.

sponsor

The main driving force behind a programme or project. Not a PRINCE2 or MSP term but equates to executive or senior responsible owner (SRO).

stakeholder

Any individual, group or organization that can affect, be affected by, or perceive itself to be affected by an initiative (programme, project, activity, risk).

swimlane

A method for documenting business process flows that separates each process step into a row (or lane) of accountability for individual roles or groups.

SWOT analysis

Acronym for 'strengths, weaknesses, opportunities and threats'. A technique to determine favourable and unfavourable factors in relation to business change or current state.

taxonomy

A classification of things, or the principles underlying such a classification. The term may be applied to relationship schemes such as parent–child hierarchies and network structures. A taxonomy might also be a simple organization of kinds of things into groups, or even an alphabetical list.

tranche

A programme management term describing a group of projects structured around distinct step changes in capability and benefit delivery.

work package

The set of information relevant to the creation of one or more products. It will contain a description of the work, the product description(s), details of any constraints on production, and confirmation of the agreement between the project manager and the person or team manager who is to implement the work package that the work can be done within the constraints.

zero-based cost centre

Similar to a cost centre, except that the division, business unit or part of the organization cross-charges other parts of the organization for some or all of its services or activities to achieve a spend of zero when its costs and income from cross-charging are added up.

Index

Index